Rights and Reason

Rights and Reason

An Introduction to the Philosophy of Rights

Jonathan Gorman

Council of Europe Convention for the Protection of Human Rights and Fundamental Freedoms, as amended by Protocol No. 11 Rome, 4.XI.1950 © European Communities 1998–2003

First published in 2003 by Acumen

Acumen Publishing Limited
15A Lewins Yard
East Street
Chesham HP5 1HQ
www.acumenpublishing.co.uk

ISBN: 1-902683-73-0 (hardcover)
ISBN: 1-902683-74-9 (paperback)

British Library Cataloguing-in-Publication Data
A catalogue record for this book is available from the British Library.

Designed and typeset by Kate Williams, Abergavenny.
Printed and bound by Biddles Ltd., Guildford and King's Lynn.

For Rupert, Claudia and Aurelia

Contents

Preface

I first came to Queen's University Belfast to lecture in social philosophy in January 1976, a time when tit-for-tat atrocities were usual. My predecessor, the late Alan Milne, had just moved to a Chair of Politics at the University of Durham, and I took over his fully worked-out courses in moral and political philosophy and in philosophy of law. He became a friend and mentor, and I took great pleasure in learning from him throughout his life. Yet I learnt, too, from his students. Philosophical studies at Queen's were polarized at that time in a way that matched community differences, but students from across that divided society had come to Alan Milne to be taught these controversial subjects. Political and legal philosophies mattered. Rights, in their various manifestations, were an important political issue. I was forced to reflect hard. I acknowledge here the great debt I owe to Alan Milne and to the succeeding generations of students who joined me in following where he had led. The reflections of the years ground the present book.

A more immediate cause of the book's writing was the encouragement received from sympathetic publisher Steven Gerrard and series editor John Shand. I am grateful, too, to the anonymous referees from North America and the UK. Theirs was not a thankless task, since I thank them all; but that is a poor return for their help. Many others have helped me, also, in sharing and shaping my thoughts about rights in many different ways. There are too many to list, but I think it very appropriate to express my gratitude here to Mr Justice Malachy Higgins for many discussions in which he has tried – I will not guess whether he would think himself successful – to keep my thoughts about rights and law attached to the real world, and to Professor Matt Kramer for setting me a constantly good example of incisiveness of thinking about rights. The core of my philosophical approach derives from reflections on objectivity and pluralism. I take pleasure in thanking Professor Cynthia Macdonald, Christopher McKnight and Professor Leon Pompa for taking those philosophical reflections seriously in many valued conversations.

There is "no quasi-object called Truth, which stays the same for all eternity",[1] holds Richard Rorty. "We hope to do to Nature, Reason and Truth what the eighteenth century did to God."[2] I was lucky to have been able to attend Rorty's seminars during his final year as an academic philosopher at Princeton – he is more than that now – but it was not until a few years later that, in a valuable discussion with Hayden White, I felt the full force – not necessarily with full agreement – of such an approach. Must human rights face the same philosophical risks as Truth and God? Read on.

Jonathan Gorman

---

1. R. Rorty, "The Continuity Between the Enlightenment and 'Postmodernism'", in *What's Left of Enlightenment? A Postmodern Question*, K. M. Baker & P. H. Reill (eds), 19–36 (Stanford, CA: Stanford University Press, 2001), 29.
2. *Ibid.*, 19.

CHAPTER 1

Introduction

The inscription on the Cenotaph in London's Whitehall says simply "The Glorious Dead". There is no doubting Western civilization's readiness to go to war, and to bear appalling losses in its prosecution. Yet even at times of greatest need, and at times when life might be held more cheaply than it is now, to believe that a cause may be worth committing suicide for, rather than merely risking death or being killed for, was to believe in a way foreign to much of Western history. Many people today see the suicidal killing of others as more characteristic of Eastern fundamentalism. It sometimes seems that such fundamentalists regard the values that they respect, and from which they act, as absolute and demanding, whereas Western values are seen as somehow less demanding and so, perhaps, less worthy.

It may well be that, as a country becomes more democratic, it becomes less ready to accept death than once it was. In the West we value peace – perhaps more than ever, just because of the horrific worldwide conflicts of the first part of the twentieth century – and we have largely achieved peace in our own lands since those conflicts. Where conflict does arise, we frequently seek to resolve it through creating continuing processes of toleration. That is a distinctive approach, and by no means as politically neutral as it might appear: as an Argentine foreign minister once said, "the idea of agreeing to disagree is a very British idea".[1] That fundamentalist or absolutist views should not be enforced on others is prescribed for our children. It is a familiar lesson from those who reflected on the evils of war.

---

1. *Today*, BBC Radio 4, 28 October (1998).

Toleration is valued as never before, and it is no surprise that many people, while perhaps regretting the passing of "standards", nevertheless believe that morality is entirely relative, and think religious choice better than religious certainty.

And yet there is, on the other hand, curiously coexisting with this relativist view, a widespread respect for rights as if they were absolute standards of morality or law. They have been described as objective trumps that all are rightly entitled to make use of.[2] Despite rights not being the whole story of our understanding of morality and law, rights in the contemporary world – and most particularly "human" rights – are in some very important sense authoritative for us. They are widely recognized as appropriate to *constrain* our individual and social choices, rather than being individually or socially chosen in the way that, in democracies, there is a choice of what religion to follow. We commonly think that widening respect for human rights marks moral progress in human affairs. If anything does, respect for human rights expresses what others might see as the moral fundamentalism of Western civilization.[3]

In public discussion, using the concept of rights can be a universal means of expressing moral issues. Sometimes this can advance our understanding – how, for example, should lying be understood? Some have considered falsehood to be the most central feature of lying. But one can deceive with selected truth. Is it deception that is central? Deception is itself a notion in need of analysis, and it may be more helpful to see a lie as offending against a *right* to a particular truth,[4] and elaborating this thought may improve our grasp of what is involved. More generally, organizing a given legal or moral problem in terms of rights, and reflection on where the rights may lie, can provide a solution, and along with that acceptance through understanding. Moral progress in human affairs and improvement in understanding are impressive achievements for any concept.

---

2. See R. M. Dworkin, "Rights as Trumps", in *Theories of Rights*, J. Waldron (ed.), 153–67 (Oxford: Oxford University Press, 1984), 153: "Rights are best understood as trumps over some background justification for political decisions that states a goal for the community as a whole." (Adapted from Dworkin, "Is There a Right to Pornography?", *Oxford Journal of Legal Studies* 1 (1981), 177–212.) See also Dworkin, *Taking Rights Seriously* (London: Duckworth, 1977).

3. "If you are looking for a modern, secular religion, you cannot do much better than the cult of 'human rights'. It has its doctrinal theorists, its practitioners and high priests, and its canonical texts", N. Malcolm, "Some Wrongs Need to be Righted", *Daily Telegraph*, 28 July (2002).

4. Clifford Longley, *Today*, BBC Radio 4, 4 Feb (2002).

Yet it is not all to the good. A contrasting point is that the concept of rights is sometimes used to express concerns that were once expressed, and arguably better expressed, without it. Accidents happen, and people naturally seek a cause and, preferably, someone to blame. The person to blame is the person, if any, whose duty it was to prevent the accident, and those affected exercise their "rights" in this context against that person. Yet the rights so exercised are not generally thought to come into being by derivation from actual duties held by other particular people, but rather to exist anyway. This offends against a familiar theoretical understanding (although not one widely shared among the public), that rights exist only in virtue of correlated duties and obligations imposed on others. Thus, against this understanding, many think that they have a simple right not to be affected by accidents, and that if an accident happens to them then they are entitled to demand redress from somebody else, and if not from a particular person then from the public at large. An increasingly litigious society is one consequence of the increasing use of the concept of rights in public understanding, and the law – although not traditionally written in the language of rights – has not been slow to oblige.

Thus the increasing use of the concept of rights is often not out of a proper respect for the rights held by others but rather a demand that the rights held by oneself should be respected. It sometimes seems that there is an incontinent generation of self-serving rights. The rights theorist Hillel Steiner remarks:

> it has now become standard practice for philosophical works on the nature of rights to begin their discussion of that subject by complaining of the vast proliferation of (often opposing) moral and political demands that come wrapped in the garb of rights.[5]

Steiner himself makes the same complaint in an earlier book on the subject.[6] The earlier claim of rights to contribute to substantive moral progress and to improvement in moral understanding is risked here for both matters. A litigious society is not obviously a good society, and it seems plain that, where one has a choice whether to exercise a right or not, it may be substantively wrong to do so.[7] Again, by casting

---

5. H. Steiner, "Working Rights", in *A Debate Over Rights: Philosophical Enquiries*, M. H. Kramer, N. E. Simmonds & H. Steiner (eds), 233–301 (Oxford: Clarendon Press, 1998), 233.

6. H. Steiner, *An Essay on Rights* (Oxford: Blackwell, 1994).

7. Reflect on Shylock's position in Shakespeare's *The Merchant of Venice*.

moral and legal difficulties in terms of the language of rights the concept of rights is forced to encompass the myriad moral and legal distinctions we ordinarily think appropriate to those difficulties, and the concept stretches to the point of confusion, as the following arbitrary list of questions shows.

Litigation is in general not free: is there a right to enforce a right without cost? Would that be a legal or a moral right? Would it depend on whether the right enforced was a legal or a moral right? Is there a difference between legal and moral rights? Is there a right to health? Does one have a right to die? Does a woman have a right to a child? Does a man have a right to a child? Against whom are any such rights held? Would a right to health block a right to patent the mapping of genes, with a possible consequential increased expense of treatment? Does one have a right to free beer? Does one have a right to free speech? Does one have a right to free computer software?[8] Is there a moral right to vote, or to break the law? There are, apparently, property rights, rights that support freedoms and democracy, the rights of the sovereign and of individual states against their subjects or citizens and against other states; there are individual rights as constitutional constraints, rights as part of a structure intended to achieve the goals of social policy (such as social welfare), rights under contracts, and human rights in their various forms. Some rights we may suppose ourselves to have only because our particular legal system gives them to us, such as a right to a state pension, but others we might suppose ourselves to have whether our laws give them to us or not, such as a right against another that he or she not injure us, or a right to benefit from a promise.[9] This selection of problems and asserted existences of both moral and legal rights, any of which could compete with any other, deliberately displays the confusion and arbitrariness characteristic of much rights talk in order to show the need for some rational ground for understanding and resolution.

We have briefly referred to current affairs, noting Eastern fundamentalism and its contrast with typical Western moral relativism. Contrasting with such relativism, human rights have been mentioned as appropriately fundamental in current Western understanding. We have noted the beliefs that establishing human rights is a substantive

---

8. The software guru Richard Stallman claims that there should be a right to free software as in the right to free speech rather than free beer.

9. Contrast with the similar elementary point, expressed without reference to "suppose ourselves", in J. J. Thomson, *The Realm of Rights* (Cambridge, MA: Harvard University Press, 1990), 1–2.

moral advance and that referring to rights permits advance in the analysis of moral and legal problems. Against this, we have noted that there has been a concurrent move towards self-serving rights and an increasingly litigious society, and also the complaint that the concept of rights is stretched to the point of confusion. The arbitrary range of questions that may be asked about rights casts doubt on both our moral understanding and our moral progress.

Yet we do seek moral progress in human affairs and an improvement in our moral understanding. Is the concept of "rights" a suitable concept to give those to us? Many of the issues jumbled together in our selection of questions are already, in practice, well understood by those professionally involved. One may practise law, and with it understand the nature and enforcement of rights under contracts, or rights held under legislation. One may study or be involved in international law and criminology, and concern oneself with problems of human rights violations. One may study or engage in political activity or policy formation where rights may well be a central issue. There is across the world a huge set of institutions and practices, international and domestic, that centre on matters of rights and human rights. Engaging in the practical questions about rights, including, as that must, both moral judgements about the various kinds of rights and a developed understanding of rights, may well involve joining or studying those institutions and practices.

By contrast, it is the task of this book to locate in an introductory way the *philosophical* issues that involve rights. Very little in twentieth-century moral philosophy was written that treated "rights" (rather than "good" or "just", or the adjective "right") as in practice the central moral concept for our Western culture, and this needs to be rectified.[10] We need to grasp more about rights than merely what is required for exercising them, protecting them or resisting or supporting their exercise by others. Rights involve social and individual choices, and where there is conflict and confusion we seek to achieve the interrelated goals of *understanding* and *justification* for what we may do. At a university or theoretical level of understanding, a number of disciplines may be associated with this, such as history, law, medicine, philosophy, politics and sociology. To locate our own

---

10. There are nevertheless some excellent works on rights. These, however, were often written by political or legal theorists, and political philosophy and philosophy of law have commonly been seen by mainstream analytical philosophers as "special" interests separate from moral philosophy itself.

study it is appropriate to begin with a sociologist writing history: T. H. Marshall.[11]

"I propose", Marshall said:

> to divide citizenship into three parts ... civil, political and social. The civil element is composed of the rights necessary for individual freedom – liberty of the person, freedom of speech, thought and faith, the right to own property and to conclude valid contracts, and the right to justice. The last is of a different order from the others, because it is the right to defend and assert all one's rights on terms of equality with others and by due process of law. ... By the political element I mean the right to participate in the exercise of political power ... By the social element I mean the whole range from the right to a modicum of economic welfare and security to the right to share to the full in the social heritage and to live the life of a civilized being according to the standards prevailing in the society.[12]

By contrast with the paragraph of jumbled questions presented earlier, we find here that rights are seemingly organized with some clarity. We will be concerned, in a way, with all the elements on Marshall's list. But does the list really advance our understanding? And does it offer any justification for the rights described? To begin with, is the list of rights correct? It would be natural to make a quick check with common-sense civic memory about this, but a philosophical concern lies in a different direction. Thus, why make a list of rights at all? Marshall's purpose is to characterize citizenship, but must rights be essentially associated with citizenship? Can citizenship not be understood in completely different terms? Why rights rather than duties, for example? Even if understanding citizenship is, implausibly, to be characterized entirely in terms of understanding rights, are there no rights that are completely separate from citizenship? Surely one could have rights if one were not a citizen at all? Philosophy typically seeks, and seeks to question, the *presuppositions* of our understanding. Querying Marshall's supposition that "rights" are the kind of thing that can be used to understand citizenship typifies this. Philosophy also seeks justification for our claims, but nothing in

---

11. Taken from the [Alfred] Marshall Lectures delivered in Cambridge in 1949, and reprinted as T. H. Marshall, "Citizenship and Social Class", in *Contemporary Political Philosophy: An Anthology*, R. E. Goodin & P. Pettit (eds), 291–319 (Oxford: Blackwell, 1997).
12. *Ibid.*, 294.

Marshall's paragraph offers justification. The rights referred to are just taken for granted as existing.

Again, why a *list* of rights? Are rights discrete things, each the same kind of thing, which can be counted and organized? And is it not odd that Marshall's list includes rights that *every* citizen is imagined to have? Are all rights like that? Rights created by contracts typically would not be.[13] Marshall's list is primarily organized according to *institutions*, with political rights associated with political institutions like parliament and local government, and social rights associated with the education system and social services. Individual rights are associated by Marshall with courts of justice by way of the right to justice. He thinks that this is "of a different order" than the individual rights themselves, but this is problematic. He supposes that courts of justice are institutions that in this context are designed to support the individual in the exercise of rights already held and that exist independently of the courts, but it is clear that in many cases it is the courts themselves that tell us whether we have such individual rights as those to free speech, thought and faith, or the right to a particular property, or to have a contract enforced.

Marshall's list of civil, political and social rights has the ring of late-1940s' social democracy in its unreflective presentation of a range of rights associated with a range of institutions, with no hint at this point that rights might have some existence as independent or universal values that were not created by human institutions. More importantly, there is no hint that individual rights might be part of an individual's *defence* against institutions or against the state. There are no "human rights" mentioned. Similarly, his list has the ring of early post-war legal theory with its unreflective sense of individual rights as existing independently of the courts' judgements, without any clarity whether that independence is due to their source in another institution of the state, such as parliament or some other legislative body, or to their source as natural values, or to some other foundation.

Certainly there are institutions in many countries that are associated with these various kinds of rights. These institutions all have histories, however, and they came into being at various times and over various periods. Marshall provides a limited history of civil, political and social rights: these rights, "in early times ... were blended because the institutions were amalgamated".[14] There was

---

13. Although consider a so called "social contract".
14. Marshall, "Citizenship and Social Class", 294.

geographical fusion as institutions spread over the ages to cover wider areas, and at the same time there was functional separation of institutions. We note with Marshall, who followed F. W. Maitland's *Constitutional History of England*, the establishment of royal power defining and defending the "civil rights" of the individual on the basis of common law. Specialist courts were created for specific purposes, and Parliament took control of national political power. The institutions concerned were so distinct that, according to Marshall, the elements of citizenship can be dated to different centuries: "civil rights to the eighteenth, political to the nineteenth and social to the twentieth ... It is only in the present century, in fact I might say only within the last few months, that the three runners have come abreast of one another".[15] Do these historical summaries solve our problems of understanding and justification? They merely repeat the doubtful association of rights with institutions. Moreover, even if we have here adequate historical explanations, we must not confuse *explanation* with *justification*. Understanding how a right may have come to be established is not necessarily a justification for keeping it, nor need it help us understand what a "right" is.

As noted, a particularly obvious feature of Marshall's list is its failure to mention *human* rights, those rights that are central to our understanding of or respect for rights as absolute standards of morality or law. It is human rights, among all rights, which are currently regarded by many as the benchmark of moral progress. It is an important corrective to Marshall's approach to note that the Universal Declaration of Human Rights was proclaimed by the General Assembly of the United Nations on 10 December 1948, a matter of months before his lectures. If it was this Declaration that he was referring to by "three runners" coming together, then he must have misread it as being a part of the history of English institutions. On the contrary, for centuries there had been a sense of such rights, or other central moral values functioning in a similar way, as existing *independently* of particular social or national institutions. It could not be a proper understanding of rights to explain or organize them only in terms of the peculiar features of national histories. Rights or other moral standards that existed independently of particular jurisdictions or cultures were necessary if jurisdictions or cultures were to be judged or compared. Pre-Reformation Europe had a common Christian authority in the Church, and the popes were able to claim a divine moral and legal[16]

---

15. *Ibid.*, 295.

authority over localized and more earthly rulers. As central religious authority fragmented there remained in the prototypes of current international law a recognition of values *independent* of the particular states. After the Second World War many leaders of Germany and Japan were tried for war crimes, and the Universal Declaration of Human Rights was in part a response to what had occurred in the war, where, as the Declaration said, disregard and contempt for human rights had resulted in barbarous acts that had outraged the conscience of mankind, and human rights had to be protected by the rule of law to avoid the need for rebellion against tyranny and oppression. The implication of this explanation is that human rights had not been *created* or *invented* by the Declaration but pre-existed it. The Declaration was a recognition and affirmation of human rights and an attempt to institutionalize international respect for them.

There has been much discussion since then about the creation of a permanent court for such crimes, and specialized tribunals have been created. More than 80 people have been accused of war crimes following the creation by the United Nations Security Council in 1993 of the specialized war crimes tribunal dealing with Yugoslavia. Former President Slobodan Milošević is now being tried for such crimes. But, again, such historical and contemporary facts and explanations do not provide *justification* for the claims made in the Universal Declaration of Human Rights. Are war crimes tribunals merely imposing "victors' justice"? Were the alleged activities "really" wrong or just wrong according to the standards of the winning side? (Should "really" be in inverted commas?) What if Milošević was acting rightly according to the law of his country at the time? Are there two different things here: acting rightly (or wrongly) according to law, and acting rightly (or wrongly) according to morality? In response to such questions the Declaration was explicitly *universal*, and it did not look only to the past; it expressed "the highest aspiration" for universal freedom of speech and belief and freedom from fear and want, and recognized the inherent dignity and the equal and inalienable rights of all members of the human family as the foundation of freedom, justice and peace in the world. The United Nations sought, through the Declaration, to promote social progress and better standards of life in a "larger freedom", and also to develop friendly relations between nations. The Declaration was intended to

---

16. Morality and legality were not clearly distinguished, and indeed it would be inappropriate in this context to try to distinguish them.

9

set a common standard of achievement for all peoples and all nations. Against Marshall, we are not to understand rights as the creation of civic institutions located in specific places and times, but rather as expressing a set of universal standards.

An outline summary of the first nine Articles will sufficiently summarize some of the kinds of rights supported in the Declaration:[17] all human beings are born free and equal in dignity and rights; they are endowed with reason and conscience and should act towards one another in a spirit of brotherhood; everyone is entitled to all their rights without discrimination on any ground; everyone has the right to life, liberty and security of person; slavery is prohibited; no one shall be subjected to torture or to cruel, inhuman or degrading treatment or punishment; all are equal before the law and are entitled to its equal protection; everyone has the right to an effective remedy in the case of violations; no one shall be subjected to arbitrary arrest, detention or exile.

Not long after Marshall's lectures, in November 1950, the European Convention for the Protection of Human Rights and Fundamental Freedoms was signed by the members of the Council of Europe. The aim of the Council of Europe, that convention declared, was the achievement of greater unity between its members, and it saw the governments of European countries as like-minded and as sharing a common heritage of political traditions, ideals, freedom and the rule of law. One of the methods by which the aim of unity was to be pursued was by the maintenance and further realization of human rights and fundamental freedoms, and protection of these was also the foundation of justice and peace in the world. A common understanding and observance of human rights was required, and they resolved to take the first steps for the collective enforcement of certain of the rights stated in the United Nations' Universal Declaration. They undertook obligations to respect human rights within the European jurisdictions, and in particular to protect the rights: to life; against torture or inhuman or degrading treatment or punishment; against slavery and discrimination; to liberty and security of person; to a fair trial; against punishment without law; to respect for private and family life; to freedom of thought, expression, assembly, conscience and religion; and to marry. In addition everyone was to have the right to an effective remedy in case of violations, and a European Court of Human Rights was established.[18] In 2000 a range of rights established

---

17. See Appendix 1: United Nations Declaration on Human Rights.

in earlier declarations was consolidated in the European Charter of Fundamental Rights.[19]

Human rights have so far here been explained in terms of declarations of universality. Yet surely one cannot justify the existence of universal standards of morality merely by declarations. What justifies the assertions made? And how universal can they be? How, for example, could the war criminals convicted at Nuremberg have been motivated by these ideal moral standards, given that there seemed to be no understanding of them or institutionalizing of them in their own lives and home institutions, since they were not "declared" until 1948? But it is disingenuous to pretend that "declaration" means "creation", as already noted; was there really no understanding of human rights in Nazi Germany?[20] On the other hand, without apparent *justification* for claims about universal rights they seem to be merely the affirmations of foreign institutions, and could the Nazi defendants rightly be blamed for not following foreign standards? The philosopher Thomas Hobbes (1588–1679) said that nothing could be right or wrong until people created a government that made laws that said so.[21] There is no morality independent of law. There are at least as many sets of laws as there are sovereign governments. There is no universal law, for Hobbes.

The philosopher John Locke (1632–1704) affirmed universal moral standards against Hobbes.[22] Locke said that the laws made by government were not valid if they conflicted with natural morality – as people sometimes say, "an unjust law is not law" – and natural morality gave everyone the right to life, health, liberty and property. The first nine Articles of the Universal Declaration of Human Rights summarized above might be seen as no more than a clarification of Locke's rights to life, health and liberty; protection of Locke's fourth right to property appears in Article 17:

---

18. See Appendix 2: European Convention for the Protection of Human Rights and Fundamental Freedoms.
19. This long document is available online. European Charter of Fundamental Rights 2000, http://europa.eu.int/comm/justice_home/unit/charte/index_en.html (accessed May 2003).
20. See the "German wife case", in H. L. A. Hart, "Positivism and the Separation of Law and Morals", in *The Philosophy of Law*, R. M. Dworkin (ed.), 17–37 (Oxford: Oxford University Press, 1977), 32.
21. T. Hobbes, *Leviathan* [1651], J. Plamenatz (ed.) (London: Collins, 1962).
22. J. Locke, "An Essay Concerning the True Original, Extent and End of Civil Government". *On Civil Government: Two Treatises*, vol. 2 [1690] (London: Dent, 1924). Otherwise known as the *Second Treatise*.

(1) Everyone has the right to own property alone as well as in association with others.
(2) No one shall be arbitrarily deprived of his property.

Yet there is more to the Declaration than an elaboration of Locke's list; other rights are also included that may be less traditional. Locke did not think it necessary to stress a right to marry and found a family, as Article 16 does, but this Article also stresses that the family is "the natural and fundamental group unit of society" and is entitled to protection by society and the state. Yet the word "family" here needs to be interpreted, and any interpretation carries a heavy weight of parochial cultural baggage. How extended may a family be? Sometimes whole tribes may be regarded as a single extended family. Is bigamy a human right? At the other extreme, would a state be offending against the Declaration if it prohibited single-parent families? The Article also guarantees that men and women are entitled to equal rights in marriage, but does this require the permission of marriage between members of the same sex? It may well seem that the greater the room for interpretation of Article 16, the less intrinsic meaning it has. The more room for human discretion, the less natural or universal meaning there can be here.

And what would Hobbes or Locke have said about Article 22? It says that everyone, as a member of society, has the right to *social security* and is entitled to the realization, through national effort and international cooperation and in accordance with the organization and resources of each state, of the economic, social and cultural rights indispensable for his dignity and the free development of his personality. Or Article 24, which (presupposing the right to work, to free choice of employment, to just and favourable conditions of work and to protection against unemployment expressed in Article 23) requires that everyone has periodic holidays with pay? It seems extraordinary that a right to periodic holidays with pay could exist naturally and independently of human political decision. If all the supposedly "human" rights are no better founded than this, then it seems we have merely added arbitrarily to the jumbled list of rights and claims to rights presented earlier. We might well ask a range of questions: how can we justify appealing to such rights as authoritative for us, either for us as individuals or as institutions or as states? How can we be motivated by, or blamed in the light of, such "independent" moral considerations, which may not be part of our culture? How are rights located in the rest of our morality and law? What rights do we have?

These issues are not a matter for the history of institutions or for political declarations. They express or presuppose our philosophical questions concerning justification and understanding, and it is the foundation for these that will frame this book.

This book is an introduction to rights, in the traditional sense in which philosophy is "introductory" to other subjects, which it introduces by presenting their foundations.[23] Philosophy has four interrelated core disciplines: ethics, logic, metaphysics and epistemology. Our interest in rights clearly falls within ethics, and the particular issues that will arise here relate closely to the other three philosophical disciplines. Logic names both the nature and the study of reasoning. Reason and its relation to moral thought has been a central issue in philosophy since ancient times, and its place in the understanding of rights will be central for us also. Metaphysics covers a range of issues, from questioning the existence of God to the nature of free will, but at its heart lie problems about the nature of reality and how external or independent, relative to human beings, "reality" is. This will be a central concern as well, and the theory of human nature is an intrinsic part of this. Epistemology is concerned with the theory of knowledge: about what knowledge (including moral knowledge) is and how claims to knowledge may be justified. Epistemology and metaphysics are linked through the simple thought that one cannot know what is not true, and what is true must in some way be real. Reason is linked to epistemology through the idea that one cannot know what cannot be justified, and reason (perhaps mathematical, perhaps experimental[24]) provides the justification. Reason is linked to metaphysics not only by way of its connection with epistemology but also by a particular understanding of what human beings are: that is, as essentially rational. We will see that this view of human nature is a crucial element in our understanding of rights. Reason is an essential feature of all philosophical disciplines since it characterizes the philosophical method of understanding in all areas. It requires clarity and exactness of expression. All these matters have a bearing on our ethical concerns and so on our concern with rights.

The existence of human rights presupposes, and they need to be understood against, a much broader background than that which is

---

23. Thus it is not this book's task to summarize current debates among rights theorists, not all of whom are addressing philosophical concerns.

24. The view that knowledge is based on reason is called "rationalism"; the view that knowledge is based on experience is called "empiricism".

specific to a particular country or a particular period of time. A common heritage of Western nations, and a contributory heritage of many countries once subject to Western empires, is the political under-standing of ancient Greece. The sophisticated moral and political philosophies of Socrates, Plato and Aristotle were developed in a context of Greek city-states with a long history of supernatural belief, and where there had always been a tendency to identify tradition or habit with what ought to be done.[25] Recording customary rules gave way to individual givers of codes of law treated as authoritative, and by the fifth century BCE the Athens of Socrates had a democracy. Yet even this democracy initially saw the laws as having an authority or independence difficult to alter. Later, however:

> new laws multiplied, the legislative process was degraded to an engine of political warfare, and even the recording of new laws became chaotic, so that it was often uncertain whether a new law existed or not, or whether a directly contradictory law might coexist with it.[26]

According to the legal historian John Kelly, one important thought arose only once among the Greek philosophers and orators who reflected about law, and that appears in a passage from Sophocles' *Antigone*:

> These laws were not ordained of Zeus,
> And she who sits enthroned with gods below,
> Justice, enacted not these human laws,
> Nor did I deem that thou, a mortal man,
> Couldst by a breath annul and override
> The immutable unwritten laws of heaven.
> They were not born today nor yesterday;
> They die not; and none knoweth whence they sprang.[27]

Otherwise, Kelly states, the Greeks "knew nothing of the idea that there exists a range of values, which, if human laws should conflict with them, render those laws invalid".[28] Even Aristotle, although dis-tinguishing "natural laws" from the positive laws commanded within states, saw such "natural laws" as laws of nature in the scientific sense

---

25. J. M. Kelly, *A Short History of Western Legal Theory* (Oxford: Clarendon Press, 1992), 9.
26. Kelly, *A Short History of Western Legal Theory*, 11.
27. *Ibid.*, 20.
28. *Ibid.*

of having universal characteristics rather than as independent values. It was not until the great construction of Roman jurisprudence that, in the writings of Cicero, we find natural laws conceived as natural values that might render invalid positive laws.[29]

It is an ancient question, then, whether any laws or rights can have an existence independent of the claims or assertions of particular jurisdictions. The modern yet almost religious belief that human rights have an eternal existence independent of human beings, but which human beings can come to know, suggests this same central philosophical question very clearly. The understanding of human rights and of rights in general essentially involves understanding the approaches to this philosophical issue, and the following chapters are framed in the light of it. On the one hand, we have "the immutable unwritten laws of heaven"; on the other hand, we have the answer that rights are given to us only by law. We cannot rest here with an intermediate suggestion, that human rights have an eternal and independent existence while other rights are given us only by law, for this unhelpfully assumes that justifications are available for both positions.

While the Greeks (apart from Sophocles) may just possibly have known nothing of the idea that there might be a range of naturally existing values, which, if human laws should conflict with them, would render those laws invalid, they certainly had the idea that there might be a range of naturally existing values. In Chapter 2 we shall examine Plato's position, and he will clarify for us the way in which such eternal moral existence might be understood. By contrast, the approach that denies that there might be naturally existing values is typically grounded in empiricism, that is, in the belief that knowledge, including knowledge of morality, should be understood as deriving solely from experience.

To contrast with Sophocles' rhetoric in favour of the "immutable unwritten laws of heaven" it is fair to present here one of the most famous passages of rhetoric against the idea of naturally existing values. The passage arises in an expression of the utilitarian moral philosophy that arose from the empiricist epistemology of the eighteenth-century philosopher David Hume (1711–1776). Utilitarianism is often expressed as the following moral principle: "an act is

---

29. *Ibid.*, 57ff. Whether these "natural values" are natural *rights* is a different question, and, in a conference paper "Human Rights – The Very Idea" (presented at Human Rights Colloquium, Corpus Christi College, Oxford, 6 July 2000), James Griffin draws our attention to Alan Gewirth's *Reason and Morality* (Chicago, IL: University of Chicago Press, 1978). The issue will not be addressed here.

right in so far as it tends to lead to the greatest happiness of the greatest number".[30] An essential point to note about this principle is that, according to it, it is the *consequences* of our actions, and *nothing else*, that determine whether our actions are right or wrong. This principle is offered as the sole standard for all moral matters. The late eighteenth-century Utilitarian Jeremy Bentham (1748–1832) made it clear that empiricism has no room for rights conceived as existing "naturally".

> Right ... is the child of law: from real laws come real rights; but from imaginary laws, from laws of nature, fancied and invented by poets, rhetoricians, and dealers in moral and intellectual poisons, come imaginary rights, a bastard brood of monsters ... Natural rights is simple nonsense: natural and imprescriptable rights, rhetorical nonsense – nonsense upon stilts.[31]

By "real laws" here Bentham means the laws of the state; those made by Parliament or other state legislatures and applied by judges. We have rights only if these positive laws give them to us. Bentham nevertheless recognized Utilitarianism as a standard of morality that is independent of the laws of the state. Yet Utilitarianism does not give us moral rights, for how a person ought to be treated depends on the consequences of that treatment, and there is nothing "fixed" or "absolute" about the answer. A claim to a so-called "right" does not even place the burden of proof on those who wish to override the "right", for everything is to be morally assessed solely on consequentialist grounds, that is, on the consequences of actions. Nevertheless, among the things to be assessed on utilitarian grounds are the laws themselves, and it is quite possible that utilitarian ends may be better achieved if certain rights are given to us by the law. Thus it is plausible to hold that the greatest happiness of the greatest number is better achieved in a state that gives its citizens the legal right to life, for example, than in a state that does not. The Utilitarians were liberals, and could recommend, on utilitarian grounds, the creation of legal rights as an efficient way of achieving moral

---

30. See J. S. Mill, *Utilitarianism*, reprinted in *John Stuart Mill and Jeremy Bentham: Utilitarianism and Other Essays*, A. Ryan (ed.) (Harmondsworth: Penguin, 1987). In what follows I capitalize the initial letters of the nouns (Utilitarian, Utilitarianism) but not those of the adjectives (utilitarian).

31. Quoted in S. I. Benn & R. S. Peters, *Social Principles and the Democratic State* (London: Allen & Unwin, 1959), Ch. 4, n. 9, from Bentham's *Anarchical Fallacies*, Works, vol. II, 523.

(= utilitarian) ends. Legal rights may thus be instituted as a means to an independent moral end. However, talking in terms of "moral" or "human" rights, on this approach, has proper use only as mere persuasive rhetoric.

Objectively, only legal rights can exist on the utilitarian approach, and these can be created only by legal systems. The legal rights a person actually has will depend upon the system in question. A right is legal if it is expressed and "protected" by a legal system. "Protected" by a legal system does not necessarily mean "enforced" by that system, for, in the event of a transgression against one's legal rights, one might receive compensation instead. Note that it would only be correct to say that rights are "recognized" by legal systems if those rights exist independently of legal systems, and on the utilitarian approach rights have no such independent existence. While, for the Utilitarian, rights do not exist independently of law, at least morality exists, in the independent existence of the principle of Utilitarianism itself. The rights the law actually gives us can therefore be criticized, if necessary, by referring to this independent moral standard.[32] Morality, understood in terms of the principle of Utilitarianism, exists as an independent standard; but rights do not.

However, not all theorists are so generous to morality – or claim so much for morality – as the Utilitarian. Hobbes held that *all* morality is grounded in law.

> The desires, and other passions of man, are in themselves no sin. No more are the actions, that proceed from those passions, till they know a law that forbids them: which till laws be made they cannot know: nor can any law be made, till they have agreed upon the person that shall make it.[33]

On this view, law is made by the "person agreed upon" or sovereign (sovereign here does not necessarily mean an individual "king", for

---

32. See T. M. Scanlon, "Rights, Goals, and Fairness", in *Theories of Rights*, J. Waldron (ed.), 137–52: "I am thus drawn to a two-tier view: one that gives an important role to consequences in the justification and interpretation of rights but which takes rights seriously as placing limits on consequentialist reasoning at the level of casuistry" (pp. 137–8). Definition of casuistry: "that part of Ethics which resolves cases of conscience, applying the general rules of religion and morality to particular instances in which 'circumstances alter cases', or in which there appears to be a conflict of duties. Often (and perhaps originally) applied to a quibbling or evasive way of dealing with difficult cases of duty" (Oxford English Dictionary, OED2 on CD-ROM Version 1.11 © OUP 1994 and © Software BV 1994).
33. Hobbes, *Leviathan*, Ch. 13.

the "Queen in Parliament" is traditionally sovereign in the United Kingdom, although today the European Union has a role in validating legislation). So much the Utilitarian might agree with. However, against the Utilitarian, it is not only rights that are made by law, but all determination of "sin", or right and wrong. Thus there is for Hobbes no independent morality by which to judge the law. For Hobbes, private self-interest alone makes people accept the sovereign's law, and we prefer any law to no law at all. Thus nothing can warrant a claim to a moral right apart from the legal system itself. The law itself determines what counts as morality, whatever the law is.

So, are there independent naturally existing eternal human rights? How are these and other rights located in our moral or legal understanding? We cannot even take for granted a distinction between law and morality, for there are different philosophical positions on this. Whether human rights are to be held to be different from other moral rights or from legal rights depends on our philosophical theory, as we have seen: Hobbes and Locke give different answers. We have already noted questions about the authority of human rights and about how we may be motivated by such moral considerations. It is not clear what natural moral rights, if any, we have, or how claims that there are such rights are to be justified. As already seen, these questions about rights do not have a completely determinate meaning without some presupposed philosophical approach, and we will explain just how various philosophies yield their different answers. To deal with these questions we will examine the approaches of Plato, Hobbes, Locke, Hume, Immanuel Kant (1724–1804) and the American jurist Wesley Hohfeld (1879–1918).

We have noted the wide range of uses of the concept of rights in contemporary Western culture. We have noted the importance of the concept in organizing our moral and legal understanding. We have noted the moral authority of human rights for us and their claim to universality. Of the many questions that may be asked, our particular philosophical concern is with the justification and understanding of claims to rights. Our initial central line of argument will involve the questions: do human rights have an independent eternal existence, and what does the "reality" of such rights involve? Grasping this will help us understand the relevance of different theories of human nature and the point of issues concerning motivation. We shall see that essentially connected to the questions about the existence and justification of rights are further issues about the relation of rights to reason, and the independent existence of reason.

Questioning the independent eternal existence of human rights is just one way of expressing the more general philosophical issue of whether any moral ideals or standards can have an independent eternal existence. As we shall see in Chapter 2, despite not using the concept of "rights", Plato, in his *Republic*, nevertheless locates this same central moral issue by asking the question "What is justice?". In Chapter 2 we will seek an understanding of two particular matters: the way in which we might understand a moral ideal to be fundamental and independent of human beings; and the way in which apparently separate issues of reason, reality, knowledge and morality articulate with each other.

We shall see that Plato understands human nature to have a threefold structure based on motivation: we can be motivated by reason, by respect for force or by desire, and different classes of people are motivated in these different ways. These three grounds of motivation are not merely that but are linked in an essential way to what it is to be of good or bad character. To be of good character is to have self-mastery by the rational part of the self. A just state is, in a related way, one that is ruled by those of such good character. Essential to Plato's position here is the claim that justice or goodness is something that is grasped through a rational intellectual understanding.

"Justice", on Plato's theory, is the "master moral concept". It expresses the sole unified standard of goodness. Other words of ethical evaluation differ only in superficial features; each expresses, as it were, a view of the same central idea: on the one hand, that moral perfection which is exemplified in the integrity of the good human character; and on the other hand, that same moral perfection which is exemplified in all the features that form a just and unified state. We may then understand rights to be authoritative just in so far as they are a way of expressing that central moral perfection.

On Plato's approach the authority of rights, indistinguishable from the authority of any other moral perfection, consists in their *truth*. He sets for us the central claim, which will guide us through to Chapter 5, that moral truth is to be understood in terms of an independent, unchanging and consistent reality known about in a special way. This truth is then interpreted "realistically", a philosophical term that in this context means that truth is seen as involving correspondence to a really existing abstract reality.[34] This truth is grasped by the exercise

---

34. In general, a metaphysical belief is "realist" when it holds reality to exist *independently of human beings*. A metaphysical belief is "antirealist" when it holds that reality is dependent in some way on us. There are, briefly, two ways of being

of reason, and can be grasped in no other way. Plato conceives knowledge as directly motivating for those who have it. Morality is thus authoritative and effective. As to what our particular rights, if any, actually are, Plato gives us no answer.

We shall see that a distinctive feature of Plato's approach was his dialectical method, whereby the truth emerged into the public space of a conversation by questioning and criticism. Essential to the effectiveness of this is the view that the people involved share the same standards of reasoning. Reason, for Plato, provides *knowledge* of the ethical or just, and the ethical is conceived as a single unchanging consistent reality that is independently authoritative for all of us who have the rational capability to know it. Morality, for Plato, is something independent, eternal and consistent, and known through the exercise of reason. Following Plato, we may understand human rights in much the same way. Plato gives us reason to believe his approach to ethics by providing an understanding of reasoning involving a theory of knowledge and also a metaphysics that includes a theory of human nature. Plato will thus locate for us the ways in which the core disciplines of philosophy relate to each other, an overview necessary for a proper understanding of the philosophy of rights. Plato will show us that there are three elements of the "reality" of the central ethical standard – and so of human rights similarly conceived – that concern us, and these will set us the book's structure: that human rights are *independent*, that they are *eternal*, and that they are *consistent*.

In Chapter 3 we will turn to the seventeenth-century thinker Hobbes, who, unlike Plato, makes explicit reference to rights in his political theory. Our earlier mention of Hobbes shows how different from Plato's position his must be, for Hobbes does not allow morality to have some independent eternal existence but rather makes morality the child of law, and law is for him a consequence of human choice. Where Plato saw human nature as having a threefold structure, with different classes of people a consequence of this, Hobbes saw everyone as equal in their fundamental characteristics. For Hobbes, all reality is material and experienceable rather than, as for Plato, abstract and intellectually apprehended. Thus we will see that Hobbes has a

---

antirealist: (i) anciently, when we hold that reality is nothing more than what we perceive it to be, so that it consists of "perceptions" or ideas in our minds – this approach is often called "idealism" instead; (ii) more recently, when we hold that we cannot "mean" by "reality" anything that completely escapes the general characteristics of human language – the dependence of reality, alternatively, *what we count reality to be*, is inescapably on us.

different metaphysics, a different epistemology and a different theory of human nature from Plato. Even reason, for him, is weak, being subordinated to the effective achievement of our desires. Nevertheless, our examination of Hobbes will show that foundational to Hobbes's theory is – as it was for Plato – an understanding of reason as setting all of humanity a common standard. Despite a very different superstructure of moral and legal understanding, Plato and Hobbes share a clear respect for the fundamental authority of reason. Both see reason as an independent and eternal standard. On the basis of such reason, Hobbes understands rights in what are effectively two different senses. First, rights may be unprotected freedoms that exist naturally. (Rights as unprotected freedoms, however, are not what we normally mean by rights, as we will see in our later study of Hohfeld.) Secondly, rights have no natural existence, but are rather a creature of rational human choice: rights are made by laws, and laws are made by those (the individual or consistent collective will) whom we choose to make them – what Hobbes calls the sovereign. Human rights as understood in the way permitted by Plato are not possible for Hobbes, yet for both Plato and Hobbes reason has independent authority as the ultimate justification in our thinking about rights.

It has long been a tradition in philosophy that reason should be in some way essential to moral understanding. It was exactly this understanding of reason that, 40 years after Hobbes, Locke used to express, with an explicitness familiar to us today, the idea of natural rights. Locke claimed for us all, in particular, the rights to life, health, liberty and property. In Chapter 4 we will find that Locke, like Plato and Hobbes, sees reason as an independent and eternal standard. For Locke, this independence and eternity are warranted by the God-given nature of reason. Hobbes thinks that the requirements of reason are something about which people may disagree, while Locke thinks its requirements are plain to all. We will thus see in Locke a presentation of natural rights as being eternal, consistent and independent of human choice. By this stage of the book, we will have come to see clearly the arguments for the alternative positions here: using in part the rationalism of Plato we can understand Locke's position as expressing objectively existing human rights; following Hobbes, by contrast, we may understand rights as created by people. Yet we will have seen that Hobbes relies on independent reason to warrant the legitimacy of the laws that create those rights. Plato, Hobbes and Locke all share the foundational view that the ultimate constraints on us are, again, *independent*, *eternal* and *consistent*.

By the end of Chapter 4 it will have become appropriate to question whether there is some independent eternal and consistent reality that underlies moral and legal understanding. We will deal with the three elements in order, examining "independence" in Chapter 5, "eternity" in Chapter 9 and "consistency" in Chapter 10. Our presentation of Locke's position in Chapter 4 will be followed in Chapter 5 by an examination of the eighteenth-century philosopher Hume's position. Hume cast doubt on the external authority of reason, and stressed experience as foundational to all knowledge and ethics. We cannot, he says, be motivated by external standards of reason, and reason cannot give us the content of any standards independent of personal desires or experience. Since reason cannot express any externally authoritative eternal standard, then natural rights as permitted by Plato and as understood by Locke cannot exist for us. The idea must be "nonsense on stilts", as Bentham later expressed it. Moreover, reason cannot supply an external standard to warrant the legitimacy of Hobbes's sovereign, either. We will see, from the contrast between the empiricism of Hume and the rationalism of Plato, that the issue of whether rights can express *independent* authoritative standards is an issue within the long-standing conflict between empiricism and rationalism.

Who is right, Plato or Hume? The conflict between rationalism and empiricism was one that, towards the end of the eighteenth century, Immanuel Kant tried to resolve, and in Chapter 6 we will present the major contribution that he made to our understanding of morality and of rights in particular. In an important way Hume was right: reason is not independent of human beings. Kant explains that reason is authoritative for us and can motivate us because it structures us as human beings and is also an essential part of our own structuring of the experienced world. Yet reason, and the morality that it underpins, while losing its metaphysical independence, does not lose its eternal character. There is a fundamental and eternal consistency both of human nature and of experienced reality. It is that consistency of reality that makes modern science possible. The world, as Hume noted, is a regular place. The success of science both supports and is warranted by Kant's rational foundation of human understanding. The character of human understanding is an essential feature of what it is to be human, and reason is thus able to express our human nature and thereby what is valuable about us as human beings. We may then understand human rights as expressing and protecting our eternal dignity and autonomy as rational human beings. Human rights, on this approach, are not *independent* but they are *universal*.

Kant's philosophy was importantly based on his analysis of human language, because the way we use language expresses the structures of our minds and so of our understanding. The rationality of the world and of morality is reflected in this. In Chapter 7 we shall see that the analysis of language has come to be central to modern philosophy. Once we have left behind the idea of rights or other moral ideals as existing independently of human beings then, following Kant, we may understand their dependent existence and content as crucially bound up with the rationality that is essential both to human nature and to the scientific world. Central to grasping the place of rights in our understanding will be an analysis of the language we use to talk about them, and this approach will also be explained in Chapter 7.

At the beginning of the twentieth century, Hohfeld made a major contribution to the "scientific" analysis of the ambiguous language of rights and duties, and in terms of this we shall be able to locate universal human rights and also those other moral and legal rights that feature in specific cultures and jurisdictions. Hohfeld offered his system as a way of making sense of the full range of practical legal concerns and as a way of solving legal problems. As we present Hohfeld's exact analytical jurisprudence in Chapter 7, and analyse the nature of his analysis in Chapter 8, we shall see that he partly sought to describe existing linguistic practice and partly sought to prescribe a corrected use of the language of rights according to eternal standards of reason. Reason was, for Hohfeld as for so many before him, an important value that should be fostered, and his analysis presupposed a Kantian respect for eternal standards of consistency.

Moral reality was originally presented by Plato as independent, eternal and consistent, and this permitted human rights to be understood in the same way. We have seen the essential role of independent and eternal standards of reason in this. By Chapter 6 we will, with Kant, have removed the early commitment to the independence of these standards and replaced it with the idea of universality. There yet remain two further difficulties: the commitment to the unchanging nature of these standards, whatever their status; and the commitment to consistency. Chapters 7 and 8 will show both of these traditional features of reason to have been accepted by Hohfeld. Moreover, that, ultimately, rights are essentially consistent with each other is a widespread modern conviction.

We shall, however, see weaknesses in using reason in this way to ground an understanding of rights. The limitations and political implications of an appeal to reason are matters to which, in the twentieth century, a number of postmodern writers drew attention, but the difficulties here were introduced by Kant, introduced, indeed, in a way inconsistent with the core of his philosophical approach. A traditional understanding of rights as eternal and as essentially consistent with each other is undermined by these difficulties. In Chapter 9 we present Kant's view that human nature and its supposedly fixed rational structures change over time and so make plausible the denial of the traditional requirement of the unchanging nature of moral standards. The attempts to ground human rights in unchanging human nature fail just because, and in so far as, there is no such thing as unchanging human nature.

In Chapter 10 we will note the further Kantian implication that reason changes over time and so permits the inconsistency of absolute moral standards like human rights. We will illustrate the idea of such a plurality of inconsistent standards by referring to Isaiah Berlin and to Ronald Dworkin, and restate their somewhat metaphorically expressed positions by arguing for the intelligibility of the idea that our moral reality, and with it our understanding of rights, may indeed be inherently inconsistent. We nevertheless respect consistency throughout: we will argue that a pluralist reality cannot be completely and consistently described within a single point of view, but that it can be if a multiplicity of points of view are adopted and tolerated. We will need to recognize different points of view if we are to encompass all our moral understanding. We will conclude the relevant parts of the arguments of the preceding chapters by observing that human rights have no independent metaphysical existence, are not plausibly universal, may with reason change over time and may be intelligibly inconsistent with each other.

In Chapter 11 we will argue that problems of the clarification of rights remain, and we will show that Hohfeld's position requires an understanding of the concepts of right and duty which is prior to his analysis. Distinguishing the meanings of moral terms from the criteria for their application, and avoiding unwanted metaphysical commitments, we shall see that three points of view for a full understanding of rights are required: that understanding rights is prior to understanding duties; that understanding duties is prior to understanding rights; and that understanding rights and understanding duties are mutually supporting.

There has been historical change over long periods of time in our beliefs about what our rights and duties are. In Chapter 12 we will present John Finnis's explanation of a change of priority of understanding from a justice-based to a rights-based approach. We will use this account to analyse the rights-based approach, in which the point of view of the beneficiary of a just situation is primary. We will look at the nature of the "individuals" who might be bearers of rights understood in this way, and examine whether groups and non-humans might have human rights. We will examine one feminist idea that rights are essentially held by individuals who are selfish and incapable of full association with others so that reference to "rights" is essentially reference to a male-based morality. We will distinguish the "interest" from the "will" theory of rights and show that the point of view of the beneficiary does not imply the will theory.

To continue towards the fuller understanding sought, in Chapter 13 we will examine duty-based and justice-based conceptions of rights. We will try to make sense of Kant's moral philosophy as a duty-based conception of rights, and will show that only part of his philosophy permits this. In so far as we follow Kant in valuing the freedom and autonomy of another person, then we shall find that his moral philosophy places rights as prior to duties, rather than duties as prior to rights. We will suggest that only if we understand morality and law entirely in terms of what can be enforced might we be able to make sense of duty as the prior concept in our understanding. We will conclude Chapter 13 by examining the view that rights and duties are in some way mutually supporting features of a just situation. This priority of justice will be explained in terms of John Rawls's *A Theory of Justice*.

The concluding chapter, Chapter 14, will begin with a summary of the argument so far. We will then note that, just as there are arguments about the content of rights, and just as there are myriad claims to rights, so there are pluralities of theories that offer some understanding of the moral and legal realm and of the places that rights may hold in it. Philosophical theories themselves conflict just as rights can do, and we will present an understanding of such conflicts by using the concept of toleration.

The proliferation of opposing rights and their theories means that rights, and particularly human rights, cannot themselves be the ultimate ground for determining the ordering of conflicting moral demands. Moreover, we are no longer in a position to insist on consistency. At this point we will examine the approach of Steiner, who suggests that rights supply adversaries with reasons to back off from interference when they have no other reason to allow the performance of the actions they wish to interfere with. He insists in his own answer on the compossibility of rights, which again begs the question in favour of consistency, but he usefully characterizes an adversarial situation in terms of three moral points of view that map onto the points of view we present in Chapter 10, where we recognize the need to make intelligible a pluralist view of moral reality by referring to an observer who is external to the contestants.

Drawing on the argument of Chapter 10, in our concluding chapter we will hold that such an external observer needs a criterion for moral truth, but that this criterion cannot have the content of *any* contestant-centred criteria for rights, for that begs the question he faces in deciding between them. We will argue by analogy with Steiner's argument, but ignoring his insistence on consistency, that, since contestant-centred criteria for rights cannot be eligible to serve as a standard of choice for the observer, it follows that any difference between contestant-centred criteria for rights cannot be regarded by the observer as relevant. For the observer, all contestant-centred criteria are then equivalent. Thus the content of a right and its justifying rights theory cannot be provided by the content of what the contestants disagree about, since the disagreement remains to be decided even when one contestant admits that the rights of his opponent provide him with a reason to tolerate the position of that opponent. Disagreement is a presupposition of toleration. Where it is rights or their theories that are disagreed about, then the very fact of conflict means that neither contestant's moral code contains a reason to *accept*, as opposed to *tolerate*, the relevant part of the moral code of the other.

Where a right is claimed that, in the pluralist situation, requires toleration, then from the point of view of the observer it is only a formal demand for freedom without further moral content that can justify that right against another. As Steiner rightly asks, the observer should ask "Who should have the freedom here?" As Kant said, "right is ... the sum of the conditions under which the choice of one can be united with the choice of another in accordance with a universal law of freedom".[35] Kant and Steiner, however, insist on universal consistency. A pluralist account of inconsistent rights and rights theories is possible by recognizing that the question "Who should have the freedom here?" is one for a specific context. We need not insist on the answer being generalizable. A narrowly understood "theory of

---

35. Quoted by Steiner ("Working Rights", 276, n. 71) from I. Kant *The Metaphysics of Morals*, M. Gregor (trans.) (Cambridge: Cambridge Universtiy Press, 1991), 56.

justice" is then required to determine by localized pragmatic procedures, which maximize freedom, which rights claims take priority in specific conflict situations. There is no other philosophy for prioritizing philosophies of rights.

CHAPTER 2

Plato

How can rights be authoritative? How can our individual and social choices be "constrained" by rights? How can we be motivated by such moral considerations? What rights do we have? How may we justify claims to rights? These questions have, at best, only a superficial clarity. More fundamental matters need to be understood in order to crystallize the puzzlements that they express. To clarify questions such as these we turn to a number of theories in moral philosophy. The first of these theories is Plato's (c.427–c.347BCE), and we will be able to find this first approach by outlining the relevant parts of the position he expresses in *The Republic*. Here we will seek an understanding of two particular matters: first, the way in which we might understand a moral ideal to be independent of human beings and so apparently capable of "constraining" their choices; secondly, the way in which apparently separate issues of reason, reality, knowledge and morality articulate with each other.

The Republic is written in the form of a dialogue, in which the main character is Plato's own teacher, Socrates. The book begins with Socrates describing his return walk to Athens from its seaport, the Piraeus. Chasing after him comes a slave boy with orders to Socrates to wait for his master, Polemarchus. On catching up, Polemarchus points out the superior number of his own companions and pretends to threaten Socrates with force unless Socrates returns with them to the Piraeus. Socrates mildly suggests that Polemarchus might be reasoned with and successfully persuaded that Socrates might continue on his way, but Polemarchus responds that persuasion will not work if he does not listen, and he will not listen. One of

Polemarchus' companions, Adeimantus, tries a different tack: he informs Socrates that a torch race on horseback will be held later. Knowing Socrates' pleasures, he refers also to the all-night festival to be held with its opportunities for conversation. This does the trick, and Socrates returns with them, saying "if it is so resolved, that's how we must act".[1] In this way, within the first page or so of *The Republic*, we find Plato's understanding of human motivation as having a threefold structure: we can be motivated by respect for force, by reason or by desire.

On his return to the Piraeus, Socrates asks Polemarchus' father, Cephalus, what it is like to be old. Cephalus has a contented old age, but observes that some of his friends, equally aged, do not. Cephalus, with Socrates' very clear approval, puts this down to character. Those of bad character have given in to their desires throughout their lives, but are now too old to satisfy them. By contrast, those of good character who have mastered their own desires throughout their lives find that, as they get older and their desires grow weaker, such self-mastery becomes even easier. It is in these ways that both the discontentment and the contentment of the old are to be understood. We, the readers, are to understand that the three grounds of motivation to which we were earlier introduced are not merely grounds of motivation but are linked in some essential way to what it is to be of good and bad character.

Socrates tries next to question Cephalus about the "goodness" or "justice" of such a contented character. Cephalus declines to discuss further and gives up the conversation to others, leaving the parting suggestion that justice consists in telling the truth and giving to others what you owe them.

The dialogue or conversational form of *The Republic* is crucial to it. Socrates, through Plato, does not give us the answer straightaway to his question "what is justice?" He makes explicit the processes of thought that lead to an answer. These processes, however, are not presented as processes of his *own* thought. It is *Cephalus* who is

---

1. Plato, *The Republic of Plato*, 2nd edn, with notes and an interpretive essay by A. Bloom (trans.) (New York: Basic Books, 1991), 327a–328b. As Bloom observes in a footnote, the expression "it is resolved" was used in the political assembly to announce that a law had been passed. That Socrates uses this expression when the determination had been made on the basis of *desire* – the wrong kind of motivation from Socrates' point of view, but a correct description of the democratic basis on which the political assembly made its decisions – shows Socrates' deliberate use of irony (*ibid.*, 441, n. 6).

asked the question, and *Cephalus*, and his successors in the discussion, who continue to be asked it. Cephalus' answer, that justice consists in telling the truth and giving to others what you owe them, is criticized by Socrates, but the criticism has a special form. Instead of merely telling Cephalus that he is wrong, or offering Cephalus reasons why he might be persuaded to think himself wrong, Socrates assumes that Cephalus is right, and draws a conclusion from Cephalus' answer, a conclusion that is presented as rightly and logically drawn according to mutually shared standards of reasoning. Does Cephalus share this conclusion? If he does not – and in the brief period during which Cephalus engages with this part of the discussion, Socrates' view is that he does not – then he has not expressed himself sufficiently accurately in the first place. The idea is that, when you say something, you mean by it both that which is explicit and that which is implicit: in other words, that which is logically implied.

Cephalus' answer to the question "What is justice?" and Socrates' response well illustrate the structure of the reasoning. Cephalus' answer – and for simplicity of explanation I shall pick only part of his answer – is that justice consists in giving what you owe. If Socrates, in asking Cephalus, is to find out what "justice" *really* means, then he will have to find out what Cephalus *really* means by this answer.[2] So Socrates asks him (and Cephalus' successors in the discussion) what exactly is implied by different interpretations of "owe". For example, does "what you owe" mean "what you have promised to return"? That would imply that it would be just or right to return a weapon to a person from whom you had borrowed it, even if the person had turned homicidal in the meantime. Does Cephalus *really mean* that it would be right to do this? He does not; but it is then necessary for him to re-express his original answer to avoid such an implication (it was at this point that he gave up). By this conversational procedure, taken over by Cephalus' successors, what is "really meant" is clarified and developed, but all the time this search for the answer consists, not in Socrates providing an answer, but in those involved in the conversation engaging in an intellectual search, governed by exact standards of logical reasoning,

---

2. Contemporary work in the theory of meaning would often distinguish very strongly between what words or sentences mean and what the people who use them mean. No such distinction is made here; indeed, it is essential that it should not be made. Further consideration of this important issue is outside the scope of this book.

into what it is that, "deep down", they really understand justice to be.[3] The logical reasoning involved in Socrates' and others' contributions to the dialogue thus comes to yield a knowledge of what justice really is, as Plato presents it here.

By this point we have begun to grasp Plato's link between the three grounds of motivation and the nature of good and bad character, and also his link between reasoned argument and knowledge of what goodness is. The implication that justice or goodness is itself something that is grasped through a rational intellectual understanding is questioned by some of Socrates' interlocutors, however; it seems obvious to them that the kind of "goodness" that Socrates is uncovering in his intellectual way is not what *they* meant by "goodness" at all. To start with, such "goodness" is not *good for you*. What is good for you is getting what you *want*, which requires having the power to do so. It is desire that counts, not reason. You don't need intellectual effort to find out what you want, nor need you share your wants. And who, of any maturity, wants the justice or goodness Socrates is seeking? You don't benefit from this rationally discovered "goodness"; you don't get rich; it cannot help you afford to pay your debts. An extremely powerful presentation is made by Thrasymachus and, a little later, Glaucon, of the view that "justice consists in the interests of the strong", and Socrates recognizes that his efforts have to be at a much deeper level than so far.

Plato presents Socrates developing, through the rational means already described, an understanding of what it is to be both a person of good character and a just society or state, and the structure of this understanding can be briefly expressed as follows: justice or goodness of character in the individual person is fundamentally identical with justice in the state. Justice, in the individual and the state, consists in keeping the parts in the proper balance. With regard to the individual self, its parts are reason, courage[4] and desire. The proper balance between these parts consists in weighing reason as superior to the other two: to be a just person, reason must master courage and desire.

---

3. I use the expression "deep down" to suggest the idea that the intellectual procedure, although involving exact logical reasoning, is not unlike recovering a long-forgotten memory. This alludes to Plato's view that such knowledge may be "recollection"; see Plato, *Phaedo*, D. Gallop (ed. and trans.) (Oxford: Oxford University Press, 1975).

4. This is an inexact translation and the implications of "courage", otherwise "spirit", can be of philosophical importance. In Ch. 1 it was glossed as "respect for force". The issues are not relevant here, however.

This is *self*-mastery, because Plato sees the rational part of the self as the true self. Different people have different characters: some people have self-mastery, with reason as their master motivation; some are mastered by courage, a somewhat unthinking although meritorious and helpful emotion; others are mastered by desire.

With regard to the state, the parts are: the class of those mastered by reason (the philosophers), the class of those mastered by courage (the military) and the class of those mastered by desire (tradespeople). That tradespeople are essentially "mastered by desire" is not some special Socratic bias on the part of the philosophical ruling class, but is a thought reflected in the bases of our modern economic understanding, a thought that applies to everyone. It is, for example, a fundamental assumption of neoclassical microeconomic theory that a person's goal is to maximize his or her own welfare, and a person's welfare depends only on his or her own consumption (with no sympathy or antipathy towards others). Each choice by a person is guided immediately by the pursuit of his or her own goal.[5] While advances in economic theory have qualified this approach in various

---

5. As summarized by A. Sen, *On Ethics and Economics* (Oxford: Basil Blackwell, 1987), 80ff. In more detail, the assumptions are: a rational economic man is, first of all, rational. "Rationality" here is understood in a special way, so that the following are true:

i. For any individual A and any two options X and Y, one and only one of the following is true: A prefers X to Y; A prefers Y to X; A is indifferent between X and Y.

ii. A's preferences among options are transitive. (This means that, if X is preferred to Y, and Y is preferred to Z, then X is preferred to Z; and if A is indifferent between X and Y, and indifferent between Y and Z, then A is indifferent between X and Z.)

iii. A seeks to maximize his or her utility, where the utility of an option X is greater than the utility of an option Y for A if and only if A prefers X to Y. The utilities of options are equal just in case the agent is indifferent between them. (In other words, more of what you think is good for you is always preferred to less.)

One becomes rational economic man rather than just rational man simply by recognizing that among the options available to us are the acquisition of commodities, so that the following is true:

iv. If option X is acquiring commodity bundle X' and option Y is acquiring commodity bundle Y', and if Y' contains at least as much of each commodity as X' and more of at least one commodity, then everybody prefers Y to X.

Finally, the following assumption is made:

v. The marginal utility of any commodity diminishes as the quantity increases. (Thus, the more you have of something, the more of it you will be willing to give up in order to get something else you want. An additional bag of gold means less to a millionaire than it does to a beggar, for example. See C. Dyke, *Philosophy of Economics* (Englewood Cliffs, NJ: Prentice-Hall, 1981), 35, 51.)

ways, the core idea is that all human beings are assumed by such theory to be motivated by actual self-interest maximization. For Socrates, by contrast, only some are so motivated. Others are motivated by reason, others still by courage. For Socrates, the proper balance between these three classes of people consists in making the reason-mastered class govern the other two: in the ideal and just state, philosopher-rulers use military helpers to govern the mass of the people.

Only a state governed by those who have self-mastery or rational self-control can ensure justice. Justice is ensured by this, and it is important to recognize that "justice" here is not to be narrowly understood. It is not just one dimension of the ethically valuable. All ethically valuable considerations, both for the state and for the individual, are covered by the concept of "justice" here. All are to be understood through the theory. There may seem difficulties: thus Plato's ideal state is undemocratic. But democracy, for him, is rule by the mass of the people, which is rule by those enslaved by their desires, which is rule by those ignorant of the good, and is thus inherently unjust. Again, Plato's state may seem totalitarian in its lack of freedom,[6] but this betrays a lack of understanding of what "freedom" really is. On Plato's view, the ideal state is one of true freedom, since it is not a state enslaved by desire. You are not free when you are a slave to your desires. Freedom is mastery by the true self, mastery by the rational self, mastery by knowledge of what is really good.

How, we asked earlier, can rights be authoritative? How can we be motivated by such moral considerations? How can our individual and social choices be "constrained" by rights? Already we can see that these questions take their significance from the background moral theory. Plato did not consider "rights" at all. But then he did not need to, given his philosophy. "Justice", on his theory, is the "master moral concept". It expresses the sole unified standard of goodness.[7] Other

---

6. See R. H. S. Crossman, *Plato Today* (London: Allen & Unwin, 1937), and K. R. Popper, *The Open Society and Its Enemies* [1945], vol. 1 (London: Routledge & Kegan Paul, 1966).

7. A detail: the meaning of the unity of the virtues is debatable; is it simply that the possession of any one of them implies that of all the others, or are they just different names for one and the same thing? Cf. especially G. Vlastos, "The Unity of the Virtues in the *Protagoras*", in *Platonic Studies*, G. Vlastos, 221–69 (Princeton, NJ: Princeton University Press, 1973). (From Plato, *Meno*, R. W. Sharples (ed. and trans.) (Warminster: Aris & Phillips, 1991), 21, n. 41.) Consistency is ensured either way.

words of ethical evaluation differ only in superficial features; each expresses, as it were, a view of the same central idea: on the one hand, that moral perfection which is exemplified in the integrity of the good human character; and on the other hand, that same moral perfection which is exemplified in all the features that form a just and unified state. We may understand rights to be authoritative just in so far as they are one way of expressing that central moral perfection, and "rights" may be in this a subordinate concept to "justice". Talking in terms of rights would then mean attending to some particular feature of justice, a feature that is unified with the rest of what justice is understood to be. Yet – while not Plato's expression of the position – "rights" may themselves come to be seen as the "master moral concept" in so far as they come to be central in our moral understanding, with "justice", in so far as that is something different, subordinate to them. We may still continue to see human rights in terms of Plato's justification.

What, then, makes Plato's understanding of justice authoritative for us? Accepting Plato's theory of human nature takes us only so far. Suppose he is right: reason, courage and desire are the three parts of the human self, with different people motivated more by one of these parts than by another, so that we can understand society as being made of three classes of people. Why should those mastered by reason get the ruling position? Why does rational self-control ensure goodness of character?

The plausibility of Plato's position derives from the plausibility of the view that you cannot be good unless you *know* what it is to be good; again, it is plausible to hold that only a state governed by those who have *knowledge* of what is really good, and in addition act accordingly, can ensure justice. It is Plato's theory of knowledge, associated with his theory of human nature, that gives his position its rational persuasiveness. Within the history of philosophy, theories of knowledge are generally classified into two kinds: empiricism and rationalism. Empiricism holds that knowledge comes only from experience. Rationalism holds that knowledge comes from reason, at least in part, and in its purest form holds that knowledge comes *only* from reason. Plato is a pure rationalist. Knowledge for him comes only from reason, and that means that knowledge of what is good or bad, right or wrong, just or unjust and so forth, also comes only from reason. To act rightly or justly, therefore, one must be motivated by such knowledge, and this requires that one be motivated by reason, which alone yields that knowledge.

The idea of the "master moral concept" goes along with this rationalist approach. There is perceived to be a single central idea embodying the moral perfection both of human character and of the just state. The various moral terms we use – goodness, justice, rights and the like – are all different ways of expressing this unified idea, and are therefore all *consistent* with each other. The standards of reason are essentially standards of consistency. The ethical forms a single internally consistent idea. Moreover, reason provides *knowledge* of this kind of thing: the idea in question is not merely something in our several heads, but something we can *share*, something *about which* we have knowledge and so something *independent* of each of us, something *unchangeable* and so *universal*. When we express that knowledge successfully then we do so in *true* sentences, and it is the consistent, unchangeable and independent idea of moral perfection that is the touchstone for the truth of what we believe here. As we work through Plato's epistemology in order to grasp his ethics we thus find a metaphysics at the heart of it.

Notice that what is known here is an independent, unchanging and consistent *reality*.[8] It is not, however, a reality like that yielded by our everyday senses. It is not something that can be seen, tasted or felt, but is rather something abstract. Its abstractness does not make it less real, however; on the contrary, it is the things that can be accessed through the everyday senses that are less real, for the everyday experienced world is in constant change. Our senses cannot be relied upon to yield eternal truth, for they constantly mislead us. We can see the distinction that Plato is getting at if we think, as he did, of Euclidean geometry. We know and can prove by reason the various character-istics of a right-angled triangle, for example, but no perfect example of such a triangle can be experienced. We might use drawings of triangles to help us in our thinking, but the perfect triangle that our geometrical conclusions truly describe exists in a world that can be accessed only intellectually. The reality expressed by such geometrical truths is nevertheless independent of us, it is eternal and it is consistent. Plato called such perfect ideas the "Forms". It is the Form of the Good that is central to his enquiry here.

Plato's conclusions thus depend on three things: (i) his theory of human motivation, which for goodness of character essentially involves motivation on the basis of the degree of knowledge of what is good; (ii) his theory of knowledge, his epistemology, his theory of

8. See also Plato, *Phaedo*.

how people can have knowledge of what is good; (iii) his metaphysics, his theory of the nature of that reality which knowledge expresses.[9] Leaving "courage" aside as not relevant to the argument at this point, Plato effectively presents to us two central conceptions of human motivation, each with its associated account of degree of understanding of what is good. The first conception is that of the philosopher, who is motivated by knowledge of the Form of the Good. Such knowledge derives from reason and not from experienced sensation or desire. Such reason gives us our true moral purposes. The second conception is that of the tradesperson, who is motivated merely by "belief" about what is good. This belief is an expression of desire and is thus supported by experienced sensation (since desire is a kind of sensation) and not by reason. For such a person, reason does not set the moral purpose but is at best a mere means to an end: the purpose of satisfying that person's desires. For the rationalist Plato, the tradesperson's belief about what is good is false. Knowledge cannot be grounded in experience, and thus desire cannot be the basis for morality. It is *ignorance* of what is good that characterizes the tradesperson's motivation, and acting wrongly is a failure of knowledge. Respect for rights, like any other way of expressing our motivation by what is moral, requires knowledge. What we know, when we have such knowledge, is the truth about some independent, fixed and consistent moral reality. Any authority that rights may have then consists in their being part of that reality, and the authority of what we say our rights are would consist in truthful correspondence to that independent, unchanging and consistent reality. Here we find one foundation for the idea of independently existing human rights.

While the tradesperson may not knowingly do wrong, can the philosopher act wrongly? Why do people act wrongly? As we saw above, Plato treats the issue as a failure of knowledge. There are two ancient views (seen in a discussion of Socrates by Aristotle in his *Nicomachean Ethics*) about why people act wrongly. The first, Socratic, view is that people act wrongly because they do not know the right thing to do. Associated with this is the following idea: if

---

9. It may be this insistence on metaphysics as opposed to epistemology that Judith Jarvis Thomson is getting at when she says: "Socrates invented the enterprise of moral theory, and what led him to do so was something theoretical, something deep: the quite general idea that while a clutter of beliefs may be a clutter of true beliefs, may even be a clutter of beliefs some or all of which are necessarily true beliefs, *knowledge* that they are true requires knowledge of what makes them true", in Thomson, *The Realm of Rights*, 31.

people did know the right thing to do, then they would *always* do it. Everyone always does what they *think* is best, and what Plato's philosophers *think* is best *is* best, since such philosophers think correctly. When people act wrongly they are mistaken about what is best. No one knowingly does wrong. The human moral dilemma is due primarily to ignorance. Philosophers, who *know*, are sure to act rightly, therefore. The second view is that people act wrongly because they cannot persuade themselves to do the right thing. Associated with this is the following idea: people usually do know what they ought to do, it is just that sometimes they want to do something different. The human moral dilemma is due primarily to desire. Even philosophers, then, might not want to do what they know they ought to do. Present-day philosophers – conscious of their weakness of will, perhaps – do not usually think of people being motivated by knowledge or belief alone. Knowing what is truly good does not ensure that one will act or govern in terms of that knowledge, for one may not desire to do what is good. By contrast, Plato's philosopher-rulers are defined by him as those who, in effect, do have this crucial motivation. Nevertheless, it is clear that self-mastery is not just a matter of reason ensuring that we have knowledge; it is also a matter of reason ensuring that we have the will to do what is good. Kant, whose philosophy we will examine later, makes this clear.

People sometimes ask, "Why should I act morally?" This is a question that typically arises if it is assumed that desire is the foundation of motivation, because it is usually taken to presuppose that we already know what it is to act morally and only our desire to do so is at issue. Only a person who did not believe that it was self-evident that we should act morally would ask for a reason to do so. But there is a dilemma here. First, if we admit the question, then we are accepting its presupposition that acting morally is not self-evidently something we ought to do. Secondly, any reason for acting morally will either be moral, or not moral. If the reason offered is itself moral, then this begs the question: if we are wondering whether to act morally, we are equally wondering whether we should accept moral reasons to do so. If the reason offered is non-moral, then it seems that acting morally is simply a way of achieving whatever it is that the non-moral reason calls upon us to do, and this is, *ex hypothesi*, not a moral matter. Morality is then subordinate to the non-moral purpose expressed by that non-moral reason. So the moralness of the "acting morally" disappears. The typical non-moral reason for acting morally, incidentally, is that it is "in one's interests" to do so; in other words, you will be punished, or otherwise disadvantaged, if you do not.

The question "Why should I act morally?" is itself not well-formed, and is somewhat like the old example of a bad legal question, "Have you stopped beating your wife?", with its false and question-begging presupposition. "Why should I act morally?" asks for a *reason*, but it presupposes that it is *desire* that motivates us. The question is muddled, and should be replaced by the central issue whether morality is based on reason or desire. Plato has presented the issue to us and has given us one answer, but only one. The matter is complex, but do not lose sight of one point: while we may not be able to guarantee good behaviour on anybody's part, we may nevertheless follow Plato in holding good behaviour to consist in acting on the basis of moral knowledge given us by reason.

We posed a number of questions at the beginning of this chapter. How can rights be authoritative? How can our individual and social choices be "constrained" by rights? How can we be motivated by such moral considerations? What rights do we have? How may we justify claims to rights? In summary conclusion, on Plato's approach the authority of rights, indistinguishable from the authority of any other moral perfection, consists in their *truth*. He sets for us the central claim, which will guide us through to Chapter 5, that moral truth is to be understood in terms of an independent, unchanging and consistent reality known about in a special way. This truth is then interpreted "realistically", a philosophical term which in this context means that truth is seen as a correspondence to a really existing abstract reality. This truth is grasped by the exercise of reason, and can be grasped in no other way; reason provides the ultimate justification, and we will see it have the same role in much of this book. Moral considerations do not "constrain" those of us who know what they are, for Plato conceives knowledge as directly motivating for those who have it. Morality is thus authoritative, even if we weak-willed beings do not always act as we should. As to what our rights, if any, actually are, Plato gives us no answer.

CHAPTER 3

Hobbes

As earlier observed in our discussion of Plato's *Republic*, in response to Socrates a powerful presentation was made by Thrasymachus of the view that "justice consists in the interests of the strong". This was developed by Glaucon, reporting what he describes as the "common opinion"[1] that justice is unpleasant in itself but is pursued for the rewards it might bring and in the hope of a good reputation. "What they say is", he continued:

> that it is according to nature a good thing to inflict wrong or injury, and a bad thing to suffer it, but that the disadvantages of suffering it exceed the advantages of inflicting it; so, after a taste of both, men decide that, as they can't evade the one and achieve the other, it will pay to make a compact with each other by which they forgo both. They accordingly proceed to make laws and mutual agreements, and what the law lays down they call lawful and right.[2]

"Taste of both" here implies that the ultimate measure of goodness is our own "taste" or, in other words, what satisfies our desires. "According to nature a good thing" amounts to the claim that, against Plato's later position, desire as a measure of "goodness" is not merely a motivational feature of the class of tradespeople but is a feature of human nature in general. It is "natural" to all of us to understand

---

1. Plato, *Republic* 358a.
2. *Ibid.*, 358e–359a; also in *Republic*, H. D. P. Lee (trans.) (London: Penguin, 1987), 104.

"goodness" or "justice" in this way; in other words, we will find that this is what we all "really mean" by it if we are trying to discover its nature through a kind of dialogue. On this view there is no room for Plato's curious intellectualized understanding of goodness as part of some abstract reality. That understanding goodness or justice in this desire-based way is natural to all of us is shown by the fact that even the supposedly "just man" would take pleasure in doing "wrong" if he could get away with it. But is this a natural fact about us all? Yes, Glaucon points out in answer; think about how one would act if one were given the means to be invisible, which ensured that one could always get away with "wrongdoing".[3]

It is in Hobbes's *Leviathan* of 1651 that we find a version of this alternative position particularly clearly spelled out. Hobbes is a materialist; according to him, we can be assured that the real world consists of material things. Experienced reality is not a false and unreliable veil that hides the perfect abstractions of Plato's intellectually apprehended world, but is itself the real world, so that experience is crucial to our knowledge of reality. It is not abstract ideas that are real and that motivate us, but material things. Moral issues are to be understood on the basis of such assumptions. As human beings we are made of material objects, the motions of which cause changes in us,[4] and our fundamental characteristics can be understood in ways that are, to us today, recognizably "scientific" in the broadest sense of that word. We can know things only as we experience them, however; we cannot be certain about what lies behind the causes we observe. By contrast, we can be sure about our own mental experiences.

Distinctive here, by contrast with Plato, is the view that there is a single theory of human nature. Whatever "human nature" may be, there is only one answer to what it is. Plato's position was effectively ambivalent about this. There is in principle nothing wrong with Plato's suggestion that we can be motivated by reason, by courage or by desire, and indeed we may wish to accept this outline psychology. Plato, however, used these notions to structure *classes of people*. Instead of holding, as we might today, that any one of us could be motivated in different ways at different times, so that human nature is a complex whole shared by us all, Plato assumed that everyone was fixed in their own master motivation. You could not educate

---

3. The story of Gyges' ring of invisibility appears in Plato, *Republic*, 359d–360d.
4. Hobbes, *Leviathan*, Ch. 6.

somebody who had a tradesperson's nature to be a philosopher: people could not change their fundamental nature and it would undermine the just society for them to try. The upshot is that there is no single human nature, but rather three different kinds, and the just society was structured to reflect these unchangeable characteristics.

Hobbes, then, has a different epistemology from Plato, a different metaphysics from Plato, and believes in a single theory of human nature. Like Glaucon, he seeks to tell us what we are "naturally" like. Unlike Glaucon, he does not give us a fairytale about invisibility to do it. Chapter 13 of *Leviathan* describes to us the "natural condition of mankind as concerning their felicity and misery".[5] "Felicity" and "misery" here mark the concentration on what satisfies and dissatisfies our desires, desire-satisfaction being our primary motivation. Yet desire-satisfaction is not to be understood solely in terms of desire, for human beings are also *rational*, but Hobbes means by this something very different from Plato. Reason is not something different from desire, which can, as Plato saw it, yield knowledge and motivate us in a different direction from desire. Reason is part of the application of desire in our actions: we are all rational in the sense that we adopt effective means to achieve the satisfaction of the desires we have. If we want something, B, and something else, A, must be done if we are to get B, then we will do A. It is in this sense that we are, all of us, rational desiring beings. This is not mere assertion, for Hobbes offers evidence about what we are naturally like. He does so in his description of what he calls the "state of nature".

In Hobbes's view we are not now in our natural state. We live in an organized society, in a state with laws, authority and many other features that are a consequence of that society. It is society itself that is unnatural, for Hobbes. He sees the natural state of a person to be the situation that person would be in if there were no government, no laws and indeed nothing that society had brought about. We have then to imagine what people would be like if all such features were absent. We have to imagine people as "individuals", then; we have to imagine a *counterfactual* situation. Hobbes's first claim is that in this "state of nature" we would all be equal, or at least a lot more equal than we are now. Most particularly we would be equal in the characteristics of "human nature". These express what we essentially are.

So many things characterize humanity: we describe ourselves as *Homo* "*sapiens*", but are we naturally wise? We may think of the

---

5. The title of Hobbes, *Leviathan*, Ch. 13.

many attributes that we have and that animals don't – our capacity for language, our science and technology – but are these things natural to us? For Hobbes they are not. The only features natural to us are those that we are born with or those that we naturally attain simply by living an individual and unsocial life. When we think of our natural characteristics of mind we must set aside "the arts grounded upon words, and especially that skill of proceeding upon general and infallible rules, called science".[6] A vast amount is thus excluded, and such wisdom as remains to each of us we are each of us equally vain enough to think that we share equally with others. Once we have excluded so much, we naturally believe ourselves equal with each other in our mental capacities. We also naturally believe ourselves equal with each other in our physical abilities since, as Hobbes says, the weakest can find means to kill the strongest. While there might be some variations in these things, they are not so great as to make us naturally defer to any other person. Our natural mental and physical equality is sufficient, then, to give us "equality of hope in the attaining of our ends", and it is this *believed* equality that matters for the argument.[7]

"And therefore", Hobbes continues, "if any two men desire the same thing, which nevertheless they cannot both enjoy, they become enemies". This conclusion both exemplifies and is justified by the view of human nature as rational and desire-led. If we want something, then we will adopt the means to achieve it. Since we are and can be motivated by no other consideration, this is certain. If another person is in our way, then we must remove them, and do whatever is necessary for that purpose. There is no special "moral" motivation that might block this conclusion.

Still, the conclusion follows only from a hypothetical premise: "*if* any two men desire the same thing ...". We might hope or imagine that people are naturally sociable enough not to want something so strongly that the death of another was a necessary means to that end. Hobbes, however, gives us more detail. He does not merely understand us as rational and desiring beings; he also tells us what our desires actually are. He recognizes that people differ in their desires and their reason:

---

6. *Ibid.*
7. *Ibid.* Note that we act on the basis of what we believe, and it does not actually matter to understanding or predicting our behaviour whether our beliefs are true; it matters only that we have them.

diverse men differ not only in their judgement on the sense of what is pleasant and unpleasant to the taste, smell, hearing, touch and sight, but also of what is conformable or disagreeable to reason in the actions of common life.[8]

Indeed, people differ widely and dangerously – this very plurality is what makes for our difficulties – but these are irrelevant details at this point, for our desires can be categorized. There are three categories of desire that actually motivate us, he says: "First, competition; secondly, diffidence; thirdly, glory". It is these that are, "in the nature of man", the "three principal causes of quarrel".

The first maketh men invade for gain; the second, for safety; and the third, for reputation. The first use violence, to make themselves masters of other men's persons, wives, children, and cattle; the second, to defend them; the third, for trifles, as a word, a smile, a different opinion ...[9]

Given that our desires are of these kinds, then the conclusion that we become enemies in the quest to satisfy them is indeed natural enough.

Our natural state is therefore a state of enmity, in other words of war, and Hobbes draws his famous conclusion:

In such condition there is no place for industry, because the fruit thereof is uncertain: and consequently no culture of the earth; no navigation, nor use of the commodities that may be imported by sea; no commodious building; no instruments of moving and removing such things as require much force; no knowledge of the face of the earth; no account of time; no arts; no letters; no society; and which is worst of all, continual fear, and danger of violent death; and the life of man, solitary, poor, nasty, brutish, and short.

But all this is a *hypothetical* and *counterfactual* state of affairs:[10] "It may peradventure be thought there was never such a time nor condition of war as this; and I believe it was never generally so, over all the world." The evidence for it, then? Let the objector to it:

consider with himself: when taking a journey, he arms himself and seeks to go well accompanied; when going to sleep, he locks his doors; when even in his house he locks his chests; and this when

---

8. *Ibid.*, Ch. 15.
9. *Ibid.*, Ch. 13.
10. "Hypothetical" means "having the form *if A then B*". "Counterfactual" can usually be expressed as "having the form *if A then B, and not A*".

he knows there be laws and public officers, armed, to revenge all injuries shall be done him ..."[11]

Also, "it may be perceived what manner of life there would be, where there were no common power [i.e. effective government] to fear, by the manner of life which men that have formerly lived under a peaceful government use to degenerate into a civil war". (Hobbes had lived through the time of the English Civil War, and had done his best to avoid it.) Finally, the international arena is an unordered and unsocial situation, with nations behaving as individuals, and we can see that they behave exactly in the described fashion:

> in all times kings and persons of sovereign authority, because of their independency, are in continual jealousies, and in the state and posture of gladiators, having their weapons pointing, and their eyes fixed on one another; that is, their forts, garrisons, and guns upon the frontiers of their kingdoms, and continual spies upon their neighbours, which is a posture of war.[12]

What, then, of justice? What of right and wrong, good and bad, rights? Hobbes says, "Justice and injustice are none of the faculties neither of the body nor mind. If they were, they might be in a man that were alone in the world, as well as his senses and passions. They are qualities that relate to men in society, not in solitude." Such moral matters do not exist in the state of nature (as they would on Plato's approach), but we can introduce the alternative which exists in society as follows.

> The desires, and other passions of man, are in themselves no sin. No more are the actions that proceed from those passions till they know a law that forbids them; which till laws be made they cannot know; nor can any law be made till they have agreed upon the person that shall make it.[13]

All moral considerations, then, are a creation within society, and have no "natural" existence. There is no natural morality, nothing to be discovered, nothing to be accessed in the way Plato suggested, whether by reason or otherwise. There are no such things as rights, then, in the state of nature. And yet such things can be brought into existence just in so far as a society is brought into existence: if we

---

11. Hobbes, *Leviathan*, Ch. 13.
12. *Ibid.*
13. *Ibid.*

agree upon a person to make laws, then laws can be made, and they will set for us the standards of right and wrong, and perhaps give us rights. Hobbes argues that it is rational for us to enter into an agreement or covenant with others in favour of a person who could make such laws, and his reasoning is straightforward. We, as individuals, are rational and desiring beings. We want gain, safety and reputation or respect from others. Safety is the most important of these, since it is a condition for satisfying the other two kinds of desire. We are rational, and will adopt the means that are necessary to satisfy these desires, in so far as that can be done. The state of nature, being a state of war, is an irrational means to these ends since, far from giving us a long and comfortable life, it actually yields a short and nasty one. Being rational, we recognize this, and realize that it is irrational to behave in the "natural" warlike way that is counterfactually hypothesized. We must give up war and seek peace.

In effect, Hobbes's argument is a *reductio ad absurdum*[14] of the hypothesized situation in the state of nature: given that we are the rational desiring beings that he understands us as being, then we could not be in a state of war.[15] If rationality is natural to us, then it seems that so must be the ordered society that we now rationally exist in. Moreover, we falsely, with Hobbes, imagine ourselves to have created our ordered society from a hypothesized irrational state of nature. If on the other hand the "state of nature" really expresses what is *natural* for human beings, then its very irrationality suggests that we are not naturally rational. Is it then correct to understand ourselves as *rational* beings? While Hobbes plainly sees the rationality of human nature as a kind of essential feature of humanity, its universality is also plainly for him to some extent a *contingency*. We can and do make mistakes, thus:

> he therefore that breaketh his covenant, and consequently declareth that he thinks he may with reason do so, cannot be received

---

14. This form of argument relies on the idea that a valid argument is one in which, if the premises are true, then the conclusion must be true. If the conclusion of an argument is self-contradictory then that conclusion cannot possibly be true, and thus we can deduce the falsity of a premise of the argument.

15. This assumes that Hobbes is right in his claim that it is rational for us to form a society. Difficulties of the so-called "prisoners' dilemma" kind suggest it may not be, but these will not be considered here. David Hume observes, "philosophers may, if they please, extend their reasoning to the suppos'd *state of nature*; provided they allow it to be a mere philosophical fiction, which never had, and never cou'd have any reality", *A Treatise of Human Nature* [1739], L. A. Selby-Bigge (ed.) (Oxford: Clarendon Press, 1888), 493.

into any society, that unite themselves for peace and defence, but by the error of them that receive him.[16]

Thus it is, for example, an error in our reasoning to seek to attain sovereignty by rebellion, primarily because rebellion is a means that relies upon the errors of others, which cannot reasonably be foreseen. Error is a widespread but variable feature of human nature. The implication is that reason, as an effective means for satisfying our desires, sets all of humanity a common *standard* rather being a universally true *description*.

To create that society which helps us satisfy our desires more effectively, we must, in the imagined situation, give up war. Hobbes characterizes this in a special way, a way that is particularly important for our concern with rights as it explicitly refers to something he calls the "Right of Nature". As our argument has moved from Plato to Hobbes, we have moved to a time where the word "right" has come into existence bearing something very like its modern meaning.[17] Hobbes's claim that there is such a thing as a natural right is plainly contrary to his claim that there is no natural standard of right or wrong, and the matter needs to be clarified. The Right of Nature is defined by Hobbes as a *liberty* of a certain kind, in particular the liberty to take whatever steps one judges necessary to preserve one's life. Liberty, otherwise "freedom", has so far been explained only in terms of Plato's theory: liberty or freedom is mastery by the true self, mastery by the rational self, mastery by knowledge of what is really good, and the avoidance of slavery to one's desires. If Hobbes defined freedom as Plato did then he would be importing into his own theory all the baggage of Plato's own approach. He does not do so: "by liberty is understood, according to the proper signification of the word, the absence of external impediments".[18]

"Impediments" are understood to be whatever can stop a person from doing what he or she wants. Since what a person wants has already been characterized in terms of gain, safety and reputation, and since safety is fundamental here as it is a condition for the other two, Hobbes particularly needs to understand "impediments" in the

---

16. Hobbes, *Leviathan*, Ch. 15. The "consequently declareth" here implies that Hobbes thinks that everyone does what they think they have "reason" to do. The analogy with Socrates' view that no one knowingly does wrong is clear (see Ch. 2).

17. The history of the word "right" is partly covered in Ch. 12. See, in particular, J. Finnis, *Natural Law and Natural Rights* (Oxford: Clarendon Press, 1980), 206ff.

18. Hobbes, *Leviathan*, Ch. 14.

context of defining the Right of Nature as those things that put safety at risk. Liberty in general is the absence of those impediments. The Right of Nature is defined as the particular liberty for each person:

> to use his own power as he will himself for the preservation of his own nature; that is to say, of his own life; and consequently, of doing anything which, in his own judgement and reason, he shall conceive to be the aptest means thereunto.[19]

In the state of nature, Hobbes says of an individual:

> there is nothing he can make use of that may not be a help unto him in preserving his life against his enemies; it followeth that in such a condition *every man has a right to every thing*, even to one another's body.[20]

The expression "right to every thing" is misleading. The universality implicit in the words "every thing" suggests that, since a right is a liberty, Hobbes understands there to be universal liberty in the state of nature, that the state of nature is a state of perfect freedom. This would mean, since liberty is the absence of external impediments, that there would be *no* external impediments in the state of nature. But Hobbes's definition of liberty in general is not a definition of the particular liberty involved in the Right of Nature. There are impediments in the state of nature, of course; it is clear that the danger to one's safety posed by other people is as strong an impediment as there could be; there is nothing to stop other people killing me. Indeed, it is precisely to *remove* such impediments that we are rationally impelled to enter an organized state. On the other hand, there are no impediments on my actions in the following sense: in the state of nature, there is nothing to stop me killing other people,[21] and it is the universality of this liberty that is intended here.

In these circumstances, having at least imagined, following Glaucon, the "taste" of both killing and being killed, it is rational for me to try to institute impediments that stop others killing me, even though those same impediments will stop me from killing others. It is rational for me, then, to give up that freedom to kill others – the Right

---

19. *Ibid.*
20. *Ibid.*, emphasis added.
21. "The weakest has strength enough to kill the strongest; either by secret machination, or by confederacy with others, that are in the same danger with himself" (*ibid.*, Ch. 13). "Impediments" warrants much closer analysis, but this is not here relevant.

of Nature – so long as others give up their freedom to kill me. Otherwise, as Hobbes says, "as long as this natural right of every man to every thing endureth, there can be no security to any man, how strong or wise soever he be, of living out the time which nature[22] ordinarily alloweth men to live".[23] To achieve the satisfaction of the desires we actually have, it is rational – "it is a precept, or general rule of reason" – for us to seek peace rather than war, which we do by laying down or renouncing the Right of Nature. The rational requirement to seek peace is Hobbes's first so-called Law of Nature. The further rational requirement to renounce the Right of Nature (as a means to satisfying the first Law of Nature) is Hobbes' second Law of Nature. Once we have an ordered society in consequence of this, it is proper to take such further steps as will reasonably preserve it, and Hobbes proceeds to a "subtle deduction" of the remainder of 19 Laws of Nature, which can be summarized as "do not that to another, which thou wouldest not have done to thy self".

The so-called Right of Nature, also called a "natural right" by Hobbes, is therefore not a "right" in an ordinary sense that we would accept today, for it imposes no obligations on others.[24] It is nothing more than a name defined to be true of a feature of a warring situation where there is no law or morality of any kind. This "right" is a mere freedom to do what we want for so long as we can get away with it. If we seek rights, as ordinarily understood, against the background of Hobbes's theory then we will find them, if we find them at all, only in the laws created by the person who has the power to do so on the basis of the renunciation of the Right of Nature that takes place in the mutually agreed "covenant" or "contract". That person it would now be proper to call, with Hobbes, the "sovereign". While we may imagine the sovereign to be a particular individual, we can also understand it to be a group with a unified will, such as a parliament. The power that is, by this contract, passed to the sovereign is a *continuing* power.

It is *unjust* to break this contract with the sovereign; indeed, the "fountain and original" of justice consists in the following third Law of Nature: "that men perform their covenants made".[25] This law

---

22. "Nature" here means one's own biological structure.
23. Hobbes, *Leviathan*, Ch. 15.
24. That rights standardly correlate with duties or obligations is a feature analysed in Chs 7 and 8.
25. Hobbes, *Leviathan*, Ch. 15.

Hobbes understands to follow logically from the first two Laws of Nature. When a person has renounced his Right of Nature:

> then is he said to be obliged, or bound, not to hinder those, to whom such right is granted, or abandoned, from the benefit of it: and that he ought, and it is his duty, not to make void that voluntary act of his own: and that such hindrance is injustice.[26]

"Just," for Hobbes, *means* "he that in his actions observeth the laws of his country".[27] The person is *said* to be obliged, we may note. The terminology of law and morals, the range of words like liberty, law, right, duty, obligation, contract, covenant, justice and so forth are all defined into existence – they are all to be understood – in terms of the structure of reasoning that Hobbes has introduced. The various Laws of Nature follow one from another as if they were lines in a geometrical proof.[28]

In a sense Hobbes has as strong a recognition of the need for consistent reasoning as does Plato, but where for Plato the end of the line of reasoning is tied to an independently existing abstract object – the Form of the Good – for Hobbes it is tied to the satisfaction of desires, desires that he has already characterized for us. While it is "unjust" to break the contract by which we renounce the Right of Nature, therefore, nothing extra is said by using the word "unjust" here beyond what has already been said; namely, that it would be *irrational* to break the contract. Moreover the validity of Hobbes's arguments here does not change with time or social circumstance, since he derives his conclusions only from essential and universal features of human nature, using perennial and independent standards of logical reasoning. The covenant with the sovereign – the social contract – is therefore something that it would be *continuously irrational* to break. "Unjust" adds nothing to irrationality: as Hobbes says, "Injustice, in the controversies of the world, is somewhat like to that, which in the disputations of scholars is called absurdity".[29] Again, "justice therefore, that is to say, keeping of covenant, is a rule of reason, by which we are forbidden to do any thing destructive to our life; and consequently a Law of Nature".[30] "Forbidden" here is

---

26. *Ibid.*, Ch. 14.
27. *Ibid.*, Ch. 4.
28. This is not a total endorsement of Hobbes's reasoning.
29. Hobbes, *Leviathan*, Ch. 14.
30. *Ibid.*, Ch. 15.

not what Kant was later to call a "categorical imperative"[31] but means here merely that, if we want to live, as we in fact do, we ought not to do something that would destroy our lives. "These dictates of reason", Hobbes concludes Chapter 15:

> men use to call by the name of laws, but improperly: for they are but conclusions, or theorems concerning what conduceth to the conservation and defence of themselves; whereas law, properly, is the word of him that by right hath command over others. But yet if we consider the same theorems, as delivered in the word of God, that by right commandeth all things, then are they properly called laws.

If we follow later writers, such as H. L. A. Hart,[32] in holding laws to be rules or standards of some kind rather than commands, then we will be all the more willing to recognize Hobbes's understanding of "reason" as both a law and a theorem.

It is as problematic for us today as it was for Hobbes to understand wherein lies the authority of reason conceived as a set of normative standards. However, it is clear that we have in Hobbes at least *two* sets of standards: first, those standards that express, independently of us many error-prone individuals, the unchanging demands of reason for consistency; and, secondly, those standards that express the commands of the sovereign, which give us such laws and rights as the sovereign thinks fit, but do so legitimately only in so far as they meet the independent, fixed and essentially consistent standards of reason.[33]

We may now put the following questions to Hobbes. How can rights be authoritative? How can our individual and social choices be "constrained" by rights? How can we be motivated by such moral considerations? What rights do we have? How may our rights be justified? The "authority" of rights needs to be understood, to begin with, in the context of the Right of Nature. To conceive of this so-called "right" as "authoritative" or as "constraining" our individual or

---

31. I. Kant, *Fundamental Principles of the Metaphysic of Ethics* [1785], 10th edn, T. K. Abbott (trans.) (London: Longmans, 1962), 37.

32. H. L. A. Hart, *The Concept of Law*, 2nd edn (Oxford: Clarendon Press, 1994). Summarily, Hart argues that law should be seen as a system of rules rather than a set of commands. The contemporary debate about what "rules" are, exactly, and how far they differ from principles, is not of relevance here; see, however, Ch. 10. See R. M. Dworkin, "Is Law a System of Rules?", in *The Philosophy of Law*, R. M. Dworkin (ed.), 38–65 (Oxford: Oxford University Press, 1977).

33. Does the ruler make mistakes? See Plato, *Republic*, 339ff.

social choices is to misunderstand it, for it is in the first place not a *constraint* but rather a *liberty*, the liberty to do *whatever* one judges necessary to preserve one's life. Moreover, far from being authoritative, it is a liberty that *ought to be given up* (since Hobbes argues that it would be irrational to exercise it), and thus the question of its justification does not arise. Note that the freedom to do as we wish is a freedom that in the state of nature reflects the fact that, even in society, "diverse men differ ... in their judgement ... of what is conformable or disagreeable to reason in the actions of common life".[34] Individuals in the state of nature have their own desires and also their own understanding of what reason requires, and we have already noted Hobbes's observation that all are prone to error.

What is required to be given up is the right to "all things", but that still leaves rights to "something" rather than "nothing": "and therefore there be some rights, which no man can be understood ... to have ... transferred",[35] for example, the right to resist assault intending death. Part of what is "authoritative" here is the desire, deemed universal, for life, but this does not *constrain* our choice but *is* our overriding choice, a choice that renders subordinate many of our other choices. What constrains our subordinate choices is the *rational demand* that we give up the right to all things. What is authoritative here is reason, which operates as an *external* impediment against the freedom to do as we wish regardless of rational error.

Consider first individual judgement about what reason requires. Hobbes understands this to be prone to error, but the possibility of error arises only because there is some external standard against which it might be measured or criticized. If reason were purely an "internal" as opposed to "external" standard, with no attempt to refer to something external, then exercising our individual judgement about what reason, so understood, "requires" would be very like trying to operate with a private language, as Wittgenstein understood that.[36] Such a standard would not constrain us at all. Hobbes's argument, by contrast, effectively understands reason as some external standard about what reason "really" requires. He certainly presumes this external standard to exist in the state of nature, for it is this that

---

34. Hobbes, *Leviathan*, Ch. 15. Recall that freedom is defined by Hobbes as the absence of *external* impediments.
35. *Ibid.*, Ch. 14. Wounds, chains, and imprisonment are included, but exceptions to the right transferred are minimized; see also *ibid.*, Ch. 26.
36. See L. Wittgenstein, *Philosophical Investigations*, 3rd edn, G. E. M. Anscombe (trans.) (Oxford: Basil Blackwell, 1968).

enables us rationally to contract our way out of the state of nature. On the other hand, he certainly presumes some internal standard also to exist, for this is what drives his argument characterizing the state of nature to the conclusion that our lives would be short and nasty. Both standards are available, then, but which of them are we to understand as naturally *motivating* us? If a purely internal standard motivates us, why would we all recognize the need to create or obey a sovereign, which is created on the basis of the external standard? Clearly the external standard is required to be able to motivate us, but we recognize the error-prone application of that standard, and this warrants transferring such judgements to the sovereign, with increased consistency an additional benefit of this, even though the sovereign may be as error-prone as the rest of us.

Richard Tuck stresses that it is men's "independency of judgement about the world" that leads to conflict, and that Hobbes's:

> proposed solution was therefore to eliminate independent judgement about matters of fact. Natural man, [Hobbes] argued, would see the necessity for everyone to transfer their individual judgement in cases of uncertainty to a common decision-maker ...[37]

Tuck's characterization of Hobbes's move as being specifically to do with "matters of fact" is unnecessarily limited. Tuck himself notes that Hobbes's sovereign could "determine the meanings of words in the public language",[38] and this implies that the sovereign can determine matters of reason as well as matters of fact. However, we do not need to rely here on what might well be an anachronistic distinction between "matters of fact" and "matters of reason",[39] for we need only note what Hobbes asserts and Tuck agrees with, which is that it is the sovereign who legitimately determines what is right and wrong, that is, "what is conformable or disagreeable to reason".[40] Now it is clear that Hobbes does not believe that reason determines the right or wrong outcome for every case, for if that were so there would be only one rational way to govern, whereas for Hobbes the rational constraints on the sovereign's power are minimal. However, since

---

37. R. Tuck, "Introduction" to T. Hobbes, *Leviathan* (Cambridge: Cambridge University Press, 1991), xvii.
38. *Ibid.*
39. A distinction that resonates for the modern philosopher in the way that it does largely as a consequence of the writings of David Hume, 100 years later than Hobbes.
40. Hobbes, *Leviathan*, Ch. 15.

legitimately determining what is right and wrong is bounded by the irrational, then the sovereign's power includes at least the determination of its own rational limits and is in any event not limited to the determination of "matters of fact". At least some independent judgements about matters of reason, as well as matters of fact, are therefore transferred to the common decision-maker.[41] Reason is nevertheless an external independent standard even for the sovereign.

While subordinate to the overriding desire for life, it is reason that is authoritative, and reason is conceived as something objective and independent of us that properly constrains our subordinate choices of action. Reason is independently real, for Hobbes; like Plato, he respects geometry "which is the only science that it hath pleased God hitherto to bestow on mankind".[42] Reason is then something absolute: something external to us. It is not a function of human choice. Our individual error-prone judgements about what reason requires will not do. Reason is eternal in its standards and is, of course, essentially consistent. Unlike Plato, however, Hobbes does not wish to interpret the abstract truths of reason in a realistic[43] way: "there being nothing in the world universal but names".[44] There are nevertheless objective and universal answers to questions about what reason requires: reason is in some sense independent of us, unchanging, universally applicable and inherently consistent.

Thus the Right of Nature is not authoritative, while reason is. Nevertheless, rights may be given to us by the laws that the sovereign passes, and such rights are authoritative just in so far as that sovereign is legitimate. The legitimacy of the sovereign is a function of the actual power of that position, a power held in virtue of the continuing rationality of our obedience and the irrationality of our disobedience. Actual power can go beyond legitimacy, because the sovereign may act irrationally.[45]

As to how we may be motivated, Hobbes's answer is in terms of our desires. It is not completely clear just how we can be motivated by

---

41. Although not all, since it is not rational to transfer *all* of our natural freedom.
42. Hobbes, *Leviathan*, Ch. 4.
43. Using the metaphysical sense of "realistic" referred to in Ch. 1, n. 34, which holds reality to exist independently of human beings.
44. Plato's "Forms" are also sometimes called or seen as "Universals". Note that it is not clear how far Hobbes can consistently be a nominalist and also hold reason to be independent of us. Are there right and wrong ways to name things?
45. It *may*, under such circumstances, no longer be rational for the subjects to obey the sovereign; but not *must*.

reason, that is, by a respect for consistency, and we will examine this in Chapter 5 when we present Hume's position. The difficulty is that reason is conceived by Hobbes as external to us, and our own individual judgements about what reason requires will not do. There are, then, certain questions that will need explaining in due course: how can we be motivated by our own judgements about what reason requires, in addition to being motivated by our desires? How can we be motivated by *external* standards of reason that require something different from our own judgement? How are reason and desire here linked? These questions still need clarification.

As to the question "What rights do we have?", there are, in Hobbes, two kinds of answer: first, we have those rights, understood as unprotected liberties, that rationally help us preserve ourselves; secondly, we have those rights, understood as correlated with obligations upon others, that the sovereign contingently gives us, if any and whatever they are.[46] Notice that there is no distinction to be drawn between "legal" rights and "moral" rights. "Human rights" in the sense we might understand that today, a sense permitted by Plato's approach, are not possible.

---

46. The sovereign has rights too, but this will not be elaborated here.

CHAPTER 4

Locke

Our search for rights began with Plato, who, despite not using the concept, framed for us a structure of understanding within which rights might be created and developed. If we accept Hobbes's approach, by contrast, we find very little further help, since Hobbes, like Plato, not only writes at a level of generality that rarely mentions the details of rights but also excludes much of what we ordinarily think about rights, stressing – where he does go into detail – the rights of the sovereign rather than the rights of the subject or citizen, for example. In particular we often think of rights – although not all of them – as independent of the state, but that approach is not permissible in Hobbes's view, since rights are essentially what the law gives us. A right to resist when attacked – even when attacked by the state – is the only independent right, but even that is not a "right" as ordinarily understood for it is only an unprotected liberty. It is reason rather than rights that is authoritative for Hobbes, as we have seen, but we cannot appeal to reason as independent of the state since we have given up to the state many of the judgements about what reason requires. A very different view about rights was expressed in 1690 by Locke, who was extremely influential in the development of democratic ideas. It is his understanding of rights that we will find far more familiar. The absoluteness of Hobbes's sovereign is here replaced by a much more limited social contract.

Locke's explanation appears in his *Second Treatise* of civil government, "An Essay Concerning the True Original, Extent and End of Civil Government", Chapter 2 of which is called "Of the State of Nature". The structure – at first sight – follows that of Chapter 13 of

Hobbes's *Leviathan* extremely closely, but we shall see that this is a superficial similarity. Locke does not work out the epistemological and metaphysical foundations of his position with Hobbes's clarity, and those foundations will not be developed here. This is not because Locke had no contribution to make about such things; on the contrary, his *Essay Concerning Human Understanding* is a major contribution to the development of epistemology. In that work Locke expresses an empiricist position of some subtlety. Locke's empiricism does not, however, clearly operate as a foundation for the thought in his *Second Treatise*, which indeed may plausibly be seen as flatly inconsistent with his empiricism. Its metaphysical presuppositions have more in common with Plato's rationalism. It is this fact that marks a major weakness, not only in Locke's position but also in our modern understanding of natural rights, as we shall see.

Much like Hobbes, Locke begins by examining what people are naturally like in the "state of nature", and again, like Hobbes, considers them to be equal.[1] They are in a state of "perfect freedom", which enables them "to order their actions, and dispose of their possessions and persons as they think fit". Just as Hobbes's conception of freedom in the state of nature was not as entire as he expressed it, so the "perfection" of freedom in Locke's understanding of the state of nature is also limited. But whereas, for Hobbes, freedom is limited by the presence of others who get in one's way, Locke understands freedom to be limited by the laws of nature.[2] Locke sees Hobbes's kind of freedom as "licence":

> but though this be a state of liberty, yet it is not a state of licence; though man in that state have an uncontrollable liberty to dispose of his person or possessions, yet he has not liberty to destroy himself, or so much as any creature in his possession, but where some nobler use than its bare preservation calls for it.

---

1. Although "age or virtue may give men a just precedency", and Locke makes clear that it is equality in jurisdiction of one over another that he has in mind in Locke, *Second Treatise*, §54.
2. My reference to Hobbes's conception of freedom here is on the basis of earlier argument as to how much freedom, given Hobbes's definition of freedom, existed in the state of nature: this was not as much freedom as Hobbes said it was. Locke in fact objects to Hobbes's definition on similar grounds: liberty is not, "as we are told, 'a liberty for every man to do what he lists'. For who could be free, when every other man's humour might domineer over him?" (Locke, *Second Treatise*, §57). Locke's understanding of freedom is somewhat more like Plato's than Hobbes's – "we are born free as we are born rational" (§60) – but it does not admit of brief summary here.

The freedom then of man, and liberty of acting according to his own will, is grounded on his having reason, which is able to instruct him in that law he is to govern himself by, and make him know how far he is left to the freedom of his own will.[3]

Recall the brevity and clarity of a relevant part of Hobbes's position.

The desires, and other passions of man, are in themselves no sin. No more are the actions that proceed from those passions till they know a law that forbids them; which till laws be made they cannot know; nor can any law be made till they have agreed upon the person that shall make it.[4]

With this we may compare and contrast a passage of equal force from Locke:

The state of Nature has a law of Nature to govern it, which obliges every one, and reason, which is that law, teaches all mankind who will but consult it, that being all equal and independent, no one ought to harm another in his life, health, liberty or possessions . . .[5]

For Hobbes, there are no laws in the state of nature (apart from reason itself, if, as we have seen, it be conceived as a "law"), but Locke here affirms that laws exist even when there is no society or organized state.

Locke tells us in detail what it is for such laws to exist: "the law of Nature would, as all other laws that concern men in this world, be in vain if there were nobody that in the state of Nature had a power to execute that law",[6] and concludes from this need for practical enforcement that the state of nature must include people who have the right to enforce it. Since everyone in the state of nature is equal, Locke concludes further that everyone has this right to punish, so that our natural rights include this in addition to the rights to life, health, liberty and property. Locke does not share with Hobbes the view that "diverse men differ . . . in their judgement . . . of what is conformable

---

3. Locke, *Second Treatise*, §63. The relationship between political freedom and the freedom of the will is an intriguing one which will not be discussed here.
4. Hobbes, *Leviathan*, Ch. 13.
5. Locke, *Second Treatise*, §4.
6. *Ibid.*, §7. For some interesting consideration of this, see R. Nozick, *Anarchy, State and Utopia* (Oxford: Basil Blackwell, 1974), particularly 137ff.

or disagreeable to reason in the actions of common life",[7] for he thinks that what reason requires is "intelligible and plain",[8] but he holds that "self-love will make men partial to themselves and their friends; and, on the other side, ill-nature, passion, and revenge will carry them too far in punishing others".[9] The state of nature is consequently "full of fears and continual dangers".[10] It is the confusion and disorder that result from these "inconveniences"[11] that justify a social contract in which each individual resigns his or her power to punish to a political community in which a united body has a single and "common established law and judicature".[12] The laws of that body are limited in that it "can never have a right to destroy, enslave, or designedly to impoverish the subjects; the obligations of the law of Nature cease not in society".[13] The ultimate sovereignty lies with the community and not with the government.

The logical form of the two compared passages from Hobbes and Locke needs to be examined. As briefly quoted, Hobbes's reads like sheer assertion, but it is nevertheless a conclusion, very plausibly drawn, from his earlier passages including, ultimately, the expression of his materialist position and his theory of meaning. Locke's passage is also part of an argument: the conclusion that no one ought to harm another in his life, health, liberty or possessions is immediately followed by this:

> for men being all the workmanship of one omnipotent and infinitely wise Maker; all the servants of one sovereign Master, sent into the world by His order and about His business; they are His property, whose workmanship they are made to last during His, not one another's pleasure.[14]

The standard explicit form of an argument preferred by logicians is: premises–inference marker–conclusion, where the "inference marker" is a word that shows that a conclusion is being drawn. "Therefore" is typically used to introduce conclusions in this format, but words like "thus" and "so" will do instead. In ordinary English, however, we

---

7. Hobbes, *Leviathan*, Ch. 15.
8. Locke, *Second Treatise*, §§12, 124.
9. *Ibid.*, §13.
10. *Ibid.*
11. *Ibid.*
12. *Ibid.*, §87.
13. *Ibid.*, §135.
14. *Ibid.*, §4.

often give the conclusion first and our reasons for it, that is our premises, last; we then use a "premise-introducing" rather than a "conclusion-introducing" inference marker. Typical of these are "for", "since" or "because". Locke has "for" to express his "consultation with reason".

The structure of Locke's argument, in preferred or standard form, is this:

Premise 1: Men are all made by one omnipotent and infinitely wise Maker.
Premise 2: Men are all the servants of one sovereign Master.
Premise 3: Men are all [God's] property.
Premise 4: Men are all equal and independent.
Conclusion: No one ought to harm another in his life, health, liberty or possessions.

The invalidity of this argument is breathtaking, and may well seem an obvious target of one of the most famous and influential passages in moral philosophy written by Hume, which the reader should see in full.

> I cannot forbear adding to these reasonings an observation, which may, perhaps, be found of some importance. In every system of morality, which I have hitherto met with, I have always remark'd, that the author proceeds for some time in the ordinary way of reasoning, and establishes the being of a God, or makes observations concerning human affairs; when of a sudden I am surpriz'd to find, that instead of the usual copulations of propositions, is, and is not, I meet with no proposition that is not connected with an ought, or an ought not. This change is imperceptible; but is, however, of the last consequence. For as this ought, or ought not, expresses some new relation or affirmation, 'tis necessary that it shou'd be observ'd and explain'd; and at the same time that a reason should be given, for what seems altogether inconceivable, how this new relation can be a deduction from others, which are entirely different from it. But as authors do not commonly use this precaution, I shall presume to recommend it to the readers; and am persuaded, that this small attention wou'd subvert all the vulgar systems of morality, and let us see, that the distinction of vice and virtue is not founded merely on the relations of objects, nor is perceiv'd by reason.[15]

---

15. Hume, *A Treatise of Human Nature*, 469.

It is indeed an elementary point of reasoning that, since the "ought" in Locke's conclusion is not supported by the "are" (plural of Hume's "is", of course) in his premises, then Locke's argument must be invalid. The common summary of Hume's position, that one cannot derive an "ought" from an "is", is formally correct,[16] although there is much more to Hume's passage than pointing out an elementary logical mistake. However, at the level of elementary reasoning two points need to be made. First, merely because an argument is invalid is no reason to hold that its conclusion is false. Locke may well be right in holding it true that "no one ought to harm another in his life, health, liberty or possessions", and many have believed him.[17] Secondly, we very commonly argue invalidly, but one important reason why we get away with it is that so much is taken for granted both by ourselves and those we are addressing. We do not need to spell out every premise, and so-called "suppressed" premises are plainly operating in Locke's work too. Philosophers, we usually think, ought to operate to higher logical standards, but it is impossible to give a reason for everything, and the acceptance of philosophical and scientific conclusions is always against the background of a shared understanding that is taken for granted and relative to which it is plausible to accept appropriate suppressed premises. It is a measure of Locke's political success that his arguments here have been so persuasive: the rights, which he claims that we all naturally have, come from reason and from God, and his argument plausibly summarizes this justification to the satisfaction of many in the audience he was addressing and to the satisfaction of many others since.[18]

This is not a measure of Locke's logical or philosophical success, however. We may observe that Locke's references in his premises to God and to reason are so general that they could at best yield only a very general ethical conclusion, while his conclusion is so very specific in its list of rights that it is plain that separate detail of justification is required for each one of them, in the absence of any obvious reason why they might hang naturally together. It is clear that Locke does not

---

16. Note that one cannot even derive "exists" from "is" without some further premise saying that one can do so.
17. Noteworthy is Robert Nozick, who builds his theory of the state on Locke's position, while commenting that Locke "does not provide anything remotely resembling a satisfactory explanation of the status and basis of the law of nature in his *Second Treatise*" (*Anarchy, State and Utopia*, 9).
18. An excellently clear summary appears in J. Wolff, *Robert Nozick: Property, Justice and the Minimal State* (Cambridge: Polity Press, 1991), 24ff.

provide the detailed argument required by his own standards of reason. Reason was for Locke, as it was for Plato and Hobbes, an eternally valid and objective standard, and it is a perennial philosophical requirement to display one's reasons with the kind of clarity and exactness anciently seen in the arguments of geometry. However tolerant Locke may wish us to be of his reasoning, it is not as if he were writing about matters that were beyond dispute. Alternative political theories were available, and we properly wish to know why a general reference to reason and to God yields exactly the rights to life, health, liberty and property. Hobbes's position is an appropriate philosophical alternative here, and we can briefly compare Hobbes with Locke to see just how much Locke could plausibly take for granted in arguing for his conclusion, by comparison with that philosophical alternative.

Plato sought to identify what was "good" for people, and we saw the alternative answers to this question provided by Socrates and his opponents, with goodness respectively understood as an independent and objective value by Socrates and as based on desire by his opponents. Two lists of what might loosely be called "values" are similarly and respectively offered by Locke and by Hobbes: life, health, liberty and property for Locke; and gain, safety and reputation for Hobbes. There is an obvious overlap between the two lists where Locke's life and health and Hobbes's safety are concerned. In both Hobbes's and Locke's organized societies, protection is intended against death and injury. Desire-led objective reason alone yields that protection in Hobbes's approach; God and objective reason provide it as claimed by Locke. In so far as we seek to believe Locke's conclusion we do not have to draw only on Locke's argument, for Hobbes offers arguments that, despite their very different philosophical kind, intend a fairly similar practical outcome.[19] Readers of Locke can plausibly take for granted Hobbes's theoretical support for the acceptability of a conclusion specifying protection for life and health, in default of Locke's own.

Again, liberty in Locke's list needs no special argument as compared with Hobbes: while liberty does not appear in Hobbes's list of desires, it is a clear presupposition of that list in the existence of the

---

19. Locke nevertheless offers detail for the "right to life" that yields different consequences from Hobbes. For example, the rights to so-called "self-ownership" are based in Locke's theory of the person, and this notion is a crucial feature of Nozick's theory in his *Anarchy, State and Utopia*. See also W. Kymlicka, *Contemporary Political Philosophy: An Introduction* (Oxford: Clarendon Press, 1990), 104ff.

Right of Nature. For both Hobbes and Locke, freedom is seen, by each in his own way, as something that has a kind of a priori value, such that it is the constraints on freedom that need to be explained. The theoretical alternative, that constraints should be taken for granted with the burden of proof placed on arguments for freedom, is not taken seriously by either of them; nor should it be.

Three concepts remain: property, gain and reputation. Property and gain are distinct concepts but are nevertheless closely related. Gain, for Hobbes, is not just wanting "more" but also means mastery of, among other entities, "cattle", a word that partly implied at his time its own etymological source: "chattels", or things *owned*. People want such mastery, but in the state of nature there is "no *mine* and *thine* distinct",[20] and this is one of the elements of the "ill condition"[21] of that state from which reason helps us to escape. "Mine" and "thine" imply property, and it is clear that protection of private property is part of what Hobbes meant by "gain". Thus Hobbes's arguments supporting his value "gain" can also be used in support of Locke's value "property". Hobbes additionally argues for "gain" understood as "more", not just as "property", but this is more than Locke needs. By contrast, Locke understands "property" to include property in one's own person, but this last overlaps with the concepts of life, health and liberty and can be supported by arguments in favour of these already given. "Reputation", finally, is to modern concerns rather obviously missing from Locke's list of rights, although present in Hobbes. For Hobbes we merely desire that others think well of us, but today we often recognize something like a right to respect from others, indeed a right – although defeasible – to be *trusted*. Trust is in any event necessary to keep Hobbes's organized society together,[22] and it is a familiar necessity for economic transactions in general. Hume and Thomas Reid (1710–1796) noted its importance, and its nature is surfacing as a philosophical and moral issue in the twenty-first century.[23] Trust is a value that, in a number of ways, conflicts with the contemporary fetish of "accountability", which reverses the burden of proof by requiring the individual to justify him- or herself rather than defeasibly assuming proper behaviour.

---

20. Hobbes, *Leviathan*, Ch. 13.
21. *Ibid.*
22. It is necessary, for example, to overcome "prisoners' dilemma" difficulties, not dealt with here. See also Hobbes, *Leviathan*, Ch. 7.
23. C. A. J. Coady, *Testimony* (Oxford: Clarendon Press, 1992); O. O'Neill, *A Question of Trust*, 2002 BBC Reith Lectures (Cambridge: Cambridge University Press, 2002).

Thus the detail of Locke's list of values – the rights to life, health, liberty and property[24] – is not in itself especially problematic by comparison with Hobbes's list of values. Such values are plausibly defensible, as Hobbes defends them, on the basis of desire-led objective reason, itself supported by a broadly empiricist materialist philosophy. What is problematic, however, is Locke's understanding of his list as a list of rights that exist *naturally* and *independently* of our natural desires and can so *limit* them as grounds of motivation. Hobbes gives no support for this. While, for Hobbes, reason exists as independent and objective, it is essentially desire-led. It is because we can experience our desires that empiricism can provide some support for moral understanding when that is grasped in Hobbes's way.[25] But empiricism cannot support Locke's understanding of rights – as Plato saw, an objective morality beyond experience can only be known by some intellectual means – and since Locke cannot look to empiricism for support and provides no alternative justification of his own, his list of rights seems rationally arbitrary, having its plausibility only on the basis of its fortuitous similarity to those we might be able to support on empiricist grounds. In so far as our modern understanding of the content of the list of rights is similar to Locke's, we face the same difficulty. The sense of arbitrariness is reinforced by the detailed range of topics covered by the various declarations of natural or "human" rights that have been made in the past 300 years in the Western tradition of political thought, and we saw some of these in Chapter 1. Moreover, if human beings do have rights "naturally", then those rights will have to be universal. But how could "property", for example, be a universal right, when the very concept of property may not be available to some alien cultures?

We may now ask of Locke the same questions that we put to Plato and Hobbes. How can rights be authoritative? How can our individual and social choices be "constrained" by rights? How can we be motivated by such moral considerations? What rights do we have? How may our rights be justified? Contrasted with the answers given by Hobbes, Locke's answers can be given in more summarized form, primarily because of the limited depth of reasoning which lies behind

---

24. Vlastos notes that Locke is sometimes thought to hold that natural rights are *absolute*, "but nowhere does Locke *say* this. Contrariwise he believes many things which imply the opposite . . . [for example] imprisonment as a punishment for crime", G. Vlastos, "Justice and Equality", in *Theories of Rights*, Waldron (ed.), 41–76, esp. 46.

25. Note that empiricism has a problem even with the objectivity of *desire-led* "reason".

them. The authority of rights derives from the authority of God and of reason. Both are objective and independent of us, existing for us in our state of nature, with their demands plain and intelligible and capable of constraining our desires through our recognition of what reason requires, as a consequence of which we may be motivated by our knowledge. Somewhat like Plato, that we have these natural rights to life, health, liberty and property is something *true*, and we can be motivated by respect for that. Truth and the authority of God go together as part of an independent, fixed and consistent reality. The need for consistency here is as strong as it is for Plato and for Hobbes. Finally, the exact rights that we have are clearly asserted by Locke, although their justification remains unclear.

Plato presents morality as something independent of us (and realistically interpreted), as eternal or unchanging in its truth and therefore universally applicable, and as essentially consistent. Hobbes presents reason as something independent of us (but metaphysically unclear), as eternal and universally applicable, and essentially consistent, and as something that warrants a very limited respect for what we may think of as morality. Locke, finally, presents morality specifically in the form of rights, and like Plato sees these rights as independently real, eternal and universally applicable, and essentially consistent in respecting standards of reason that are also conceived as independently real, eternal and universally applicable. All, despite their differences, argue their philosophies on the assumption of an independently real, eternal and universally applicable standard of reason. Plato and Locke permit human rights to be grounded on reason; Hobbes does not permit independent human rights at all, but for him reason nevertheless constrains such rights as the sovereign may legitimately permit or exercise. Our obedience to the sovereign, and so respect for such rights as the sovereign may institute, is rationally required according to an independent standard. None of these three philosophers sees any difficulty in supposing human beings to be motivated by such considerations.

CHAPTER 5

Human motivation

We have seen that, for Plato, Hobbes and Locke in their different ways, any authority that morality may have for us, and so any authority which "rights" may have for us, consists in its unchanging and independent status and in its essentially rational or consistent nature, foundation or content, however that may be known. In addition, whichever of the detailed conclusions of these philosophers we accept, reason has a capacity to motivate us. It is now time to question the presupposed "independence" of morality or reason that these philosophers use in their various approaches.

Plato's theory of human motivation essentially involves motivation on the basis of the degree of knowledge of what is good. A weakness in this for present-day philosophers is that it seems appropriate to respond in the following way: knowing what is truly good does not ensure that one will act or govern in terms of that knowledge, for one may not desire to do what is good. Rational self-mastery is not just a matter of reason ensuring that we have knowledge of the good; it is also a matter of reason ensuring that we have the will to do what is good.

Hobbes presents an alternative: it is not Platonic abstract ideas that are real and that motivate us, but material things. As human beings we are made of material objects, the motions of which cause changes in us, and these form our own mental experiences, which include our desires. Our will involves reason guiding the moves we make to satisfy our desires. It seems that we *can*, although – against Plato – not *must*, be motivated by respect for what is true. Perhaps equivalently, it seems that we can, although not must, be motivated by respect for what is rational.

We have seen a difficulty with Hobbes's position here. When Hobbes says that geometry or reason is bestowed on mankind by God he cannot mean that reason is a universal feature of human nature, for he says that all of us are prone to error. Rather, reason sets an external *standard* that we may or may not achieve. Moreover, this is not a standard that is universally straightforwardly available, since our errors do not lie only in a failure to do what we know reason requires of us; we also err in our judgement of what reason requires. We may then apparently be "motivated" to the satisfaction of our desires either by reason itself or by our own judgement of what reason requires. Both are apparently natural to us, as we have seen: motivation by what reason really requires takes us out of the state of nature by way of a social contract, whereas motivation by our own erroneous judgement of what reason requires leads us to war in an attempt to satisfy our natural desires. It is unclear whether we ought to take both as properly able to motivate us. In either event, we are also motivated by our desires.

How we can be motivated by *external* standards of reason that require something different from our own judgement of what reason requires may seem to be explicable once we are in society. Thus one apparent way of doing this is by appealing only to our desires, and the sovereign is in a position to do this by imposing on us costs and benefits, punishments and rewards. We might say that how much a person has a respect for what reason demands is a contingency, and that a person who has no respect for what reason demands is somebody who is forced to respect it by the sovereign, who puts unavoidable obvious costs in his way. But we are then not motivated by *external* reason at all, but only by our desires – desires to avoid the imposed costs – even if the outcome contingently coincides with what reason demands. Note also that the sovereign too may be in error. Moreover, a solution merely in terms of social enforcement will not do, for external standards of reason are required to motivate us out of the state of nature, and without them the argument does not take us as far as a situation of social enforcement. Our internal error-prone standards might leave us in a state of war. The difficulties remain: how does reason – internally or externally judged – relate to motivation?

There is not, in Locke, so clear a contrast as in Hobbes between being motivated by our own judgements about what reason requires and being motivated by what reason itself requires, since what reason requires is "intelligible and plain" and is thus readily and universally available.[1] Our rational errors lie not so much in discovering what reason requires as in a failure to do what we know reason requires of us. Thus the ground of our giving up, in the state of nature, the right to punish is that such motivations as self-love, partiality to one's friends, ill-nature, passion and revenge will often prevent us from acting in accordance with the clearly seen demands of reason. Generically, then, for Locke, "desire" may motivate us instead of "reason". How this is possible is not explained.

It is Hume who clarifies the issue here. "Nothing is more usual in philosophy", he says:

> than to talk of the combat of passion and reason, to give the preference to reason, and to assert that men are only so far virtuous as they conform themselves to its dictates. ... on this method of thinking the greatest part of moral philosophy, ancient and modern, seems to be founded.[2]

This is fallacious, he continues, and he offers proofs "that reason alone can never be a motive to any action of the will; and secondly, that it can never oppose passion in the direction of the will".[3] Hume bases his arguments on his theory of the mind, which is itself a clarified version of the broadly empiricist approach adopted by Hobbes and, in his epistemological writings, by Locke.

Hume is as firmly empiricist as Plato was rationalist. Not only does all knowledge come from experience, but all the contents of the mind, everything of which one is aware, come from experience. Experience is whatever the senses deliver to us, and we should note that the "senses" here are not restricted to sight, hearing, smell, touch and taste, but also include whatever we might "internally" sense, the "passions": thus I may *feel* angry, or ill, or desire, or aware of myself as walking. If there were a sixth external sense, then that would not be excluded by Hume; the number of senses we have is itself a matter of experience. "A passion is an original existence",[4] but, by contrast, when we think, or imagine, or – most importantly here – reason, then within our minds we are operating with the thoughts or ideas that the experiential sources have given to us, and these ideas are not the "original existences" themselves but mere derivatives of them.

---

1. Locke, *Second Treatise*, §§12, 124.
2. Hume, *A Treatise of Human Nature*, 413.
3. *Ibid.*
4. *Ibid.*, 415.

The ideas in our minds are nothing more than copies of or abstractions from our experiences, and are ultimately caused by those experiences. It is essential to Hume's philosophy that "motivation" is to be understood as that which *causes* us to act, and indeed causation – appropriately understood in empirical terms – is one of the foundation principles for understanding the operations of the mind.[5] Only an "original existence" can be causally effective. Reasoning is something we do with ideas in our minds, and it is merely an operation that associates these abstractions one with another. It has no causal power in itself. Reason "judges of truth and falsehood",[6] by comparing correspondence between thoughts and experiences. All that abstract reasoning can do is help us to form judgements about how to act, perhaps by pointing out to us what causes what.

> 'Tis from the prospect of pain or pleasure that the aversion or propensity arises towards any object . . . It can never in the least concern us to know, that such objects are causes, and such others effects, if both the causes and effects be indifferent to us.[7]

Reasoning does not motivate, then; it is our passions that do that, informed by beliefs about causes and effects that reason may point out to us. And if reason cannot motivate, it cannot oppose motivation by our desires, for it has no causal force. "We speak not strictly and philosophically when we talk of the combat of passion and of reason. Reason is, and ought only to be the slave of the passions".[8] Passions can be "contrary to reason" only in so far as they are accompanied by, for example, some false opinion.

> 'Tis not contrary to reason to prefer the destruction of the whole world to the scratching of my finger. ... a passion must be accompany'd with some false judgement, in order to its being unreasonable; and even then 'tis not the passion, properly speaking, which is unreasonable, but the judgement.[9]

---

5. See D. Davidson, "Actions, Reasons and Causes", reprinted in *The Philosophy of Action*, A. R. White (ed.), 79–94 (Oxford: Oxford University Press, 1968), 79–94. See also M. Smith, "The Humean Theory of Motivation", *Mind* 96 (1987), 36–61.
6. Hume, *A Treatise of Human Nature*, 417.
7. *Ibid.*, 414.
8. *Ibid.*, 415.
9. *Ibid.*, 416.

What motivates us here is the *passion*, not reason;[10] and the apparent conflict between passion and reason is actually a conflict between violent and calm passions, with "custom and repetition" an important cause of changes in our passions.[11] When we think of people as "reasonable" we are really thinking of them as being primarily motivated by calm passions, which are perhaps more apt, as shown by experience encapsulated in custom, to succeed in meeting their interests. Moreover, and particularly against Hobbes, our desires are not limited to the selfish desires of gain, safety and reputation (although it may be excusable to think so): "the voice of nature and experience seems plainly to oppose the selfish theory".[12] There are natural *virtues* as well as artificial or socially created ones,[13] such as "limited generosity"[14] and "sympathy".[15] Against Locke, by contrast, for Hume respect for property is a social and not a natural virtue.[16]

Reason should therefore not be seen as something that has its own causal or motivating force, for desire alone is what moves us. Reason can help us formulate our judgements about what, for example, may be effective in satisfying our desires, but cannot go beyond this. Note that it is consistent with Hume's theory of motivation, although not with his theory of knowledge or of the mind's contents, that reason might yield, as Plato claimed, substantive knowledge of a world beyond experience. This is because, in principle, we might be motivated by desire for objects intellectually accessed. Hume's epistemology, however, in addition to removing reason as source of motivation, also tells us the content of what reason can supply. For Hume, all substantial matters of knowledge are yielded by experience. Reason can only compare and contrast ideas that derive from experience. Reason cannot give us access to Plato's transcendent moral values, therefore, precisely because such things are not given in experience. Reason is in itself empty of all empirical content, and is therefore empty of all content. It cannot be a motivating force; nor

---

10. Passions may be violent or calm. It is not relevant here to outline Hume's recognition that we may confuse a "calm passion" with "reason".
11. Hume, *A Treatise of Human Nature*, 422.
12. D. Hume, *An Enquiry Concerning the Principles of Morals*, sect. V [1752], in *Hume's Ethical Writings*, A. MacIntyre (ed.) (London: Collier-Macmillan, 1965), 63.
13. Hume, *A Treatise of Human Nature*, 474–5.
14. *Ibid.*, 494.
15. *Ibid.*, 574ff.
16. *Ibid.*, 489.

can it supply any information about what morality requires. We can be morally motivated only by our passions, and only our passions and other experiences can provide the content of whatever morality might require. Can we, then, experience rights? Only as Hobbes conceived them, as a way of instituting the commands of the sovereign, which amounts to saying that we have rights only if the sovereign gives them to us. Rights have no "original existence", and can be no more than just one way of expressing the sovereign's desires or commands. We do not experience them as Locke wished to understand them in his political writings, as objective and independent truths or entities that exist naturally. We can experience, relevantly in this context, only such things as our felt responses to things we like or dislike, which may include the sovereign's punishments or rewards.

Hume's answer to the question of how we are motivated thus offers clarification of some difficulties in the approach of the earlier philosophers. It does so, however, at a cost; any fondness we may feel for rights or indeed morality in general as some kind of independent yet direct constraint on our own or on the sovereign's actions will have to be given up. The fundamental move that drives us to this conclusion is Hume's empiricism, however, and Plato at least does not accept this epistemology. The nature and role of reason in human motivation is a crucial issue that divides Plato and Hume. We cannot be directly motivated by rights as independently real, eternal and universally applicable, nor by reason similarly understood, if Hume is right. Hume's empiricism makes Locke's rights untenable. We can see that the understanding of rights depends crucially on the epistemology, metaphysics and associated theory of human nature that we accept. There remains a choice to be made here between rationalism and empiricism, a choice that is necessary for our further understanding of rights. Moreover, there is more both to morality and to motivation than has been disclosed so far.

CHAPTER 6

Human value

Given Hume's approach, we cannot be directly motivated by rights as independently real, nor by reason similarly understood. We can be motivated only by desire. Moreover we are not to understand the content of any moral claim, including a claim to a moral right, as involving some reference to an independent moral reality. And yet the human capacity for rationality – that essential feature which we supposedly all have to *be* reasonable – is imagined by Plato, Hobbes and Locke to consist at least partly in a respect for standards of reason that are in some way external to us, however they are known. It is this that is often thought to make us characteristically human and distinct from other animals. Even the materialist Hobbes sees reason in this way. Reason, furthermore, in some way necessarily constitutes or expresses or is involved in – even if only minimally – morality. We face here a polarization of alternatives: the conflict between empiricism and rationalism. It is Kant who tries to resolve that conflict,[1] and he does so through a complex presentation of a theory of our human nature and our relationship to reality.

At this point we need to understand that the theory of motivation effectively – so far – has *two* central functions in moral theory and, within that, for the theory of rights. First, a theory of motivation acts as a constraint for any acceptable theory of morality in the following way: a theory of morality must not be conceived to make demands on us that we cannot understand or know about or be motivated to

---

1. See I. Kant, *A Critique of Pure Reason* [1787], 2nd edn, N. Kemp Smith (trans.) (London: Macmillan, 1929).

follow.[2] Secondly, a theory of motivation is an essential feature of the theory of what it is to be a human being. Such a theory tells us what kinds of entities we are; it acts as a theory of human nature and in so far as human beings are morally valuable or have rights just because they are human beings, then the theory of human nature tells us what it is that is valuable about them. The nature and role of reason, the fundamental issue that divides Plato and Hume, is not just an issue of how we *know* what is good, and it is not just an issue of how we can be *motivated*, it is also an issue about what is valuable about us as human beings.

Kant clarifies these issues further.[3] First, an early difficulty needs to be noted and set aside. On Kant's approach, the "theory of human nature" that embraces the matters so far explained is made both broader and narrower, in the following ways. We have seen that a theory of human nature can be essentially involved in theories of ethics. Kant says, however, that he does not work from a "theory of human nature" but from a theory of "all rational beings".[4] It is proper to ask: how far does the set of "all rational beings" relate to the set of all human beings? Kant is quite clear: the set of all rational beings includes all human beings but may in theory go beyond it. Kant's theory of human nature is to be understood as a theory of all rational beings, then, and plainly this could have a broader application. Kant does not speculate further; despite his explicit point, he continues to write about rational beings as if he were writing only about human beings. Nevertheless, we observe that a door to possibilities has been opened, and we should note the possibility that there might, in some morally important sense of "irrational" and "rational", be both irrational human beings and other rational animals. Constraints on the discussion of the possibility of rights for animals have their foundations here. If there are irrational human beings then the "theory of all rational beings" is, in an important sense, narrower than the "theory of human nature"; if there are other rational animals then the "theory of all rational beings" is wider. If there were a serious dislocation between "human beings" and "rational beings", then to which set would morality apply or for which set should we develop our understanding of morality? Yet despite the door to alternatives

---

2. Plato does not believe that his tradespeople can be motivated by the moral demands that arise for philosophers.

3. Most usefully here, in Kant, *Fundamental Principles*.

4. *Ibid.*, 5, 29, 51.

that he has briefly opened, for Kant there is an essential link between rationality and morality and human nature, and he is not alone in that supposition, as we have seen. He develops his arguments as if there were no dislocation between "human beings" and "rational beings". Reason, in Kant's view, characterizes what it is to be a valuable human being, as well as characterizing the nature of our knowledge, including our knowledge of morality, and also the structure of our motivation.

We have expanded our understanding of moral theory to include the problems of how we know what is good, how we can be motivated and what is valuable about us as human beings. "Moral agency" is a useful expression in this context: to be a "moral agent" is to be the kind of entity that can act on the basis of moral considerations. A theory of moral agency draws on two other theories: a theory of motivation; and a theory providing the moral standards on which we are to act. These theories must be consistent, for as we have seen it is no use requiring us to be motivated by moral considerations that we cannot be motivated by. Reason operates in Plato's philosophy in these two ways: his theory of human nature puts together in a consistent manner a theory of how we are motivated and a theory of how to have knowledge of the good. As such, his theory of human nature is a theory of what it is to be a "moral agent".

A theory of human nature of this kind is limited in its presentation, and it is helpful to introduce here a further expression: "moral object". Like Plato's, Kant's approach has "reason" as its central feature. However, reason explicitly operates, for Kant, in three ways and not two: it accounts for the motivation of moral agents; it is the foundation for knowledge about morality; and it also characterizes that to which moral action and knowledge is addressed. It tells us what is morally deserving about another person. Utilitarianism similarly involves these three elements but, unlike Kant, in terms of desire rather than reason: desire motivates us; desire-satisfaction or pleasure provides the standard of goodness; and maximizing the desire-satisfaction of others expresses what it is to treat them in a moral way. The third element here embraces Kant's and the Utilitarians' views of what it is to be a "moral object", what things should be valued and why. The three functions of a moral theory explained here are plainly and importantly linked with each other in the theories introduced so far, but there is both moral and pedagogic merit in distinguishing the term "moral object". Understanding motivation may not make you good; understanding how you know what is good may not make you good; but putting matters in terms of "moral objects" requires you to address your attention to other entities and what is valuable about them, and that is at least beginning to be good.[5] Thus to be a "moral object", in this context, is to be an entity that is deserving of some kind of moral consideration, an entity on the receiving end of moral action, an entity recognized as valuable in some appropriate way. Such recognition is very typically expressed in terms of a person's "rights", "just entitlements" or "welfare".[6] Plato did not deal with rights, and in particular did not distinguish this third important feature of moral language. The question "What is valuable about another person or entity?" did not clearly arise on his approach. For Kant, however, it does.

In current debate about the understanding of rights, the "interest" theory is distinguished from the "will" theory, and the present approach with respect to these theories needs to be clarified here. The interest theory of rights holds that a right essentially protects the right-holder's well-being or interests, and it may seem that understanding rights as expressing what is valuable about another person expresses an interest theory. By contrast, the will theory holds that a right's protecting an interest is neither necessary nor sufficient for its being a right, and that it is a person's competence to choose whether a right should be enforced that constitutes the essence of their holding a right.[7] The expression of this contrast presupposes that a person's interests can be specified independently of their capacity for choice. The move to thinking of rights as expressing what is valuable about another person is neutral between these positions, however, since what is valuable about another person may be taken to consist in their capacity for choice rather than in their interests. Moreover, it should not be assumed that a clear contrast can be drawn between these two positions, for it is possible to hold a position in which our interests are simply identified with our capacity for choice. Kant particularly values choice – the human will – as the essence of what is valuable about us, as we shall see.

---

5. This approach contrasts with that of John Rawls, for whom "the principles of justice are not derived from the notion of respect for persons, from a recognition of their inherent worth or dignity", *A Theory of Justice* (Oxford: Oxford University Press, 1972), 585. Such notions are "not suitable" (*ibid.*, 586).

6. This is intended to leave open the question of how far a person's "rights", most obviously human rights, should be identified with or distinguished from their "welfare", for example. See also Ch. 12.

7. For further analysis see M. H. Kramer, "Rights Without Trimmings", in *A Debate Over Rights: Philosophical Enquiries*, M. H. Kramer, N. E. Simmonds, H. Steiner (eds) (Oxford: Clarendon Press, 1998), 7–111.

Kant uses a religious source to exemplify a crucial feature of his philosophy of human understanding.

> Even the Holy One of the Gospels must first be compared with our ideal of moral perfection before we can recognise Him as such; and so He says of Himself, "Why call ye Me (whom you see) good; none is good (the model of good) but God only (whom ye do not see)?" But whence have we the conception of God as the supreme good? Simply from the idea of moral perfection, which reason frames *a priori*, and connects inseparably with the notion of a free-will.[8]

There are here a general point and a specific point, which both need to be explained. In general, in Kant's view, you must already have the idea of something before you can experience it as a thing of the kind that you experience it to be. We experience things as things of a certain kind, and experiences are intelligible to us at that level. But experiences are not just "given" to our senses in this intelligible form (as an empiricist like Hume would see it), but are the structured outcome of both an unintelligible or "blind" input and also a rational input provided by the experiencing self's fixed structure of understanding.[9]

The structure of the mind's understanding frames experiences against a background of space and time and in terms of such fundamental categories as objects, processes and causation. It is within this framework that the ordinary concepts of everyday understanding have their place. The fundamental categories are "a priori": they exist in the mind "from the first", and rather than being derived from experience they are a condition for all possible experience. "For 'right' can never be an appearance; it is a concept in the understanding."[10] They characterize the unchanging framework of all possible human knowledge and understanding, and are shared by all human beings; equivalently, they are shared by all rational beings. The structure is essentially a rational structure, just as human beings are essentially rational. The idea of moral perfection exists in the mind somewhat like these universally shared a priori categories, although it

---

8. Kant, *Fundamental Principles*, 30.
9. "Concepts without intuitions are empty; intuitions without concepts are blind" (Kant, *A Critique of Pure Reason*: see the "Transcendental Aesthetic"). "Intuitions", for Kant, means the raw or unstructured part of experience, something not experienced in itself.
10. Kant, *A Critique of Pure Reason*, A44.

has its own peculiar status. This involves the specific claim that moral perfection is inseparably connected by reason to the notion of free will. Three things are here essentially linked: moral perfection, reason and free will.

Kant is clear and explicit. "Nothing", he says:

> can possibly be conceived in the world, or even out of it, which can be called good without qualification, except a Good Will. . . . A good will is good not because of what it performs or effects, not by its aptness for the attainment of some proposed end, but simply by virtue of the volition, that is, it is good in itself.[11]

This links the will to moral perfection. Yet not just any exercise of the will constitutes a free or good will, but only its exercise as governed by reason.[12] The will is fully free when it naturally follows reason, and it is then also good and, moreover, the only perfectly good thing. The rational autonomy of the will is the supreme principle of morality.[13] The rational will is the only unqualified good thing, for Kant, and this means that within his theory this idea of the "good will" operates as the "master moral concept", as the idea of justice did for Plato. Again like Plato, other words within the ethical category are derivative from this central notion and offer no theoretical rivalry.

In consequence, while it is common for us to evaluate particular actions as "right", this can only be derivative from an evaluation of the goodness of the will involved. The moral worth of actions then lies in the moral intention underlying them rather than what is actually carried out: "in order that an action should be morally good, it is not enough that it conform to the moral law, but it must also be done for the sake of the law, otherwise that conformity is only very contingent and uncertain".[14] Kant asks us to recognize that the

---

11. Kant, *Fundamental Principles*, 10–11.
12. ". . .we assume it as a fundamental principle that no organ for any purpose will be found but what is also the fittest and best adapted for that purpose" (*ibid.*, 12). "For as reason is not competent to guide the will with certainty in regard to its objects and the satisfaction of all our wants (which it to some extent even multiplies), this being an end to which an implanted instinct would have led with much greater certainty; and since, nevertheless, reason is imparted to us as a practical faculty, i.e. as one which is to have influence on the will, therefore, admitting that nature generally in the distribution of her capacities has adapted the means to the end, its true destination must be to produce a will, not merely good as a means to something else, but good in itself, for which reason was absolutely necessary" (*ibid.*, 14).
13. *Ibid.*, 71.
14. *Ibid.*, 5.

goodness of the rational will consists in intending to comply with the moral law for its own sake:

> an action done from duty derives its moral worth, not from the purpose which is to be attained by it, but from the maxim by which it is determined ... on the principle of volition by which the action has taken place, without regard to any object of desire.[15]

This is one's rational duty, and duty is to be understood precisely as willing for the sake of the law: "Duty is the necessity of acting from respect for the law."[16] This "necessity" is a *rational* necessity; the good will is a rational will. The "maxim" or "principle of volition" that drives the good will is purely rational and involves no inclination or desire: "Now an action done from duty must wholly exclude the influence of inclination."[17]

The rationalist basis of morality, for Kant, is expressed in the universal and consistent nature of the principles that govern the good will, respect for which is what makes it a good will. It is an essential feature of morality that it is unchanging and consistent, and it is an essential feature of the rational structure of the understanding that it is unchanging and consistent. Our moral duty does not vary with the contingencies of our desires or our situation.

> Everyone must admit that if a law is to have moral force, i.e. to be the basis of an obligation, it must carry with it absolute necessity; that, for example, the precept "Thou shalt not lie", is not valid for men alone, as if other rational beings had no need to observe it.[18]

The absolute and unconditional nature of moral requirements mean that all empirical matters must be excluded from them, just because, as Plato also saw, experience does not deliver reliable and eternal truths. The contrast between absoluteness or the categorical character of the moral law, and the contingency or hypotheticality or conditionality of lesser requirements, is stressed by Kant:

> now all imperatives command either hypothetically or categorically. The former represent the practical necessity of a possible action *as means to something else* ... The categorical imperative

---

15. *Ibid.*, 18–19.
16. *Ibid.*, 19.
17. *Ibid.*, 20.
18. *Ibid.*, 4.

would be that which represented an action as necessary of itself without reference to another end.[19]

The moral law is a categorical imperative, indeed *the* categorical imperative.

Respect for the moral law cannot involve respect for any empirical element or content of such a law. Such respect, with all such content excluded, can only be respect for the abstract conception of such laws. This amounts to a respect for the universality and consistency of reason itself. "The pre-eminent good which we call moral can ... consist in nothing else than the conception of law in itself, which certainly is only possible in a rational being".[20] Again:

> the basis of obligation must ... be sought ... *a priori* simply in the conceptions of pure reason. ... in as far as it rests even in the least degree on an empirical basis, perhaps only as to a motive, such a precept, while it may be a practical rule, can never be called a moral law.[21]

Thus the good will is not a will that acts out of respect for a particular set of moral laws, or even all moral laws, but a will that acts out of respect for the *general conception* of such laws, that which all such laws have abstractly in common, without their empirical content: "the will is conceived as a faculty of determining oneself to action in accordance with the *conception* of certain laws. And such a faculty can only be found in rational beings."[22] "Rational beings alone have the faculty of acting according to the *conception* of laws, that is according to principles, i.e. have a will."[23]

To specify the moral law is not to provide some list of particular commands, then, but to specify a general principle of respect for the consistency that rationality requires. Essential to the notion of consistency is that there should be no variation of the "principle of volition" with changing circumstance, so that the principle must be understood to be universally valid. Thus respect for the moral law is essentially respect for the universality of its application: "I am never to act otherwise than so that I could also will that my maxim should become a universal law."[24] Again, "there is therefore but one

19. *Ibid.*, 37 (emphasis added).
20. *Ibid.*, 20.
21. *Ibid.*, 4.
22. *Ibid.*, 54 (emphasis added).
23. *Ibid.*, 35 (emphasis added).
24. *Ibid.*, 21.

categorical imperative, namely this: Act only on that maxim whereby thou canst at the same time will that it should become a universal law" and "the imperative of duty may be expressed thus: Act as if the maxim of thy action were to become by thy will a Universal Law of Nature."[25] Kant illustrates the application of this principle to a number of concrete situations, arguing, for example, that it would be inconsistent with duty for a man to take his own life, or make a false promise, or leave his talents undeveloped or have no concern for the distress of others.[26] We see in these illustrations the operation of reason in showing us our duty, that is, providing knowledge of what ought to be done, and also the operation of reason in structuring the good will.

Yet moral requirements are not determined purely by respect for the categorical imperative. This imperative is initially conceived and presented by Kant as a command addressed to a particular person. Such a person is supposedly enjoined by it, for example, not to make a false promise or ignore the distress of others, because of the inconsistency that such proposals would supposedly yield if universalized. Yet this inevitably presupposes some contingency. Suppose, for example, there were only one person, only one rational being, existing in the universe. This would have an immediate effect on the supposedly universalizable claim that that person ought not to ignore the distress of others, for there are no others. For Kant, the principle of volition governing my actions should be such as could consistently be a universal law of nature, where "law of nature" is particularly understood to be an imperative that guides more than one person. The contingency that there are many people is built into the apparently pure abstractness of the categorical imperative. That imperative, supposedly empty of contingency, in fact expresses *explicitly* merely one fundamental feature of Kant's moral philosophy, which is that nothing is perfectly good except a good will. The imperative also *implicitly* presupposes a second fundamental feature of Kant's philosophy, which is that there is more than one good will.

The essential and sole goodness of the good will, and the contingency that there is more than one, bypass the abstraction of the categorical imperative. Respect for reason is not merely respect for it in the nature of one's own principles of volition but respect for it in other people also, and this yields a more immediately substantive

---

25. *Ibid.*, 46.
26. *Ibid.*, 47–9.

moral result than the abstraction of the categorical imperative.[27] "Rational nature exists as an end in itself",[28] says Kant, and this tells us how to treat other people. "So act as to treat humanity, whether in thine own person or in that of any other, in every case as an end withal, never as means only."[29]

> Now I say: man and generally any rational being exists as an end in himself, not merely as a means to be arbitrarily used by this or that will, but in all his actions, whether they concern himself or other rational beings, must be always regarded at the same time as an end.
>
> Beings whose existence depends not on our will but on nature's, have nevertheless, if they are irrational beings, only a relative value as means, and are therefore called things; rational beings, on the contrary, are called persons, because their very nature points them out as ends in themselves, that is as something which must not be used merely as means.[30]

Again, "for all rational beings come under the law that each of them must treat itself and all others never merely as means, but in every case at the same time as ends in themselves", with its crucial consequence:

> Hence results a systematic union of rational beings by common objective laws, i.e., a kingdom which may be called a kingdom of ends ... Morality consists then in the reference of all action to the legislation which alone can render a kingdom of ends possible.[31]

In this move of Kant's we recognize that the consistency of the moral will is not a matter of the consistency of the principles and considerations that in some sense exist inside each individual. Our attention is directed away from what might be supposed to be some Cartesian private space towards the legislation that would express or constitute a "kingdom" or state in which all action was not only based upon consistency within individual wills but was also based upon respect for others just because they are rational beings. Each person, as a rational being, respects the moral law and in so doing effectively legislates for all others. The rational consistency that is required is

---

27. Kant distinguishes the "form" and the "matter" of principles of volition here; *ibid.*, 65.
28. *Ibid.*, 56.
29. *Ibid.*
30. *Ibid.*, 55.
31. *Ibid.*, 62.

therefore a consistency throughout the community and not just within each individual. It immediately follows that the rights that all people have in that ideal state, rights that exist in virtue of the duties that all people have in that state to respect others as rational beings, must form a consistent set. "Now morality is the condition under which alone a rational being can be an end in himself, since by this alone is it possible that he should be a legislating member in the kingdom of ends."[32] People are respected in that ideal state *as legislating members*, so that "*Autonomy* then is the basis of the dignity of human and of every rational nature", consisting of both "freedom and self-legislation",[33] and this involves a will that "could never contradict itself".[34]

As already seen, Plato presents morality and Locke presents rights as independent or naturally existing, as eternal and universally applicable, and as essentially consistent. Hobbes presents reason in a similar way. Hume's empiricism holds that there cannot be knowledge of such considerations and neither can human beings be motivated by them. It is ultimately this empiricism that lies behind Bentham's claim that talk of natural rights is "nonsense on stilts". Kant's moral philosophy now reinstates a form of rationalism in which people can know how they ought to act and moreover can be motivated by that knowledge. There is an essential link between morality and reason, so that morality is eternal, unchanging and consistent, and independent of human *inclination*. Yet morality and reason are not independent of *humanity*; they are not to be understood as having some *separate* metaphysical existence, but are to be seen as necessarily linked to what human beings, conceived as rational beings, essentially are. It is the structures of our own understanding that are foundational to rights. It is those structures that have the traditional characteristics of being eternal in their form and inherently consistent. Human nature is eternal and unchanging, just as are the scientifically founded laws of nature that express for us the rational structure of the experienced world.

Thus Kant's position enables us to offer intermediate answers to the questions posed earlier. He provides a moral philosophy that gives us the principles governing our duties, and that characterizes the entities to which we owe those duties. Those entities, in virtue of the duties we have to them, have rights against us to the performance of those duties. These duties are universally and equally held, and in

---

32. *Ibid.*, 64.
33. *Ibid.*, 65, 83.
34. *Ibid.*, 66.

consequence the rights that exist in virtue of them are also universally and equally held. All rights are consistent with each other: they are "compossible".[35] Their "authority" for us is clearly explained, and the way in which we are motivated by such moral considerations is clearly explained. Rights are a way of expressing and protecting our dignity and autonomy as rational human beings, and the content of those rights is that which is necessary and sufficient for this purpose. Both legal and moral rights are being explained by Kant here: it is moral rights that are foundational, and these express also legislation for the "Kingdom of Ends".

We have seen that "theories of human nature" in the moral context should explain three things: moral motivation, moral standards and moral objects. It is important to appreciate that these three are in principle very different matters. It is a major confusion of thought to suppose that it is the theory of moral agency – whether in terms of capacity for moral knowledge or motivation – that necessarily grounds people's status as moral objects. Plato did not offer an account of moral objects at all. In one line of argument, Kant thought that people should be treated as "ends in themselves", on the ground that they were essentially rational moral agents; on this view, a person's "rights" depend on their being such agents, and are built merely on the "duties" of others. We shall examine Kant's position on this in more detail, in Chapter 13. For Bentham and John Stuart Mill (1806–73) it is a person's capacity for pain and pleasure that both motivates them and grounds their status as moral objects; Utilitarians do not speak of "rights" but only of the "rightness of actions". While what we say about a person, considered as the object of moral action, must not be incompatible with the theory of what it is to be a moral agent, it need not be, and had better not be, the same. Would it be acceptable, without further excuse, to kill a person so long as they were unconscious and did not feel the pain? Or torture a conscious person, a child, or an animal lacking a capacity for Kantian moral agency? We say no; but for persons and other entities who are missing the characteristics of moral agency (whatever those characteristics are), even present-day theories of justice are poor at justifying or explaining such persons' status and limitations as moral objects.

---

35. To use the term derived from Leibniz and insisted upon in this context by Hillel Steiner: "Prevention is a relation between the respective actions of two persons such that the occurrence of one of them rules out, or implies the impossibility of, the occurrence of the other. If both such actions can occur – if they are *compossible* – then neither prevents the other", *An Essay on Rights*, 2, 33.

CHAPTER 7

Hohfeld's analysis

Following Kant, we need no longer understand reason, human rights or other moral ideals as existing in some way independently of human beings. Rather, we are to see human nature, the natural world and the world of morality as all structured in terms of reason. Reason both provides the ultimate justification for our fundamental moral standards and frames our understanding of them. The reasoned detail of Kant's moral philosophy requires that we act from duty, and the rights of others are to be understood in terms of whatever correlates with those duties.

Kant's arguments concerning the rational structures of the human mind were based particularly on his analysis of the structures of human language.[1] The way we use language expresses our understanding of the world and of our moral status and duties within it, and so expresses the rational structures of our minds. In the twentieth century the analysis of language came to be central in philosophical understanding, and such analysis has permitted a major advance in our understanding of rights. This analysis of language continues the Kantian approach beyond the determination of general structures to involve a fine-grained analysis of particular concepts. At the present stage of our argument we are working with Kant's position in holding that it is the structures of our own understanding that are foundational to rights. Human nature is eternal and unchanging and essentially rational. Our ultimate moral standards – expressed for us as human rights – are thereby universal, eternal and inherently

---

1. The deduction of the categories, in *The Critique of Pure Reason*.

consistent, although they are no longer seen as metaphysically independent.

We seek next to advance our understanding of rights, within the broad foundations just expressed, by presenting a detailed conceptual analysis of rights. While understanding based on this approach is usually regarded as part of the analytical tradition in philosophy, "analytical" is a problematic term.[2] The analytical tradition of philosophy started in Austria and Germany in the late nineteenth century and came to be developed primarily in English, being in due course shared between North America, the British Isles, Australasia and some Scandinavian countries. It is a continuing tradition and was most influential during the first 75 years[3] of professional academic philosophy in the twentieth century.

In this tradition, university study in philosophy standardly covers a certain range of subjects. First, we may note the study of the history of philosophy, which initially takes as canonical texts and arguments drawn from at least the following philosophers: René Descartes (1596–1650), Locke, George Berkeley (1685–1753), Hume and Kant. It is a tradition that aims for the highest quality of logical reasoning and that makes epistemology foundational for the rest of philosophy. Earlier philosophers, particularly Plato and Aristotle, are typically read in the light of these interests.[4] Unlike other post-Kantian philosophical traditions, it is a tradition that takes the empiricist scepticism most clearly expressed by Hume as centrally problem-posing, although empiricist solutions are not insisted upon. Like Kant,[5] particular philosophers may take rationalist positions on the various issues, although the burden of proof in the tradition is such that arguments based on empiricist assumptions have a central place. The centrality of epistemology both reflects and expresses a concern with the limits of our understanding of the natural world, and in consequence the nature and limits of scientific understanding – usually assumed to be a successful enterprise – have set the agenda for

---

2. There will be an analysis of "analytical" in Ch. 8.

3. In recent years there has been a marked increase in discussion between different traditions in philosophy, sufficient to require a professional philosopher to understand more than his or her own tradition.

4. It is common in this tradition to study no philosophers between Aristotle and Descartes.

5. Kant's "dogmatic slumber" was roused by Hume: Kant, *Prolegomena to Any Future Metaphysics* [1783], P. G. Lucas (trans.) (Manchester: Manchester University Press, 1953), 9.

many philosophers in this tradition. The theory of existence also has a central place, although it is often – but not exclusively – driven by the ontology of mathematics and science. In addition to studying particularly its own canonical figures[6] in the history of philosophy, the university study of philosophy in this tradition therefore stresses study in logical reasoning, epistemology and metaphysics.

Moral philosophy is missing from the list so far, although it has always been – in a sense – a central part of the standard philosophy curriculum in this tradition. For the first seven decades of the twentieth century, it was standard to write as if – and sometimes to claim explicitly that – philosophers had no expertise whatever about substantive moral concerns. In consequence moral philosophy in this tradition, until roughly 1970, was regarded only as a branch of epistemology and metaphysics, and in terms of practical moral advice was seen as merely transmitting to a new generation the older substantive positions, such as those of Kant or the Utilitarians.[7]

Understanding these core philosophical subjects of logic, epistemology, metaphysics and ethics in the twentieth century developed in a major way through a concentration on language deriving from the logical positivists of the "Vienna Circle" (see below), American pragmatism and the later work of Wittgenstein. The outcome is that for this tradition there is also a post-Kantian canon in the history of philosophy: Mill, Gottlob Frege (1848–1925), Bertrand Russell (1872–1970), Ludwig Wittgenstein (1889–1951) and W. V. O. Quine (1908–2000), at least. The post-Kantian canon for this analytical tradition continues to be broadly empiricist in its agenda, although again it is not a condition of accepting the tradition that one should be an empiricist.[8]

The philosophical attitudes of the analytical tradition were particularly influenced by the empiricism and positivism of the Vienna Circle, a group organized by Moritz Schlick (1882–1936), which met from the 1920s until the late 1930s, and which expressed philosophical beliefs derived from the Austrian physicist and philosopher Ernst Mach (1838–1916). On Mach's view, our best scientific theories are justifiable only by reference to our sensations, and are acceptable

---

6. The canonical figures involved overlap with the canonical lists of other traditions in philosophy, although the same philosophers are often read in different ways.
7. The substantive moral and political philosophies beginning with Rawls's *A Theory of Justice* became influential from the 1970s onwards.
8. This outline historical account of the analytical tradition in philosophy is supplemented by a more exact account in Ch. 8.

only in so far as they continue to apply successfully to the world. Mach's position was thus an extension of Hume's empiricism: every-thing we know must be derived from our experiences.[9] This approach involves attempting to build our entire understanding using only the building blocks of the immediately perceived data of the senses. We have already observed the sceptical impact of this Humean approach on our understanding of human rights.

But Mach's – and so the Vienna Circle's – position was not only empiricist in Hume's atomistic way but also strongly positivist. Epistemological positivism[10] holds that science alone provides proper knowledge, but the Vienna Circle – who were known as logical positivists – held more than this: they believed that science was the only proper way of saying anything at all. They attempted to show that only scientific sentences are meaningful, because only scientific sentences are verifiable. The point of this was to find a criterion that would distinguish proper science from metaphysical, moral and other speculation by showing everything but scientific sentences to be meaningless as true descriptions of the world. The idea of sentences referring to *independently existing* human rights that might be known by philosophical means is nonsensical. Science discloses no such things in the universe. Moral judgements were typically understood as expressions of emotion, and certainly not as the kinds of thing that could be true or false.[11] Even philosophers should abide by the rules of language used in science. Since on the positivist view science alone achieves knowledge, philosophy can make no substantive contribu-tion to knowledge,[12] and philosophers are left merely to analyse the meanings of sentences for the sake of pedagogical clarification. Analysing the language of rights is then the appropriate activity for philosophers of rights. Conceptual analysis is not just a part of philosophy but the whole of it.

The approach thereby sets for philosophy a standard of clarity and exactness of meaning, a standard modelled on the clarity and

---

9. Hume's "atomism" was rather unthinkingly assumed by positivist philosophers of science until the work of W. V. O. Quine.
10. Not to be confused with legal positivism, for which see Hart, "Positivism and the Separation of Law and Morals".
11. See A. J. Ayer, *Language, Truth and Logic* (Harmondsworth: Penguin, 1971), Ch. 6.
12. The supposition that philosophy is not substantive ignores the fact that it is a substantive philosophical claim, necessarily associated with the positivist position, that science alone – and indeed science conceived in a particular way – achieves knowledge.

exactness of meaning to be found in scientific sentences. Analytical philosophers thus tend to be more austere in their language than their more speculative predecessors. They are so in order to keep a tight rein on meaning and take less risk in saying something false. The original logical positivist approach was afterwards notorious for its failure to find a self-consistent criterion of meaningfulness and also for its failure to find, in the theory of meaning, a criterion for science. Despite these failures, the general attitudes of the Vienna Circle, embodying empiricism, the philosophical centrality of science and the requirement for philosophy to keep to a scientific exactness of meaning, have remained strongly influential in the analytical tradition.

In 1919 two articles from the *Yale Law Journal* written by Hohfeld were published in book form as *Fundamental Legal Conceptions as Applied in Judicial Reasoning*.[13] This work was an exercise in analytical jurisprudence and reflected the philosophical attitude apparent in logical positivism: the idea that by scientific standards of meaning the truth is revealed. The book's "Introduction" by Hohfeld's Yale colleague W. W. Cook says of it that "its chief value lies in the fact that by its aid the correct solution of legal problems becomes not only easier but more certain. In this respect it does not differ from any other branch of pure science."[14] Much was owed to this work by twentieth-century analytical theorists of both moral and legal rights, and much is owed by practising lawyers also, if only because so many were trained to believe it.

A particular feature of Hohfeld's approach should be noted here. In Chapter 1 we asked whether there is a difference between legal and moral rights. Beyond mentioning there the different approaches of Hobbes, Locke and the Utilitarians, our subsequent argument has mainly addressed the issue of how far we may understand human, moral or natural rights as expressing some eternal and consistent reality independent of human institutions or choices. Thus, in so far as there may be a distinction between moral rights and legal rights, the argument has concentrated upon moral rights. With Hume we questioned the independence of such rights, and with Kant we came to understand the intrinsic rational connections between our own natures and institutions and the moral standards that are to govern them. Analysing the language of rights in our actual institutions is a crucial move towards the

---

13. W. N. Hohfeld, *Fundamental Legal Conceptions as Applied in Judicial Reasoning*, W. W. Cook (ed.) (New Haven, CT: Yale University Press, 1919).
14. W. W. Cook, "Introduction", in Hohfeld, *Fundamental Legal Conceptions*, 3.

further understanding of rights. In so far as there may be a distinction between moral rights and legal rights, we find in Hohfeld a particularly explicit analysis of legal rights: of rights in the language of the law. We therefore find we are attending to a particular jurisdiction rather than to morality or law "in general". Hohfeld attended to a US jurisdiction, although his claims extended to other English language jurisdictions in the common law tradition. His reasoning nevertheless has implications beyond this. The relationship between legal and moral rights will be discussed further in Chapter 8.

In terms of the development and teaching of law, Hohfeld's work was a milestone, sometimes perceived as almost arrogant in its claims; Hohfeld begins with a brief yet learned presentation of what at the time were classical explanations – often authoritative yet divergent – of the notions of trusts and other equitable notions, and holds them all – and moreover the understanding of all other jural interests – to be inadequate. One of the greatest hindrances to our understanding of and our successful solution of legal problems, he says, "arises from the express or tacit assumption that all legal relations may be reduced to 'rights' and 'duties'".[15] Legal questions are much more complex than such binary choices permit, although Hohfeld's developing argument shows that he thinks the failings are not so much due to reducing legal relations to "rights" and "duties" as due to reducing them to simplistic versions of these. The notions "right" and "duty" are ambiguous, and "chameleon-hued words are a peril both to clear thought and to lucid expression".[16] Legislation using such terms was confused, and lawyers had indiscriminately used them in their discourse. Hohfeld disambiguates these notions and presents four kinds of rights and four kinds of duties in a newly exact logical structure. The four kinds of rights are named as right, privilege, power and immunity. The four kinds of duties are named as duty, no-right, liability and disability.

The terminology here is not quite as useful as it might be. It is odd, for example, to find "right" effectively occurring twice, appearing first as a vague term that in ordinary legal use indiscriminately covers such things as privilege, power and immunity, and appearing for a second time as an exact term that forms part of the clarifying analysis. Again, it is odd to find "duty" effectively appearing twice in the same way: as Hohfeld notes,[17] "duty" is the correlative of "right" even

---

15. Hohfeld, *Fundamental Legal Conceptions*, 35.
16. *Ibid.*
17. *Ibid.*, 38.

when "right" is used in its "broad and indiscriminate" way. Hohfeld partly observes this, and, without renaming his conceptions, occasionally speaks of the more exact understanding of a "right" as a "claim", an understanding that had some support from legal authorities. Later writers often use the expression "claim-right" to perform the same task, and I shall do the same here. Curiously, the identical difficulty with the word "duty" appearing twice appears not to have been commented on. I shall not offer a different word to express the exact understanding of "duty", for the presentation of Hohfeld's position can be made largely in terms of "right" and does not require it.

Hohfeld analyses the four senses of each of the vague concepts "right" and "duty" in terms of a structure of the logical relationships between his more exact notions, some of which he then illustrates with practical legal examples. Hohfeld's structure is shown in Table 7.1.

Table 7.1 Hohfeld's structure of logical relationships

Jural opposites:	right [claim-right]	privilege	power	immunity
	no-right [no-claim-right]	duty	disability	liability
Jural correlatives:	right [claim-right]	privilege	power	immunity
	duty	no-right [no-claim-right]	liability	disability

This hints at a much clearer understanding of the vague concepts of "right" and "duty", but is nevertheless still opaque, largely because of the unexplained nature of the notions of "opposites" and "correlatives". As L. W. Sumner remarks, "To a philosopher's eye the most obvious [limitation] is Hohfeld's failure to analyse any of his conceptions."[18] I shall present some of these terms, in order, initially, to explain the nature of Hohfeld's logical relationships. Hohfeld begins his own explanations with "jural correlatives". I shall do the same, and we will find that explanations of "jural opposites" arise in the context of this.

---

18. L. W. Sumner, *The Moral Foundation of Rights* (Oxford: Clarendon Press, 1987), 19.

Imagine, with Hohfeld, a situation where a person, X, has a right against some other person, Y, that Y should stay off X's land. This vaguely named right is particularly to be understood as a claim-right. This seems an elementary situation, but it could be simplified further than Hohfeld presents it. More simply, X might have a claim-right against Y that Y should stay off *some* particular piece of land. Need it be X's land? We might typically think here of X *owning* the land in question, but of course he need not do so. We can imagine X having the claim-right against Y even if X does not own the land. Thus, Y might have *promised* X not to go on the land, and X might have the claim-right in virtue of that promise. Is it property or promising that is the issue here? Neither. When we think of the claim-right in question, we need, for exactness of understanding, to extract it from irrelevant details about how the claim-right came about or on what basis it is justified.

In the situation where X has a claim-right against Y that Y should stay off certain land, Hohfeld points out that we normally understand in virtue of that very situation that Y is under a *duty* towards X to stay off that land. Again, where Y is under a duty towards X to stay off certain land, we normally understand that X thereby has a claim-right against Y that he stay off that land. For Hohfeld, the relationship between X's claim-right against Y and Y's duty towards X in such a context is thus that of a "correlative". If two things are "correlative" then they have a *mutual* relationship. "Claim-right" is in effect a technical term that is to be understood in such a way that the mutual relationship with the appropriate sense of "duty" exists. However, Hohfeld takes for granted what that relationship is exactly.

Grammatically, one way of marking how two words may be correlatives is that they are "regularly used together",[19] but that is certainly not true of "right" and "duty", however vaguely or exactly understood they are. Thus entire legal systems may be expressed in the terms of the language of duties rather than of rights, and vice versa, with one being used largely to the exclusion of the other; indeed, the general change from the language of duties to the language of rights within the law (if not in politics) was a notable feature of twentieth-century legal developments.[20] We will examine the implications of

---

19. Definition of "correlative" in the *Oxford Encyclopedic English Dictionary* (Oxford: Clarendon Press, 1991).
20. The point is not that politics does not use the language of rights, but that it had previously used the language of duties less than did the law.

changing points of view between the language of rights and the language of duties in Chapters 11, 12 and 13. As we noted in Chapter 1, it has been widely remarked that there is, in the contemporary Western world, a proliferation of claims for various rights, whereas people are rather less ready to bring their duties to public attention.[21]

A second mark of the way in which two words may be correlatives is that they are "so related that one implies the other",[22] which we understand to mean that *each* implies the other, and it is clear from his article that this is roughly what Hohfeld has in mind. So, "claim-right" and "duty" are correlative just in so far as "each implies the other". But this too cannot be right, for neither implies the other any more than "white" implies "black"; on the contrary, we might well think of "right" and "duty" as *opposites*, and, indeed, the top half of Hohfeld's table comes close to saying that.

What is actually meant by Hohfeld's view that "claim-right" and "duty" "imply each other" is that, thinking of the land example above, "X has a claim-right against Y that p" implies that "Y has a duty towards X that p" and "Y has a duty towards X that p" implies that "X has a claim-right against Y that p". Thus it is not that the particular *concepts* "claim-right" and "duty" are correlatives, but only that certain *sentences* are correlatives, sentences in which these terms *may* – although certainly not *must* – be embedded. With these assumptions taken for granted, "claim-right" and "duty" are roughly concluded by Hohfeld to be "jural correlatives".[23] This conclusion is a mere short-hand that becomes even less helpful as we move to the other elements of the vague meaning of "right", and it is this inexplicitness of reasoning that makes Hohfeld's table initially so opaque.

Single words will not do: the mutual implications between so-called "correlatives" can only be understood properly by making explicit the contents of the rights and duties involved and the particular people concerned who bear them. The structures of the sentences that express these rights and duties, with the order of the placeholders within them, are crucial to their meaning and to their logical implications. It is elementary that "X has a claim-right against Y that p" is very different from "Y has a claim-right against X that p". Yet do they not have the same logical form? They do, but the form is neither expressed by these sentences nor by Hohfeld's table (Table 7.1).

---

21. O'Neill, *A Question of Trust*.
22. Definition of "correlate" in the *Oxford Encyclopedic English Dictionary*.
23. Hohfeld, *Fundamental Legal Conceptions*, 36.

Hohfeld's "X" is the *name* of an imagined particular individual, as is his "Y" the name of some *other* imagined particular individual. To express logical form, these placeholders have to express *variables* and not names. With X and Y purely understood as variables, "X has a claim-right against Y that p" is *identical* to "Y has a claim-right against X that p". The sentence preceding this one may seem odd to those unused to semi-formal reasoning, and it may seem odd to some logicians too. The oddity is not logical, however, but is due to its flouting the following obvious but rarely expressed convention also used in algebra: do not change the symbols used for variables in the course of the argument.

In the situation considered, the particular person named X has a claim-right against the particular person named Y that Y not go on a certain piece of land. As we have seen, it may well be that the land does not belong to X, and we have extracted this claim-right from such irrelevancies. The point of removing such irrelevancies is to avoid blocking what we can imagine. So freed, we can recognize that it may happen that, not only does X have a claim-right against Y that Y not go on the land, but that Y also has a claim-right against X that X not go on the land. The one claim-right does not imply the other, but this is a possible situation. We can imagine that both X and Y are security guards who patrol the perimeter of the land, neither permitted to enter the land himself but each having the claim-right to stop anyone else – including each other – from entering. (They may even jointly own the land, and have agreed that the situation be like this, so that we understand the claim-right is clearly theirs and not that of some company that employs them.) In virtue of this possibility, it is clear that X's claim-right against Y that Y does not go on a certain piece of land may result from a very different situation from one in which the very same claim-right is held by X against Y, but the land does belong to X. In this last situation X has a claim-right against Y that Y not go on the land, but X is typically at liberty to go on it himself.[24] X's right to go on his own property is therefore a very different right from his claim-right to keep Y off it.[25] Here we meet Hohfeld's second sense of the vague word "right": right as "privilege". It is a privilege in Hohfeld's terminology that X is able to go on his own land, and "X has the privilege of

---

24. Not always; the prevention of livestock disease, for example, may block the property owner from going on his own land.

25. Again, despite being the property owner, X may nevertheless not have the right to prevent a livestock disease inspector from going on X's land.

going on his own land" implies the absence of a duty on X to stay off the land. "The privilege of entering is the negation of a duty to stay off."[26] "Privilege" and "duty" are jural *opposites*. Expressed slightly more exactly, "X has the privilege of going on his own land" implies "X has no duty to stay off his own land", and we may observe that the latter also implies the former.

Where X has this privilege, Hohfeld says, Y has no right to stop X from entering, and this latter concept Hohfeld calls a "no-right", meaning, "no-claim-right".[27] "Privilege" and "no-claim-right" are then jural *correlatives*, according to Hohfeld, as Table 7.1 shows. Yet this second pairing displays more clearly the apparent oddity in Hohfeld's approach. By "correlatives" we understand that two things are related in that each implies the other. There are two simple ways in which implication can happen. At the level of words or concepts, we might say that one word implies another if it includes that other in its meaning. "Bachelor", then, implies "man". This is not, however, a *mutual* implication, since "man" does not imply "bachelor". Only a synonym would provide mutual implication at this level. Moreover, this is not the level at which Hohfeld is operating his correlativity, since we have already seen it to be obviously false to suppose that, as a word, "claim-right" implies "duty" or vice versa. The second simple way in which two things might imply each other is at the level of the sentence, and we have seen how this works with Hohfeld's first pair of correlatives. Strictly, it is not that "claim-right" and "duty" are correlatives, but rather that the sentences "X has a claim-right against Y that p" and "Y has a duty towards X that p" are correlatives. Each, it is claimed, implies the other, supposedly in a simple and immediately recognizable logical step that assumes that "X" and "Y" are names and not variables.

Yet this is not the situation that arises for "privilege" and "no-claim-right". Once again, these do not mean the same thing. In other words, neither implies the other. We have to construct the appropriate sentences into which they are to be fitted if we are to discover the correlativity here. Hohfeld himself tells us that the appropriate sentence for privilege is "X has the privilege of entering on the land". This implies, he also tells us, that "X does not have a duty to stay off".[28] We have observed that this latter sentence also implies the

26. Hohfeld, *Fundamental Legal Conceptions*, 39.
27. *Ibid*.
28. *Ibid*.

former. With this mutual implication between the two, it turns out that "privilege" and what we might call "no-duty" are jural correlatives. (This is not surprising, since we have noted that "privilege" and "duty" are jural *opposites*.) Yet Hohfeld offers "privilege" and "no-claim-right" instead. Why? Hohfeld's reasoning is that "the correlative of X's privilege of entering himself is manifestly Y's 'no-right' that X shall not enter".[29] Far from being manifest, this cannot be formally correct reasoning, for the simple reason that the sentence "X has the privilege of entering on the land" *makes no reference to Y at all*, and can therefore formally imply no sentence in which Y plays any significant part. Rather than accuse Hohfeld of an elementary logical mistake, we may recall from our study of Locke's position the importance of suppressed premises.

In this context Hohfeld has to be taking for granted some suppressed premise that warrants a reference to Y in his conclusion. Hohfeld seems to think here that searching for a "correlative" for a sentence whose subject is X is searching for an implication of that sentence where the subject is Y. "Correlatives" of X-based sentences are required by him to be understood as essentially Y-based. (If we examine Table 7.1, we shall also observe, by contrast, that jural "opposites" of X-based sentences are themselves X-based sentences.) Hohfeld plainly thinks of rights of Xs in general – and not just of claim-rights in particular – as necessarily involving some reference to other particular people, Ys, "against whom" the rights are held. This is a common assumption:[30] Steiner, for example, makes the following claims:

1 Rights are constituted by rules. (The rules constituting *moral* rights are standardly taken to be those of *justice*.)
2 Rights signify a bilateral normative relation between those who hold them (their subjects) and those against whom they are held (their objects).
3 These relations entail the presence or absence of constraints on the conduct (performances and forbearances) of objects.
4 These constraints consist in objects' duties (obligations) or in their disabilities (lack of capacities to alter subjects' normative relations with objects) ...

---

29. *Ibid.*
30. That does not make it correct. As Sumner says, "We also need not share Hohfeld's assumption that the subject and object of a relational duty must be distinct individuals" (*The Moral Foundation of Rights*, 25).

... most accounts of what rights are, accept features (1) to (4) on this list[31]

Accepting particularly Steiner's features (2–4) for rights in general, then, just as a claim-right involves specification of three things – the person(s) who has (have) the right; its content; and the person(s) against whom it is held – so the same must be assumed to be true for a privilege, given that it is a kind of right. The sentence "X has the privilege of entering on the land" cannot then be properly complete in its explicitness, for it is missing any specification of those against whom it is held.[32] Making explicit a suppressed premise analogous to Steiner's (2–4), together with the refinement in our understanding of what Hohfeld means by "correlative", will indeed yield Y-based sentences.[33] Only these, for Hohfeld, can be the *relevant* set of correlatives for his table. The fact that "X has the privilege of entering on the land" and "X does not have a duty to stay off" are also logical correlatives is irrelevant, and no more than a re-expression of the jural opposites "privilege" and "duty".

These irrelevant correlatives are nevertheless an inexplicit part of Hohfeld's reasoning. "X has the privilege [against Y] of entering on the land" implies "X does not have a duty [to Y] to stay off". Given the correlativity of "claim-right" and "duty", then "X does not have a duty [to Y] to stay off" implies "Y does not have a claim-right against X that X stay off" (and vice versa). So, in Hohfeld's shorthand, X's privilege is correlative with Y's no-claim-right. Says Hohfeld, "thus far it has been assumed that the term 'privilege' is the most appropriate and satisfactory to designate the mere negation of duty".[34] It is X's duty that is negated here, and with that is implied the "mere negation" of a right of Y's in the matter. Thus the jural correlative of "privilege" is "no-claim-right".

Yet why not say, for example, that, in virtue of X's privilege of entering his own land, Y has a *duty* not to stop X from doing so? Here Hohfeld is right. He seeks to clarify the concepts involved. In the case

---

31. Steiner, *An Essay on Rights*, 56–7.
32. Are these particular people X, Y, etc.? Or is it *anybody*? The former are usually characterized as rights *in personam*, and the latter characterized as rights *in rem*. See Hohfeld, *Fundamental Legal Conceptions*, 81–2.
33. Actually, it will only do this if it is a right *in personam*, for Y is a *name* and not a *variable* in Hohfeld's analysis. Hohfeld's table involves reasoning that confuses names and variables.
34. Hohfeld, *Fundamental Legal Conceptions*, 44.

of the ownership of property by *X*, a complex bundle of rights and duties are in practice typically held "against" other people such as *Y*. As we have seen, *X* may have the claim-right against *Y* that *Y* not go on his land. *X* may also have a second claim-right against *Y* that *Y* not stop *X* from exercising *X*'s privilege to go on his own land. But this second claim-right is not the same as the privilege itself. The absence of a claim-right on *Y*'s part to stop *X* from going on the land is a different thing from the presence of a duty on *Y*'s part: either a duty to stop *X* or a duty not to stop *X*.

The remaining columns of Hohfeld's table are constructed and understood on similar lines. Just as right, privilege, no-right and duty are logically interrelated, so power, immunity, disability and liability are logically interrelated. One needs only to understand one from this second set of jural concepts to be able to understand the rest. Think, first, with Hohfeld, of "power" as "*X* having an ability to do something". The obvious jural opposite of this is *X*'s "disability" of doing so. A "power" is a kind of right, and rights are held against others. Imagine another person *Y* against whom the power is held: we are then to understand *Y* being under a "liability" to *X* in the matter, so that "power" and "liability" are jural correlatives. If *Y* has no such liability, then *Y* is immune to the relevant exercise of power: "liability" and "immunity" are jural opposites. If *Y* has such immunity, then *X* has a disability of exercising the power against *Y*, so "immunity" and "disability" are jural correlatives.

A brief example from Hohfeld will enable us to complete the explanation of his table.

> In *Booth v. Commonwealth*,[35] the court had to construe a Virginia statute providing "that all free white male persons who are twenty-one years of age and not over sixty, shall be *liable* to serve as jurors" ... It is plain that this enactment imposed only a *liability* and not a *duty*. It is a liability to have a duty created.[36]

There is a clear difference between owing a person a duty and being merely liable to owe that person a duty, as in this jury case. The duty is only owed when the power is exercised so as to create the duty. Yet is this so different from the exercise of a claim-right? Cannot a claim-right holder *choose* to exercise that right? In the case of *X*'s property, should we say that *X*'s claim-right against *Y* that *Y* not go on a certain

---

35. *Ibid.*, 44, n. 85 – original reference to (1861) 16 Grat., 519, 525.
36. Hohfeld, *Fundamental Legal Conceptions*, 59.

piece of land only imposes a duty on Y if X chooses to exercise that right, and that if he does not then Y is merely under a liability? This may indeed partly be so, and this may enable us to understand the "rights" of a property-owner all the more clearly. In addition to those already discussed, we find that powers are typically included. Powers impose liabilities; one may have the power to exercise a claim-right, but the claim-right only exists in so far as the power is exercised in favour of its existence, precisely because Y's duty only exists if that claim-right is exercised. Otherwise only the liability of Y to X exists. We need, with Hohfeld, to distinguish the existence of powers from the existence of claim-rights, and this will include distinguishing the existence of powers to create or exercise claim-rights from the exist-ence of claim-rights. Having a vague generality of "rights", in particular property rights, can include all of these more exact things, each understood in terms of the logical relationships that Hohfeld specifies. Many similar comments and appropriate lines of reasoning can be constructed using the resources of Hohfeld's table (Table 7.1). Using it, we can begin to see, for example, the many relationships with others that the "simple" holding of property might involve. It may then be appropriate to understand the table not only as offering a conceptual scheme in terms of which legal questions can be answered or in terms of which moral or human rights issues may be expressed, but also as offering a conceptual scheme in terms of which many complex social relationships can be understood.

The complexity of detailed understanding of rights that Hohfeld's system permits can nevertheless come at some cost to simplicity. It is difficult to deny that learning the meaning and application of Hohfeld's table with its many implications, both explicit and implicit, is a fairly hard intellectual task. Finnis points out that lawyers often talk of rights not as relationships between some particular persons, the things they have a right to and other particular persons against whom those rights are held, but more simply as relationships between particular persons and the things they have a right to. Using Finnis's example, a person, A, may have a right to £10 under some contract. Initially the contract may make another person, B, liable to pay the £10, but later, if (for example) the contract is assigned to another, a further person, C, may be liable to pay the £10 instead. Assignment then changes the situation from one set of Hohfeldian relationships to another different set, but, Finnis suggests, understanding the situation in terms of such changing Hohfeldian detail is at the cost of recognizing the essential unity of the situation over time, a unity that is represented and preserved in the non-Hohfeldian description of the core situation as being one in which A has a right to £10.[37]

Yet while we must not lose sight of such unity, which may perhaps be helpful in the understanding of some *human* rights (which may be held against *everybody*), it is plain that talk of "unity" is little more than an expository shorthand: the Hohfeldian detail is necessary for expressing the changing legal reality to which the assignment of the contract gives rise, and the Hohfeldian system fully recognizes and indeed presupposes, in this context, the ongoing centrality of the contract itself. From a Hohfeldian perspective, the "core situation" is not one in which A has a straightforward right to £10, but one in which A has a right to £10 *under the contract*, and one cannot fully understand what that means without understanding the changing detail about the duties of those against whom A's right is held, detail that the Hohfeldian system permits but that lawyers' shorthand can obscure.

As we follow Hohfeld's route we can develop greater clarity of understanding, even though much in this area was not fully specified by Hohfeld. For example, does the sentence "X has the claim-right against Y that p" imply "X has the power to *create* a claim-right against Y that p"? Almost certainly not; for example, buying property and the claim-rights that go with it is expensive. It would be nice if I could simply *create* such claim-rights without paying for it, but I do not have the power to do so. Yet does X having a claim-right against Y imply "X has the power to *exercise* a claim-right against Y that p"? Even here, not necessarily. Certainly some rights may not be waived; for example, I cannot waive my right not to be killed by another, and therefore do not have the power either to create this right or to waive it. Yet, as a landowner, I can waive my right against Y not to enter on my land; I do have the power here to exercise the right or not.[38] Is that a power to create the right, after all, since the correlated duty only exists if I exercise the power? Yet to "waive" a right seems to presuppose its existence before being waived; it is, perhaps temporarily or with some other limit, to revoke something already there. In that case the correlated duty is also in existence prior to this revocation. Thus, in the case of a claim-right, we might think that its correlated

---

37. Finnis, *Natural Law and Natural Rights*, 201–202.
38. There are limits here: while, as a landowner with a mortgage, a person may have the claim-right to stop others living on his or her land, he or she cannot waive it to such an extent that others may claim possession without offending the rights of his or her mortgage company.

duty is in continuous existence unless revoked; while, in the case of a power, we might think that some correlated duty only comes into existence when the power is exercised.

All this suggests a series of logical connections between claim-rights, duties, powers and liabilities that is not fully apparent in Hohfeld's table, where the first two columns and the last two columns are presented by Hohfeld as free-standing and with no inter-connections. We might, then, seek much more than Hohfeld offers in his table,[39] and a number of philosophers have done so, often making full use of the latest developments in applied modal logic.[40] No further development will be offered here. Whatever the exact details of all the logical relationships may be, what might be called the Hohfeldian research strategy is sufficiently clear in its aim to specify and if necessary stipulate[41] a scheme of exact concepts, mutually supporting each other by logical implication, and together sufficiently expressing the vague notions of "rights" and "duties" in a form intended to make full sense of the entire category of our practical concerns. Such concerns may be either moral or legal, although Hohfeld's interest was primarily with the latter.

---

39. Hohfeld was aware that analysis beyond his table was required and embarked on further argument that was not fully developed at his early death.
40. See I. Pörn, *The Logic of Power* (Oxford: Basil Blackwell, 1970); Sumner, *The Moral Foundation of Rights*, 19, 28 (comment and yet further reading).
41. A point stressed by M. H. Kramer, "Rights Without Trimmings", 23.

CHAPTER 8

Hohfeld's analysis analysed

What exactly does it mean for Hohfeld's scheme of "exact" concepts to be an "analysis" of fundamental jural relations? According to Hohfeld we can use his system to solve legal questions, as his editor Cook observed. For example, where a person has property rights of a certain kind, we can *deduce* that someone else has the appropriate correlative duties. More generally, with complex situations we can deduce a series of relationships involving claim-rights, privileges, powers and immunities, and their opposites and correlatives. Hohfeld quotes Bruce Wyman's (1876–1926) work *Public Service Companies*, as follows:

> The duty placed upon every one exercising a public calling is primarily *a duty* to serve every man who is a member of the public. . . . It is somewhat difficult to place this exceptional duty in our legal system . . . The truth of the matter is that the obligation resting upon one who has undertaken the performance of public duty is *sui generis*.[1]

And Hohfeld comments on this, "It is submitted that the learned writer's difficulties arise primarily from a failure to see that the innkeeper, the common carrier and others similarly 'holding out' are under present *liabilities* rather than present *duties*".[2]

---

1. B. Wyman, *Cases on Public Service Companies, Public Carriers, Public Works, and Other Public Utilities*, 2nd edn (Cambridge, MA: The Harvard Law Review Association, 1909), §§330–33.
2. Hohfeld, *Fundamental Legal Conceptions*, 57.

As Cook says, these kinds of solutions to legal questions are "correct" solutions:[3] the *truth* of the matter lies not with Wyman but with Hohfeld. But what makes them correct? Given the truth of presupposed assertions about a person's legal rights, further legal and social truths can then be deduced. These conclusions, it bears stressing, are understood as *true*, as *correct* answers. In terms of Hohfeld's analysis, their truth requires the soundness of the legal reasoning involved, presupposing his clarification of the meanings of the terms used in that reasoning. This is imagined to be a "scientific" approach, describing a relevant part of reality just as does a scientific theory. But truth requires more than consistency of reasoning, and what does the "truth" of the sentences involved in Hohfeld's reasoning amount to?

Their truth does not consist in some sentence-by-sentence correspondence to some metaphysically independent legal or moral "reality" that stands outside jural systems or actual moral practices. We saw, in our continuing argument towards Kant's position, that rights do not have an independent metaphysical existence, but may be structured in virtue of an essential link to rational human nature and our moral institutions. It may be that sentences about *human* rights are made true by derivation from universal features of human nature, as Kant claims, but it is plain that Hohfeld's analysis of rights is specific to a particular language and a particular jurisdiction and particular time. As we shall see later, the meaning of "rights" has changed over time. Nothing in what Hohfeld says suggests that general features of human nature are involved here, and the attempt to generalize what he says to other times, cultures or jurisdictions would be plainly incorrect.

So it is neither an independent metaphysical existence nor a temporally and culturally universal language or practice that might make Hohfeld's assertions about rights true. Yet neither is it plain that they are true merely in so far as we, in our local situation, *believe* them to be true, for surely not anything we believe will be true. What, then, would make Wyman wrong and Hohfeld right? One suggestion is that our psychology is organised in terms of the language we learn, so that our choices of what to believe are not so free as we might imagine. Our rights or duties might then be understood as the collective psychological response of individuals ingrained by "millennia of conditioning".[4] Yet that cannot be right, either, for, given Hohfeld's

---

3. Cook, "Introduction", 3.
4. Kelly, *A Short History of Western Legal Theory*, 369–70, referring particularly to Axel Hägerström.

analysis, it is often only careful and deliberate legal or moral reasoning that tells us what our more subtle rights, duties, powers and immunities might be. Moreover, while Hohfeldian reasoning will be based, for example, on presuppositions about some rights from which some other duties are derived, the initial assumptions of that reasoning will to a considerable extent reflect established law or established moral practice, and this too can be very deliberately "chosen" or created. Can just any law or moral practice be established? In so far as our rights exist in virtue of a Hohfeldian set of rights sentences being true,[5] then we still need to understand what the truth of Hohfeld's analysis amounts to.

Sumner is helpful here.[6] We have noted Humean objections to natural rights; Sumner too expresses a range of objections to natural rights, drawing on Bentham's approach to do so. He characterizes Bentham's main argument as follows: "(1) there can be no rights without laws; (2) there can be no natural moral laws; therefore, (3) there can be no natural rights".[7] Premise (1) here is supported by the view that rights are claim-rights that correlate with duties, so that they exist only in so far as there are laws imposing those duties. Bentham's argument for (2) derives from his view that laws require a legislator and there is no natural legislator, but Sumner replaces this rather unsatisfactory account with the more modern view that laws exist in so far as they are valid within a legal system, and "the existence of the system as a whole is a matter of its being sustained by conventional social practices of compliance with and acceptance of its rules on the part of those to whom the rules apply".[8] In so far as we understand a legal system in terms of Hohfeldian concepts with their deductive links, then our legal rights form a system that identifies the jurisdiction in question.

As Hans Kelsen (1881–1973) put the most extreme logical form of this, "the state itself is a complex of norms".[9] Kelsen offered a "pure science of law" in which norms are validated within a single consistent system in terms of a basic norm or "Grundnorm".[10] Sumner's

5. This might be interpreted as the "ontological commitment" of what we say in this context. See W. V. O. Quine, "On What There Is", in *From a Logical Point of View*, 2nd edn, W. V. O. Quine, 1–19 (New York: Harper & Row, 1961).
6. Sumner, *The Moral Foundation of Rights*, esp. 108, 111ff.
7. *Ibid.*, 112.
8. *Ibid.*, 113.
9. Kelly, *A Short History of Western Legal Theory*, 356.
10. R. Cotterrell, *The Politics of Jurisprudence* (London: Butterworths, 1989), 106–10. See also Pörn, *The Logic of Power*.

Benthamite objection to natural rights suggests that we should see Hohfeld's account as expressing or describing a legal system, understanding by that a rule-governed social practice. Such an answer is most obviously appropriate to *legal* rights within a specific jurisdiction. Is there a distinction between legal and moral rights? In so far as Hohfeld's scheme may be interpreted as analysing the language of *moral* rights, then the "moral system" to which it relates will not necessarily be identified with a particular jurisdiction. A moral system may reflect a social practice that does not map upon a particular jurisdiction. A particular instance of differential mapping occurs with "natural" or – better – *human* rights, understood now in non-metaphysical or Kantian terms. Since human rights are, whatever else they are, *universal*, then the moral system expressing them must be universal too. Given Hohfeld's general approach, human rights should then be understood to exist in terms of universal conventional social practices, of which perhaps the entire world might be philosophically persuaded.[11]

The dispute between the natural law theorists and Bentham, Sumner points out, is over whether there can be *non*-conventional rule systems that can create rights. Bentham says no, drawing on his own empiricist assumptions of a Humean kind. By contrast, the natural law theorists like Locke are committed to saying yes. An important point that Sumner stresses is that Bentham's position is not that no non-conventional rule systems exist. The rules of reasoning, which we have already supposed to be in some sense "independent" of us or non-conventional, would be like this.[12] Bentham's point would be that such rules *conferring rights* cannot exist. They cannot do so, on Sumner's Humean extension of Bentham's argument, because we cannot explain how such rules can give moral reasons for action in the absence of social convention. There would have to be a social convention requiring, in effect, that any such independent natural rules should be followed.

Yet cannot Hohfeld's analysis still reveal truths just as science does? Bentham and Hume may be correct, in part: we may wish to accept that we cannot be directly motivated by non-conventional rule systems and that only social convention, operating perhaps through desire, will motivate us to follow non-conventional rules. But that does not prevent

---

11. Rawls, *A Theory of Justice*, 21.
12. "The rules of arithmetic or natural deduction", as Sumner puts it (*The Moral Foundation of Rights*, 114).

non-conventional rule systems, like reason, from having some independent or Kantian existence, and if it can be so for reason, why not for rights? Or is it not so for reason? Is an appeal to reason not so objective after all? The answer to that will take us through to Chapter 10. As a first step, Hohfeld's analysis itself needs to be analysed.

Hohfeld says of his analysis:

> Eight conceptions of the law have been analyzed and compared in some details, the purpose having been to exhibit not only their intrinsic meaning and scope, but also their relations to one another and the methods by which they are applied, in judicial reasoning, to the solution of concrete problems of litigation.[13]

Thus his understanding of the meanings of the terms analysed is that they have an "intrinsic" meaning, and are also those that are actually used in real judicial situations that deal with real legal problems. There is a wealth of references to actual legal usage by Hohfeld in support of his analysis, and yet there are also a "considerable number of judicial opinions" that "afford ample evidence of the inveterate and unfortunate tendency to confuse".[14] Hohfeld, while certainly finding much in the law reports in the way of judicial support for his analysis, is *selecting* those that support his position: he is *judging* the judges,[15] as in the following.

> Lord Westbury, in *Bell v. Kennedy* (1868), L.R. 1 H.L. (Sc.) 307: "Domicile, therefore, is an idea of the law. It is the *relation* which the *law creates* between an individual and a particular locality or country." [Compare the confusion in the discussion of the same subject by Farwell, J., in *In re Johnson* [1903] 1 Ch., 821, 824–825.] Contrast the far more accurate language of Chief Justice Shaw, in *Abington v. Bridgewater* ....[16]

Hohfeld's analysis is not a simple description of legal usage, then. Indeed, he offers a way of speaking that is clearly not familiar to all

---

13. Hohfeld, *Fundamental Legal Conceptions*, 63.
14. *Ibid.*, 27. Hohfeld's examples of legal confusion do not come from public law (for example, law governing the separation of powers and the powers of the state), points out Nicholas Bamforth, who argues that courts frequently refer to rights in public law cases in ways which do not easily fit a Hohfeldian analysis. See Nicholas Bamforth, "Hohfeldian Rights and Public Law", in *Rights, Wrongs and Responsibilities*, M. H. Kramer (ed.), 1–27 (Basingstoke: Palgrave, 2001).
15. A pleasant alliteration, derived from S. Lee, *Judging Judges* (London: Faber & Faber, 1988).
16. Hohfeld, *Fundamental Legal Conceptions*, 35, n. 24.

legal colleagues of his time: "Those Yale men say rights-powers-privileges-and-immunities as a single word, the way the rest of us say son-of-a-bitch".[17] But if the analysis is a false *description* of the ways in which all legal people think and judge, then what makes it correct? We have here a semi-formal linguistic system with a range of concepts used in sentences that have certain logical relationships with each other. What is the status of this linguistic entity? Does it describe how language is used? Partly it purports to do so, and is selectively supported on that basis; on the other hand, it also sets a standard for how language ought to be used in a legal context. Yet the notions involved can also be regarded as moral notions – is this a different descriptive or prescriptive task? It was precisely a range of difficulties of this kind that affected the approach of the logical positivists, who saw science as the only way of achieving knowledge. We need next to examine these difficulties. Cook's description of Hohfeld's analysis as not differing from any other branch of pure science reminds us of how close Hohfeld was to the developing analytical philosophy of his time.

The word "analytical", in the context of contemporary analytical philosophy, is ambiguous in a number of ways. It can mean merely that the philosophy in question is "analytical" just in so far as it insists on clarity of meaning, with no more being implied. It can mean more: that the "analytical" philosophy in question insists on clarity of meaning and also embodies a certain theory of "clarity" of meaning. Sometimes "analytical" in this context implies that the embodied theory of "clarity" of meaning is one that holds that expressions in a natural language are essentially vague and must be readily translatable into the terms of a formal or symbolic – preferably classical – logical system.[18] Yet sometimes "analytical" in this context implies that the embodied theory of "clarity" of meaning is one that takes natural language, with all its subtleties and distinctions, as inherently exact, so that concentration on ordinary usage will resolve philosophical

---

17. A. L. Corbin, "Foreword" to Hohfeld, *Fundamental Legal Conceptions*, x. See also John Finnis's point about lawyers' talk (*Natural Law and Natural Rights*, 201–202).
18. This is broadly Carl G. Hempel's view. See his *Philosophy of Natural Science* (Englewood Cliffs, NJ: Prentice-Hall, 1966). Isaiah Berlin (whom we shall introduce in Ch. 10), while an empiricist, consistently rejected the philosophical desire to "translate many *prima facie* different types of proposition into a single type", as he put it in his essay "Logical Translation", in *Concepts and Categories: Philosophical Essays* [1960], I. Berlin, 56–80 (Oxford: Oxford University Press, 1980), 57.

difficulties and even, following the later Wittgenstein, dissolve them.[19] These are the main views, although there are others.[20] While a strong degree of attention to linguistic meaning is essential to the analytical approach, the term, apart from the implications just noted, is sometimes taken to imply in addition a belief in empiricism, which, as observed earlier, is very influential within the tradition, although often in an extremely weak sense.[21] Sometimes, however, the word "analytical" is taken to imply empiricism very specifically of a Humean kind, and it is then sometimes assumed that an analytical philosopher believes particularly in mechanism[22] and atomism,[23] or even determinism. Sometimes empiricism in a strong but more general sense is taken to be implied, permitting the non-Humean holistic

---

19. This is also the position of the Oxford philosopher J. L. Austin, not to be confused with John Austin, author of *The Province of Jurisprudence Determined* (London: John Murray, 1832).

20. R. G. Collingwood, who was strongly against positivism, suggested that philosophers should choose their vocabulary according to the rules of literature. See his *An Essay on Philosophical Method* (Oxford: Clarendon Press, 1933), 207. Philosophers in the analytical tradition have nevertheless rarely warmed to the suggestion that one cannot be literal and must therefore embrace the metaphorical. For an insistence on the literal and an explanation of the metaphorical see Davidson, "What Metaphors Mean".

21. For example, most philosophers in the "analytical" tradition would require knowledge claims to be justifiable, so in a minimal sense they are sceptical, and their scepticism would be a consequence of an empiricist attitude rather than, for example, being driven by a Cartesian and rationalist "method of doubt". Note that it is possible to be a positivist – to believe that science is the only way of achieving knowledge – without also being an empiricist, for one might hold a non-empiricist philosophy of science.

22. Hume's "mechanism" involved the claim that, space and time apart, the only fundamental relation that exists between all the things that exist is a causal relation. The view is that the world consists of many things in causal relationship with each other, a world that we are supposed to know about on the basis of experience. Hobbes anticipated this. One needs to leave the analytical tradition to find serious philosophical criticism of this idea. Hegel's philosophy is a useful corrective, and Hegel's treatment of mechanism is carefully examined at length in B. T. Wilkins, *Hegel's Philosophy of History* (Ithaca, NY: Cornell University Press, 1974), Ch. 2.

23. Frank Ankersmit, for example, characterizes "analytical" philosophy as assuming "that language is the principal condition for the possibility of all knowledge and meaningful thinking" and that philosophers should accept "the so-called *resoluto-compositional* method", that is, that "philosophy of language ought to start with an investigation of the behavior of logical constants, proper names, et cetera, and of the meaning of words and propositions," and work up to the solution of complex issues on these atomistic foundations; *History and Tropology: The Rise and Fall of Metaphor* (Los Angeles, CA: University of California Press, 1994), 2.

empiricist pragmatist Quine, for example, to count as one paradigm of an analytical philosopher.[24]

Again, when contemporary philosophy is described as "analytical", it is sometimes the logical positivist characterization of philosophy, with all its presuppositions, that is referred to. Opponents – and indeed sometimes friends – of analytical philosophy often incorrectly assume that philosophers who take problems of meaning seriously and write and reason according to exact standards must thereby also believe that science alone achieves knowledge. Thus various degrees of weak or strong positivism are sometimes taken to be implied by the term "analytical". Moreover, some opponents of analytical philosophy specifically oppose what are asserted to be its positivist presuppositions and illegitimately derive from that a further opposition to any methodological requirement of exactness of meaning. Thus any insistence on clarity and exactness of meaning is often associated by opponents of analytical philosophy with the positivist view that science is central.[25] There are, then, a multiplicity of connotations of the term "analytical" in the expression "analytical philosophy". Within the analytical tradition, the attention that analytical philosophers pay to the exact understanding of what they are themselves doing is such that confusions about the many connotations of the word "analytical" fortunately do not arise too often.

The philosophy of science created within the logical positivist tradition developed over a number of decades, but has yielded what is still known to many as the "standard" account. This account involves analysing the logical and epistemological status of scientific theories on the basis of empiricist assumptions, and the conclusions are briefly these: a scientific theory consists of a series of sentences that have the logical form of a universal conditional, that is, "Whenever A then B". Not every sentence with such a form counts here, for *definitions* have that logical form but are excluded. The universal conditionals in question are not those defined to be true but are those the truth of which is derived from experienced evidence.[26] Once we have formulated such scientific generalizations, then we can predict a future B given a present A, or we can explain a past B by reference to an earlier A, and so forth.

---

24. See, for example, W. V. O. Quine, *Word and Object* (Cambridge, MA: MIT Press, 1960).
25. "Postmodern" attacks on analytical philosophy often embody this view.
26. It is not relevant here to present the problem of induction.

The exact details of this model are not important other than to illustrate the kind of thing a model of science can be. What matters is that we have some model. Given a model of science, and adding to it the further positivist assumption that science is the only way of achieving knowledge, we may then wish, if so philosophically inclined, to conclude two things: that the model of science represents or correctly summarizes actual scientific thought and/or practice; and that the model of science sets a standard for correct thought and/or practice for other disciplines, such that the appropriate reality[27] will be truly described if that model is followed. Hohfeld was not the first to model his approach to law on science, and indeed there is more to being "scientific" in the legal context than being logically exact, for exactness permits accurate prediction in both law and science. That judicial decisions should be predictable is an important practical concern, and, as Roger Cotterrell remarks, "the theme is often traced to an 1897 speech in Boston by Oliver Wendell Holmes, ... [who] declared: 'The prophecies of what the courts will do in fact, and nothing more pretentious, are what I mean by the law'".[28]

The application of the standard analysis of science to other disciplines is intended as straightforward. It follows from the positivist assumption that anything that purports to provide knowledge yet that does not match the standard analysis simply fails to provide knowledge at all. Moreover, if we believe the position of the earlier logical positivists, as explained earlier – that their analysis is a criterion of meaning as well as a criterion of science – then anything that fails to meet the standard is meaningless as well as empty of knowledge. The result is brutal: swathes of disciplines collapse on the basis of this criterion, and not just speculative metaphysics as hoped but much else, very probably even science itself. Subsequent work took two approaches, which presupposed one or other of two views about the status of the model of science, one seeing it as prescriptive and the other as descriptive. These two approaches were founded on different conceptions of the nature of philosophical analysis, approaches that we see run together in Hohfeld's own presentation. The philosophical issues concerning the status of Hohfeld's analysis are a very close analogue of these issues in the philosophy of science.

---

27. Is legal reality different from scientific reality? That is an issue to be taken seriously, but it will not be addressed here.
28. Cotterrell, *The Politics of Jurisprudence*, 191, giving as his reference O. W. Holmes, Jr, "The Path of the Law", *Harvard Law Review* 10 (1897), 457–78, at 461.

It was explained above that analytical philosophy requires at least clarity and exactness of meaning, and that there are two main views about how this should be understood. On one view, derived particularly from logical positivism, it is assumed that ordinary language is inherently vague, and any claim to exact knowledge that is to be taken seriously needs to be readily translatable into the terms of a rational model, itself best expressed in terms of a formal deductive system. The logical positivist philosophy of science then expresses or models in these terms our necessarily scientific rationality. Applying this to philosophy of law, we should "rationally reconstruct" what lawyers and judges do. We should note the purpose(s) of law, and show how this (these) rationally ought to be attempted in the light of a scientific model that sets the standard. This approach takes the model of science as prescriptive for lawyers and judges, and the analytical philosopher of law, on this approach, is concerned with what legal reasoning ought to look like. The approach is conceptually stipulative, and Hohfeld's analysis is sometimes taken as stipulative in this sense.

On the second analytical approach to philosophy of science or of law, which derives its conception of analysis – although very rarely with any explicitness – from the later work of Wittgenstein,[29] it is assumed that ordinary language has the fullest possible range of exact literal and rhetorical resources, and that concentration on ordinary usage will resolve philosophical difficulties. Analytical philosophy of law is then conceived as exact ordinary language analysis of what is meant by certain distinctively legal modes of expression, method, evidence and so forth. On this view we need to grasp what legal reasoning is rather than what it ought to be. We need to grasp what actually counts as legal reasoning, and it is lawyers and judges themselves who may well be held to be the proper and best assessors of this. On this approach, analytical philosophy of law is supposed to provide a theoretical or summary description of what lawyers and judges do, and can be falsified by the linguistic "facts", facts that embody, for example, what is "correctly" – typically by judicial standards – called a "right" or a "duty". Recall that some courts are more authoritative than others, and that if meanings and correct reasoning are to be stipulated into correctness then the House of Lords or the US Supreme Court exemplify the kind of people

---

29. That is, from his *Philosophical Investigations*, rather than from his *Tractatus Logico-Philosophicus* [1922] (London: Routledge, 2001), which was more "logical positivist". Only in more recent studies of Wittgenstein does the view of him as having expressed two distinct philosophies begin to break down.

to do it, not Hohfeld or the logical positivists. Hohfeld's own deference to legal authority here is as apparent in his work as is its a priori stipulative nature; hence some confusion.

The difference between these two analytical approaches to philosophy of law can be summarized in terms of differing standards of "correctness" here. There is no doubt that the standards set by science as understood within logical positivism would contradict some lawyers' views about what counts as good legal reasoning. On the first analytical approach, it is so much the worse for legal reasoning, since the standard of correctness is set by the scientific model. On the second analytical approach, it is so much the worse for the scientific model, since the standard of correctness is set by the best understanding of lawyers. Jurisprudents and philosophers of law have not always been clear about which side of this debate about the nature of philosophical analysis they were actually on.

While a rump of old logical positivism remains, the understanding of philosophy of science was revolutionized by the publication in 1962 of Thomas S. Kuhn's *The Structure of Scientific Revolutions*.[30] Kuhn, primarily an historian rather than a philosopher of science of the standard kind, noted that historical research revealed that science in the past had not operated in ways that accorded with the requirements of the standard empiricist model.

> The more carefully [historians] study, say, Aristotelian dynamics, phlogistic chemistry, or caloric thermodynamics, the more certain they feel that those once current views of nature were, as a whole, neither less scientific nor more the product of human idiosyncrasy that those current today ... myths can be produced by the same sorts of methods and held for the same sorts of reasons that now lead to scientific knowledge.[31]

Kuhn suggested that scientists normally operated against the vague background of an accepted general understanding of the world or "paradigm", an understanding that framed not only the answers to scientific questions but also the questions that it was thought appropriate to ask.

Part of the process of such "normal" science was to articulate with explicit clarity the detailed implications of the paradigm, and this

---

30. T. S. Kuhn, *The Structure of Scientific Revolutions* (Chicago, IL: The University of Chicago Press, 1962).
31. *Ibid.*, 2.

detailed development might well include in part some of the exact features suggested by the logical positivists. However, the history of science disclosed not one scientific paradigm but many. Paradigms did not persist but went through a period of rise and fall and replacement. When a paradigm collapsed it did so not for the reasons suggested by logical positivists but for a variety of pragmatic – such as social or psychological – reasons. Kuhn claimed that a period of "revolutionary" science followed the recognition that an existing paradigm did not command confidence, and in this period scientists cast around for a new approach that, despite being very poorly articulated in its initial form, might offer hope of further understanding in the future. The history of science therefore did not disclose the greater and greater accumulation of knowledge but rather a pattern of revolutionary changes between periods of normal science. Apart from a period of revolution, the best science at any particular time was produced against an unquestioned background of accepted presuppositions.

Kuhn's work was fascinating to many disciplines and widely influential, indeed perhaps more influential than most works of philosophy in the twentieth century, no doubt because it so clearly undermined the long-established positivist attitudes in philosophy and undermined in particular the standard empiricist philosophy of science.[32] A certain vagueness of expression on Kuhn's part allowed for a wide range of implications to be drawn.[33] We have noted that there are two different approaches to analytical philosophy. On one approach, analytical philosophy requires clarity of meaning in the sense that proper understanding is best expressed in the terms of a formal rational model typically exemplified by scientific theories. On the other approach, analytical philosophy takes natural languages as inherently exact, in such a way that ordinary language use is a paradigm case of correct use. The contrast between these two approaches yields a contrast between two analytical approaches to philosophy of law, as we have seen, where the standard of correctness is on the one

---

32. Ironically, Kuhn's work was also issued as a volume in the *International Encyclopedia of Unified Science*. The "unity" of science was normally taken to involve the acceptance of positivism and the consequent imposition of scientific models on, for example, history or the social sciences.

33. Thus Margaret Masterman claimed that 21 different senses of the word "paradigm" appeared in Kuhn's book; M. Masterman, "The Nature of a Paradigm", in *Criticism and the Growth of Knowledge*, I. Lakatos & A. Musgrave (eds), 59–89 (Cambridge: Cambridge University Press, 1970). Kuhn himself was not the best judge of the meaning of what he said.

hand set by the scientific model, and on the other hand set by the best understanding of lawyers and judges. On the first approach, philosophers of science were initially taken to be speaking for science itself in trying to impose on others their model of science. The positions of those others were rhetorically weak, given the generally undoubted successes of natural science.

But for those who accepted Kuhn's position – and even for those who did not – this approach could no longer be accepted. The positivist philosophers of science were seen as speaking for themselves, not for science, since science – conceived as the real judgements of real scientists in the real world as disclosed by the history of science – did not fit their model any more than the other disciplines did. Science could not be seen as an authoritative accumulation of "facts". Positivist philosophers of science were therefore forced to face a dilemma paralleling that which the practitioners of other disciplines had hitherto faced: given a conflict between real science and their own rational model, which should be taken as pre-eminent? The rhetorical high ground that had previously been theirs was theirs no longer. Even the most obstinate positivists could no longer rely on science itself for support, and as empiricists they were in no position to rely on pure reason alone.

Yet, while moving away from imposing on legal understanding the deflated positivist model of science, it is too quick to turn to the "facts" of legal discourse or practice in the same way that Kuhn turned to the "facts" of the history of science, for Kuhn's arguments were powerfully relativistic. There are no scientific "facts", for what we count as true and what we do not is always relative to some background paradigm, and paradigms change. Moreover, the grounds for their change are not grounds that necessarily disclose some movement in the direction of truth, but are typically sociological in nature.

Relativism, a very old philosophical problem, is also a very new one in the postmodern world, and it is continually fuelled by disagreements among the plurality of historical approaches that the ongoing history of historiography discloses. Whatever the importance of history either to philosophy of science or to philosophy of law, no philosopher could for long think that understanding science or law involved a simple appeal to the historical "facts" of actual practice. Even Kuhn's position, it was eventually seen, did not and could not involve an appeal to "facts" from the history of science, but involved the development of a model for understanding the history of science itself. Thus it is too simple to draw a contrast between philosophy of

112

law as prescriptive for and descriptive of legal understanding, as if the "facts" of legal practice and terminology were independent of the theories about it. The contrast should perhaps be seen as being between different *models* of legal reasoning: perhaps one based on successful natural science, however that is understood, and the other – "best legal judgements" – expressing the legal profession's own best model, its interpretation of its own practice over time. Nor is there any reason to think that there are merely two choices here, or only one model within the legal profession.[34] In any event, models or interpretations are unavoidable.

The upshot of Kuhn's approach at this point is that which model is the most appropriate to legal reasoning is a pragmatic question, and moreover that it should not be assumed that only one model should be used. There may be a multiplicity of legal approaches, or paradigms. Once we are aware of the existence of different paradigms, frameworks, models or interpretations,[35] then we immediately face the question of *choice*, with the further implications of relativism that lie behind that. While the possibility of choice between models does not imply that one model is no better than another, we at this point have no clear rational basis for preferring one to another; moreover, there may perhaps be a moral or political or other kind of evaluative choice in choosing one over another. Hohfeld cannot merely *stipulate* his way out of difficulties here.[36]

Hohfeld's theory, then, is an attempt to summarize some features of an existing social – in particular linguistic – practice, conjoined with a recommendation that certain further refinements be universally adopted by his profession. There is not here either a description of metaphysically independent rights or a simple description of rights talk. While there are descriptive elements in his theory that we may take to be "true", theoretically these amount to little more than a reminder of how certain past judges or jurists had reasoned. Some of this reasoning was "good" reasoning and some "bad", by Hohfeld's lights, with his assessment being made not on the authority of the court in question but by an appeal to clarity and consistency. The

---

34. See Lee, *Judging Judges*, for the view that each judge brings his or her own philosophy of law to decision-making.

35. These should not be assumed to be the same thing.

36. As Matthew H. Kramer seems to suggest; note that it is a moral choice to be as slavishly logical as Hohfeld (and Kramer) seem to require, as we shall see. The logical clarity of Kramer's presentation of Hohfeld's position nevertheless deserves praise. Kramer, "Rights Without Trimmings", 23.

stipulative recommendations of Hohfeld's table are similarly justified by him by an appeal to clarity and consistency, by the need to "think straight" in relation to all legal problems.[37] Here the "truth" of Hohfeld's analysis reflects what he takes to be the eternal and universal standards of reason, rather than the particular features of a local social practice.

Hohfeld's theory is not evaluatively neutral, then,[38] in its appeal to clarity and consistency, nor does it avoid appealing beyond the local to the universal. Hohfeld carries through that Kantian commitment to rationality in his analysis of language. Clarity permits predictability, and that is widely recognized as a value that the courts and the legal profession should foster.[39] Yet the recommendation of consistency that Hohfeld's approach presupposes is problematic. The original Platonic understanding of morality as independent, fixed and consistent has, through development towards Kant's moral philosophy, changed to a sense of morality – and of human rights in particular – as primarily universal rather than independent, yet still unchanging and consistent. Some moral rights, however, may not be universal but rather localized to a particular culture. Legal rights, by contrast, are merely those accepted within the legal practice of a particular jurisdiction and these may or may not overlap either with the moral rights of local cultures or with universal human rights. As a matter of political reality, localized moral rights and particular legal rights may, despite their distinction from human rights, be justified by their supporters in terms of the universal justifications that are properly available only for human rights themselves. In terms of our overall concern with such matters as an international understanding of human rights that can be independent of particular jurisdictions or particular cultures, it is the universal features of such rights that give them their justification and that need to be analysed. The unchanging and universal demands of reason that are presupposed by Hohfeld and that are essentially involved in morality here need to be evaluated, and it is Kant himself who displays the weakness of reason.

---

37. Hohfeld, *Fundamental Legal Conceptions*, 25.
38. Although it may well be normatively neutral between the will theory and the interest theory of rights; see Kramer, "Rights Without Trimmings", 65.
39. On the other hand, peace-making is valuable too, and the fudges of diplomatically achieved agreements – which have their place in legal practice – are not necessarily well-served by insisting on clarity.

CHAPTER 9

Change

Recall Kant's moral philosophy. He explains the unchanging rationality of the principles that govern our duties, and characterizes human nature as valuable in virtue of its essentially rational characteristics. Fundamental rights and duties are universally and equally held, and all rights are consistent with each other in a "Kingdom of Ends". Reason is fundamental. Reason gives intelligibility. Reason sets the standards. And reason expresses the essence of what we ourselves really are. This unchanging, universally shared and consistent standard that essentially applies to the human condition ensures the applicability and acceptability of his theory.

Yet we disobey. We do not now live in a world in which everyone's autonomy is respected and in which everyone acts in a way that meets the requirements of Kant's categorical imperative. Why not? And does it matter? In general, moral ideals or legal standards are logically independent of actual behaviour: it is no refutation of either the ten commandments or the 30 miles per hour speed limit that they are frequently disobeyed.

However, when commenting on Plato's position, we noted two central approaches to the analysis of what it is to act wrongly. On the Socratic view, acting wrongly is due to ignorance of the right thing to do. We are to make sense of the nature of acting wrongly in terms of the intellectual apprehension of the Form of the Good. The philosophers among us, at least, always act as they ought in virtue of their character as rational beings, which ensures that they know the Form of the Good. If, with Kant, this is not limited to the philosophers but, instead, we are all rational beings, then it may well seem that we will all act as we should. On the other, non-Socratic view, we might know the right thing to do, but might nevertheless act wrongly due to a failure to desire the right thing rather than a failure of knowledge. Here the understanding of human nature in terms of desire is an essential part of understanding why we act wrongly. According to one Christian approach, we believe that humanity is "fallen from grace". Human beings are primarily disposed to evil in some form; while knowing what God requires, all of us are sinners. We may hope, Christianity tells us, for salvation, but in practice that is likely to be in the life hereafter. Our fundamental disposition to sin and so to need forgiveness characterizes humanity more truthfully than the supposition that we are rational beings who actually act as we ought. Understanding what it is to act wrongly depends, in these examples, on our prior philosophy.

That people do not always do what they ought to do thus raises a particular problem for Kant's moral philosophy since that philosophy is essentially connected to a view of human nature. We cannot just hold that the "Kingdom of Ends" is an ideal, which, like a speed limit, has validity independent of our actual behaviour. Kant has to recognize that the facts of human moral disobedience show that we are each of us not as rational as the ideal that his theory expresses. While we saw earlier that Kant raised the possibility of distinguishing human beings from rational beings, he wrote his philosophy as if there were no significant practical distinction. However, moral imperfection shows that there is indeed a serious dislocation between "human beings" and "rational beings", and this in itself suggests that Kant's moral theory may not be as universally applicable or acceptable as first appears. Moreover the impact of this point has serious implications for Kant's position. If I act wrongly, then I do not act rationally. If I do not act rationally, then I do not have a rational will. If I do not have a rational will then I do not have a good will. If I do not have a good will then I have no essential and unconditional value, since *only* a good will is unconditionally good. I then deserve no respect as an end. I may be acceptably treated as a means. And this is true for everyone else also. A central standard from Kant's moral philosophy then fails, given a dislocation between human beings and rational beings.

This is a depressing thought, perhaps; but Kant's intellectual world of the Enlightenment was characterized by optimism about the human condition. For aeons, humanity had lived a precarious existence at the mercy of natural and social forces that were neither understood nor controlled. The universe was a mysterious and dangerous place, made more bearable perhaps by belief in a benign God, but mysterious and dangerous none the less. Yet generations of slowly developing scientific understanding had begun to make light what had once been dark, and in Newton's laws of nature the very heavens had had their motions circumscribed and thereby tamed. The universe revealed its rationality and regularity in all things large and small, and the demonstration of humanity's ability to understand how nature worked and might be controlled yielded huge intellectual optimism.

The world is to be understood as a rational place. We can understand it, and can use our understanding to control it. As we have seen, Kant tells us why this is so: the rationality of the universe is not some alien characteristic but reflects the rationality that we ourselves bring to all knowable experience. Reason is both within us and outside us. It is no wonder that we can understand the universe. Knowledge of reality is no longer the prerogative of God.[1] Just as the essentially rational nature of our own understanding has surfaced in our new knowledge of the universe, so we may expect our essentially rational nature to develop also. This development occurs in two places: first, in our moral *understanding* – itself instantiated by the new existence of Kant's own theory; secondly, in our moral *behaviour*. This optimism has been rightly characterized as a belief in the so-called "perfectibility of man".[2] Our present falling short of perfection reflects not so much something like original sin as a second approach: the fact that the human race is still progressing.

In 1784, in a Berlin journal, Kant published a brief essay on the a priori principles that underlay our understanding of human progress, entitled "Idea of a Universal History from a Cosmopolitan Point of View".[3] This essay consists of nine sections, each with a title that consists of a proposition that is reasoned for in the section that it heads. Putting the nine titles together into a single text, we find the following argument produced:

---

1. Against Vico's "verum-factum" principle (*The New Science*, 1725–1744), which in this context says that what God has made, only God can know. See L. Pompa, *Vico: A Study of the "New Science"* (Cambridge: Cambridge University Press, 1975); P. Burke, *Vico* (Oxford: Oxford University Press, 1985), 78.
2. John Passmore's book uses this title: *The Perfectibility of Man* (London: Duckworth, 1972).
3. Extract from I. Kant, "Idea of a Universal History from a Cosmopolitan Point of View" [1784], W. Hastie (trans.), in *Theories of History*, P. Gardiner (ed.), 22–34 (New York: The Free Press, 1959). The essay has also been published as "Idea for a Universal History with a Cosmopolitan Purpose", H. B. Nisbet (trans.), in *Kant: Political Writings*, 2nd edn, H. Reiss (ed.), 41–53 (Cambridge: Cambridge University Press, 1991). Page references that follow are to the Gardiner collection.

All the capacities implanted in a creature by nature are destined to unfold themselves, completely and conformably to their end, in the course of time. In man, as the only rational creature on earth, those natural capacities which are directed toward the use of his reason could be completely developed only in the species and not in the individual. Nature has willed that man shall produce wholly out of himself all that goes beyond the mechanical structure and arrangement of his animal existence, and that he shall participate in no other happiness or perfection than that which he has procured for himself, apart from instinct, by his own reason. The means which nature employs to bring about the development of all the capacities implanted in men is their mutual antagonism in society, but only so far as this antagonism becomes at length the cause of an order among them that is regulated by law. The greatest practical problem for the human race, to the solution of which it is compelled by nature, is the establishment of a civil society, universally administering right according to law. This problem is likewise the most difficult of its kind, and it is the latest to be solved by the human race. The problem of the establishment of a perfect civil constitution is dependent on the problem of the regulation of the external relations between the states conformably to law; and without the solution of this latter problem it cannot be solved. The history of the human race, viewed as a whole, may be regarded as the realisation of a hidden plan of nature to bring about a political constitution, internally, and, for this purpose, also externally perfect, as the only state in which all the capacities implanted by her in mankind can be fully developed. A philosophical attempt to work out the universal history of the world according to the plan of nature in its aiming at a perfect civil union must be regarded as possible, and as even capable of helping forward the purpose of nature.

Summarizing, since the world is a rational place, everything it contains must have its own purpose and also be best fitted for its own purpose, and we, being rational, can work out what this is. Therefore everything in the course of time will achieve its own purpose and become perfectly what it is meant to be. The capacity for reason that is essential to human beings will also in due course achieve its own perfection. Since rational perfection yields moral perfection, moral perfection will also be achieved in the course of time. We know that this development does not occur in our own short lifetimes, and so –

since we are assured of its happening – it has to occur in the human race as a whole over the course of its history. We can then see this history as progression to a perfect state consisting of a perfect moral community wherein all rights are consistent with each other and mutually respected. What is the alternative to this conclusion? It is unacceptable – indeed, self-contradictory, since the world is constructed in accordance with reason – to suppose that the world is not, after all, governed by reason. Optimism rather than pessimism about human nature is rationally warranted.

Kant's philosophical successor Georg W. F. Hegel (1770–1831) was politically conservative. He elaborated Kant's philosophy of history; since at any one time the progress of historical reason is developed from what is necessarily a less moral and less rational previous state, we have to be careful. Rather than risk relapsing into the worse moral state that we have just left, we must preserve the rational enlightenment so far achieved, and defend it. Hegel's younger followers used similar reasoning to argue in the opposite direction. Tomorrow must be better, so let us get rid of today as fast as possible. This revolutionary political response to the march of history was a major feature of Karl Marx's position. In his essay Kant had explained how nature will use the antagonism between human beings in order to achieve the final perfect state. "Man wishes concord", he said; "but nature knows better what is good for his species, and she will have discord",[4] and "Nature works through wars".[5] The generations of killing carried out in the name of historical progress were claimed to be justified by the inevitable achievement of the final perfect state, a state that Kant affirmed.

Once one accepts, as Kant does in his philosophy of history, that human nature changes over time, then there is no theoretical bar to accepting that human nature may change with place also, or indeed vary with other features. Kant's younger contemporary Johann Herder (1744–1803) emphasized the importance of national character; human nature is not unified but diversified, so that each race has a separate fixed set of fundamental characteristics. Neither Kant nor Herder saw the misuses to which part of their thought might be put, but those who experienced the rise of Fascism and Communism in the twentieth century saw the dangers clearly. As the Oxford philosopher R. G. Collingwood (1889–1943) warned, this dividing up of human

---

4. Kant, "Idea of a Universal History", 26.
5. *Ibid.*, 28.

nature "means that the task of creating or improving a culture is assimilated to that of creating or improving a breed of domestic animals. Once Herder's theory of race is accepted, there is no escaping the Nazi marriage laws".[6]

Superficially, we may see Kant's main moral philosophy as expressing the standards of rational moral perfection that humanity will achieve at the end of history in the final perfect state, standards against which we may now be measured and relative to which we recognize our actual current disobedience. It is almost as if Kant took Plato's Form of the Good and turned it from a really existing but abstract eternal reality into a really existing but only future reality. However, this does not solve the problem; Kant's belief in his philosophy of history that human nature changes over time has very serious implications for his philosophy. We have already noted that, given that only a good will is unconditionally good, the fact of our disobedience marks us as irrational and so as not deserving unconditional respect as ends. If we will be morally and rationally perfect in the final state, then we are not so now – we cannot be, given that we need to undergo historical change before we can achieve it. None of us, at our own stage of historical time, is as moral or rational as we might be. Moreover, it follows that we are not as fully human as our descendants will be in the course of the generations, precisely because the essence of humanity is perfect rationality. Human beings now, even if not those human beings at the end of history, may then be acceptably treated as a means. Future human beings' rights must be respected; ours – if we deserve any, given our nature – need not be. Time travellers – if they are possible – will not meet anyone in the past who has human rights. This is inconsistent with what Kant's main moral philosophy is normally taken to imply.

Moreover, Kant's philosophy of history tells us that we will eventually arrive at the final morally perfect state, but it will be at a bloody cost, since nature works through wars. Since the march of history is a rational development, it follows that it is also a moral development – Kant's philosophy of history is essentially a theory of *progress* – and the justification lies in the perfect moral end that is achieved. Again we have a conflict between this conclusion from Kant's philosophy of history and the conclusion of his work in moral philosophy, where the idea that the end might justify the means is completely unacceptable. Nor is this just a matter of conflict between

---

6. R. G. Collingwood, *The Idea of History* (Oxford: Oxford University Press, 1946), 92.

two parts of Kant's theory; appealing to our ordinary moral judgements, we recognize that, whatever Kant's theories may say, the ideas that (i) people are *now* worthy of respect (despite their disobediencies), and indeed have *rights* in virtue of that, and that (ii) generally the ends do not justify the means, express central moral values for us.

The serious implications of and for Kant's approach here go beyond a mere inconsistency between what he says in his moral philosophy and what he says in his philosophy of history, and go beyond a mere inconsistency with some of our current moral values. The claim that human nature changes over time, added to the claim that morality consists in being rational, which particularly involves valuing the human self as an unconditional end, and added to the claim that reason is understood as the essential constituting feature of human nature, implies that morality changes over time and that reason changes over time. That morality changes over time is not a view that Kant fully recognized, either in his main moral philosophy or in his philosophy of history. Again, that reason changes over time is also not a view that Kant took fully seriously, either in his main moral philosophy or in his philosophy of history. Yet if human nature changes over time and the other elements do not then we must insist upon dissolving Kant's connection between human nature and morality and his connection between human nature and reason. Some major Kantian assumption(s) must be denied. It was Kant's successors, rather than Kant himself, who noticed these things.

While, logically, there are a range of possible ways in which we may dissolve the inconsistencies that follow if we accept the view that human nature changes over time, in practice many of Kant's successors were willing to keep links between human nature, morality and reason, and accept the implications that – against Kant – both morality and reason did indeed change over time also. Hegel in particular produced a theory of such change. Apart from Hegel's position, however, we can recognize the view that accepting moral change over time naturally leads to moral relativism. Just as human nature may be imagined to change with time, or with place, or with race, or with culture, so morality too is often supposed to change in the same way. While we are typically unwilling today to believe in more than one human nature, we are much more willing to adopt the view that morality is not an absolute or single standard, as Kant thought, but varies, typically with different cultures. Nor do we believe that there is a final perfect state displaying an absolute standard, and in this we show our consistency.

This position forces us to recognize that human rights must be relative, too; they are perhaps just a contemporary feature of post-war international goals that derive from particular Western traditions, whose cultures have the status they do because of the economic and military power currently associated with them. We earlier argued, with Kant, that human rights, which may be taken to express the foundation of our current moral values, cannot be seen as metaphysically independent moral values, and they then lose such justification as this status might give them. They may then be humanity-dependent, unchanging and universal. Universality would then be the foundation of their justification. We now argue, against Kant, that, given Kant's own assumption in his philosophy of history that human nature changes over time, human rights are not unchanging and universal either. Like legal rights, which are contingently located in particular jurisdictions, and like moral rights, which are contingently located in particular moral cultures, human rights are just another contingent set of standards. The attempts to ground human rights in unchanging human nature must fail just because, and in so far as, there is no such thing as unchanging human nature.

Yet Kant's original epistemological and metaphysical position – that human nature does *not* change – still has an authority for many of his successors and for many philosophers today. That our experienced world is a function not only of an external input but also of a mental input is, in some form or other, very widely shared. Kant's interpretation of this as involving *unchanging* structures of the mind, of human nature, is again widely accepted. Here we typically do not allow that human nature varies with time, place, race and the like, and we may then understand human rights as the absolute and unchanging values protecting the way we eternally are. As described at the beginning of Chapter 1, Western cultures uncertainly embrace both moral relativism and a belief in unchanging human rights. On one hand we may insist on a common human nature throughout time and place, and give no credence – let alone ethical credence – to the extremes of racism and the like that the alternative seems to permit. On the other hand we find a belief in Darwinism – or at least in evolution, if not in Darwin's explanation of it – very widely accepted. According to this, human nature has developed and therefore changed over time. Did evolution stop with the rise of consciousness? Is the mind–matter distinction – which an affirmative answer to this question seems to imply – plausible? No change; and yet change? That we live with such inconsistency takes us to the next important point.

122

CHAPTER 10

Inconsistency

We have seen that, if human nature changes over time, and if human nature is essentially connected to morality through what is valuable about it, then morality changes over time too. But there is a further implication. If human nature changes over time, and reason is understood as the essential constituting feature of human nature, then reason changes over time too. The same conclusion follows from the views that morality changes over time, and that morality is constituted by reason. While a widespread belief in moral relativism demonstrates the acceptability of the idea that morality may change, the idea that the standards of reason may change is much less familiar to us. Plato's Form of the Good was presented by him as *independent*, *eternal* and *consistent*. We have throughout used this to characterize the apparent authority that human rights have for us. We have now seen arguments against their independence and eternity and in consequence against their universality, but consistency remains a dogma, one expressed in the claim that human rights – or, indeed, rights more generally – must be *compossible*. All rights are compossible just when all rights can be exercised at the same time, that is, that the action of one person exercising a right does not make impossible the exercise of rights by others.[1]

If reason requires at some time that we believe something, and reason changes, then it may require at some later time that we believe

---

1. Prevention is a relation between the respective actions of two persons such that the occurrence of one of them rules out, or implies the impossibility of, the occurrence of the other. If both such actions can occur – if they are *compossible* – then neither prevents the other.   (Steiner, *An Essay on Rights*, 2, 33)

something else. The point may be made clearer in the following way. Just as human nature may be imagined to change with time, or with place, or with race, or with culture, so reason (understood as essentially and mutually constitutive of human nature) may be supposed to change in the same way. A later belief may be inconsistent with an earlier belief. "What reason requires" is not then a consistent set of truths. If we lose the assumption of consistency then we have no ground for supposing that the moral demands on us are consistent. In particular, we may have rights that are inconsistent with each other. That moral "reality" expressed by our justified claims to rights is then an inconsistent reality. Such a position is often described as "pluralist".

The idea that reality – even moral reality – might be inconsistent may well seem extraordinary. Yet it is an idea that is often presupposed. We can illustrate it with Ronald Dworkin's presentation of the 1889 case of *Riggs v. Palmer*.[2] A man murdered his grandfather. The grandfather's will named him as heir. Should he inherit? The court must enforce laws and contracts, and the grandfather's valid will was clear. Yet the court must also ensure that common law maxims are followed, and no one is thereby permitted to profit from his own wrong. In fact the murderer was not permitted to inherit. We have here, for Dworkin, a conflict of legal *principles*. "We say that our law respects the principle that no man may profit from his own wrong, but we do not mean that the law never permits a man to profit from the wrongs he commits."[3]

Where principles conflict they must be "weighed", for Dworkin. We are not to treat "no man may profit from his own wrong" as a *rule* that, where it conflicts with other rules, either permanently overrides them or is permanently overridden by them. Rules are different from principles. By regarding this expression as a *principle*, Dworkin is saying that its relationship to conflicting principles is not fixed, and is a matter that has to be weighed on a particular occasion. The idea is that these and other such principles lie on some legal or moral shelf ready to be taken down as occasion demands and applied to particular cases. A decision in a particular case will resolve the conflict, following the "weighing" of the principles and the removal of one for the occasion, and so remove the inconsistency. The principles are then returned to the shelf after use. Yet what is on the shelf is the legal or

---

2. Dworkin, "Is Law a System of Rules?", 38–65.

3. *Ibid.*, 46.

moral reality, and here we find inconsistent principles. It should not be supposed that this situation is different for rights, for it is not. The grandson may have a *right* under his grandfather's will to inherit, while other possible inheritors may at the same time have a *right* that he should not, given that he murdered the grandfather.[4] Only one of these rights can be enforced in a particular case, but both exist.

With the passing away of mainstream historicism in the Western world we have moved to what is sometimes called a "postmodern" position, where the Enlightenment view that truth is independent of us, fixed and consistent is denied; where the historicist view that truth is independent of us and developing towards a fixed and consistent conclusion is denied; and what is asserted is that truth is not independent of us, that the search for consistency is itself totalitarian, and all is purposeless change. Morality and human nature do not encompass eternal independent and consistent truths. Nor, of course, do rights. Kant's view that our rights must be compossible may then be seen as a totalitarian imposition of universal consistency.

A philosophical difficulty lies in attempting to make sense of these ideas. If "anything goes" then we lose all sense of morality, but our moral understanding embodies at least some minimal sense of the possibility of claims to rights being true, and of the possibility of reasoning in reference to them. We need to locate with more accuracy what can be meant by the idea of our moral or legal shelf truly containing inconsistent rights or other principles about which we can reason. At the moment we have no more than a metaphor.

Among those who have tried to express the idea of inconsistent moral reality in an intelligible way, Isaiah Berlin is prominent. In his famous lecture "The Hedgehog and the Fox"[5] he presents "hedgehogs" as seeing everything as part of a single whole, and as seeking truth in synthesis, generality and simplicity, while "foxes" look for more and more differentiation and detail, and seek truth in analysis, particularity and multiplicity.[6] Berlin, seeing himself as a fox, believes that there are many different conflicting moral points of view, each offering a comprehensive view of life. If each of these many different

---

4. Readers who have mastered the chapter on Hohfeld's analysis will recognize that the possible rights in this situation are far more complex than this.

5. I. Berlin, *The Hedgehog and the Fox* (London: Weidenfeld & Nicolson, 1953). I have presented some of the following material in "On Hedgehogs and Foxes", *Philosophical Inquiry* 21 (1999), 61–86.

6. The word "analysis" here has the sense of "breaking things up into their many parts".

moral points of view is truly comprehensive, then we may observe that each moral point of view must account also for the values of opposing moral points of view. We have to suppose that each comprehensive moral point of view, as Berlin understands that notion, typically takes a certain moral value as primary. Each comprehensive moral point of view then has to deal with the moral values of conflicting points of view in one of three ways: by explicitly denying the conflicting values; by explaining those other values away; or, at best, by accepting those other values but holding them as essentially secondary to its own primary value. The difference between conflicting moral points of view means that conflicting values are differently weighted in each. Conflicting moral points of view are therefore incompatible with each other at least in terms of what each point of view claims as the primary value. For example – to refer to one of Berlin's favourite conflicts – a comprehensive moral point of view that puts the value of political freedom first is incompatible with a comprehensive moral point of view that puts the value of political equality first. Berlin's pluralist position implies that it is wrong to unify these different values in a single moral theory. The attempt to impose on the world a "unified" comprehensive moral point of view is totalitarianism, and this is in itself wrong. Totalitarianism is bound to be wrong, for no comprehensive moral point of view is ever really unified, but is rather an improper triumph of some values over those others with which it is inconsistent.[7] In a similar way we must not take some rights as triumphing over others, or indeed rights in general as "trumping" other moral or legal demands.

Some philosophers will wish to interpret Berlin's position in the same way as common sense suggests we should approach conflicting theories in science. So when we say that there are many conflicting comprehensive moral points of view, these philosophers will regard each such moral point of view as an attempt to represent moral truth. Conflict between different moral points of view will then imply a failure to represent moral truth correctly on the part of one or more of them, and imply also that some means of deciding correctly between the different moral points of view has to be found. When we eventually hit upon moral truth, conflicting moral points of view will be superseded. We should then seek a comprehensive moral point of

---

7. Totalitarianism is not a simple matter of the state refusing to allow for freedom of association, as Roger Scruton has it in his *A Dictionary of Political Thought*, (London: Macmillan, 1983), 466.

view that makes a better job of moral understanding than the failed and conflicting moral approaches of the past. A single comprehensive moral point of view will replace the many. It would be a mark of final moral truth that moral conflicts are resolved in the one true theory. While it is true that there are many different moral points of view, this is a mark of failure and not success in representing "moral reality". The compossibility of rights is required, on this approach.

But it is clear that Berlin does not understand his claim in this way. When he says that there are many conflicting comprehensive moral points of view, he is not to be taken as referring merely to actual conflicts between different *theories* about moral reality. He is referring to the "moral reality" itself. Berlin's pluralistic view is that moral reality is inherently and essentially inconsistent. That being so, any attempt to formulate moral understanding into a single consistent moral theory is a move away from understanding the nature of morality and not a move towards it. "It is impossible to choose a single set of values and live by them without running into contradictions"; there are no "rational solutions to moral questions".[8] There is, in the light of this, no reason to think that our rights form a consistent set as Kant claimed. On the contrary, on this approach, many claims to rights may be legitimately made and yet they may be inconsistent with each other.

Both Dworkin and Berlin use the idea of "weighing" in this context, and neither go much beyond a metaphorical expression of what is involved. Berlin's own arguments are not as clear as they might be, and will not be summarized here. Ultimately Berlin takes the wrongness of imposing consistency on morality as self-evident. It is indeed difficult if no support is provided for this foxlike philosophical claim that moral reality is essentially inconsistent. But then it is doubtful if any philosophical position can be *proved* to be correct. What is more problematic is that the entire position may be completely unintelligible, since truth itself may be seen as essentially a consistent unity. Such an objection presupposes something we have already examined: a more general belief in a determinate reality akin to that of Plato, who casts a long shadow. Belief in a determinate reality is a common-sense view about the nature of reality that supposes that reality exists as some fixed or unchanging logically

---

8. A. Smith, "Thoughts for the Day", review of I. Berlin, *The Proper Study of Mankind: An Anthology of Essays*, H. Hardy & R. Hausheer (eds) (London: Chatto & Windus, 1996), *Observer*, 23 February (1997).

consistent conflict-free entity that is independent of us and of the beliefs we have about it.

If we adopt an empiricist cast of mind like Berlin's, we will ask how far experience yields such an understanding of reality. The notion of metaphysical independence has already been examined and discarded. Again, empiricism is unable to show that the common-sense realist conceptions of unchangeability or universality are derivable directly from experienced reality; our beliefs and conceptual schemes are "underdetermined" by our experience. Berlin concluded, like many other twentieth-century empiricist philosophers, that facts are classified and arranged against the background of a general conception of the world.[9] Kant concluded this much, but for him – outside his philosophy of history – the classification of experience is against the background of fixed structures of the mind: a feature of unchanging human nature. For many twentieth-century empiricists, by contrast, organizing reality through the classifications of our language is something human beings can consciously do by choice.[10]

A postmodern position, such as Michel Foucault's (1926–84), also typically supposes freedom of choice in what to believe about reality. As he says:

> "truth" and similar expressions are devices to open, regulate and shut down interpretations. Truth acts as a censor – it draws the line. We know that such truths are really "useful fictions" that are in discourse by virtue of power (somebody has to put and keep them there) and power uses the term "truth" to exercise control: regimes of truth. Truth prevents disorder, and it is this fear of disorder (of the disorderly) or, to put this positively, it is this fear

9. Berlin, "The Purpose of Philosophy", in *Concepts and Categories: Philosophical Essays*, I. Berlin, 1–11 (Oxford: Oxford University Press, 1980), 8.

10. There nevertheless have to be limits. Quine opens *Word and Object* with a quotation from James Grier Miller: "ontology recapitulates philology". The content of Quine's book makes it clear that "philology" does not have its older sense of the study of classical learning and literature, but that it means rather the scientific investigation of the laws and principles of language. Language is a social institution based on overt behaviour. Quine argues that there are no determinate ways of translating different languages into each other, and reference to a shared world is inscrutable. Ontology, however, cannot recapitulate philology, for philology has its own ontology. We cannot set up the world of language without presuppositions of that exercise, and a pragmatic approach to that world has more presuppositions still. The main ontology that Quine himself presupposes is that many people exist, who can choose what to believe.

of freedom (for the unfree) that connects it functionally to material interests.[11]

So, why not believe inconsistent things? Is logic merely a normative system that I can disobey? Is it a social practice or game whose rules can be broken? Or does disobedience entail unintelligibility, so that pluralism makes no sense? Note that it is not *truth* that supposedly constrains us here, as Foucault would have it, but *logic*.

A better approach to making the pluralism of moral truth intelligible involves the idea that reality is an *essentially contested concept*. An "essentially contested concept" was Bryce Gallie's idea; he applied it to things like democracy, but never to reality itself.[12] Here we shall develop Gallie's idea in a direction to which he did not apply it and that he might not have approved. We will apply his notion to reality, which we will take to include moral reality and so to apply to the issue of how far we can truthfully or really have inconsistent rights. In the case of an essentially contested concept, we are to understand that there is disagreement about what counts as real, and furthermore that it is essential to understanding the meaning of the word "real" that one recognizes that such disagreement about its application exists. A similar point can be made for "true"; here I shall run the argument with "real". Note the similarity between this and Berlin's conception of *moral* pluralism. For Berlin, it is a failure to understand morality if one fails to grasp the necessary disagreements about the application of moral terms.

Gallie's notion, while liked by political scientists, was disliked by most analytical philosophers, being seen as merely restating a feature of practical moral and political contexts without offering a proper analysis of it. Moreover, it was itself widely thought to be unintelligible. There was no clarity to the idea, it was said. Gallie's own analysis of an essentially contested concept as being "appraisive", "internally complex" and as "permitting a number of possible rival descriptions of its total worth" was certainly not helpful. Some clarification that minimizes metaphors is required here.

To *contest* the application of the word "real" is to presuppose that the application of "real" by one's opponent in the contest is inconsistent with one's own application of "real".

---

11. I derive this useful quotation from K. Jenkins, *Re-thinking History* (London: Routledge, 1991), 32; Jenkins quoted it from M. Foucault, *Power/Knowledge* (New York: Pantheon, 1981), 131–3.
12. W. B. Gallie, "Essentially Contested Concepts", *Proceeedings of the Aristotelian Society*, 56 (1955–56), 167.

Moreover, if the application of "real" is *essentially* contested then the contest over its application cannot end so long as "real" is applied at all. This entails that no compromise between the contestants is possible and moreover that no win is possible for either would bring the contest to an end. A compromise or a win would imply that the contest was a mere contingency rather than essential.

The previous two short paragraphs embody the heart of the difficulty. Note the mode of voice used to express each point. The first of the two short paragraphs refers to "one's opponent" and "one's own application of 'real'". The contest between the two opponents is here expressed from the point of view of just one of them. Reading the first of the two paragraphs with appropriate understanding requires that one hypothetically adopt or identify with the position of one of the opponents.

By contrast, the second of the two short paragraphs refers to "the contestants" in a way that makes it clear that the contest between the two is expressed from the point of view of an outsider to the contest. Reading the second paragraph with appropriate understanding requires that one hypothetically adopt or identify with the position of such an outside observer.

Imagine there are only two of us left in the world contesting the application of the concept "real". Then one of us dies. The contest does not end, for, given that the word expresses an essentially contested concept, the survivor fails to grasp the meaning of "real" in applying only his own conception of it. The survivor has to continue to adopt the points of view of dead contestant(s), in addition to his own, if he is to have a full understanding of "real". There are conflicting points of view here, even if there is only one person left to hold them. I do not minimize the psychological difficulty in embracing two conflicting points of view at the same time. People can, however, switch between points of view over time. They have not thereby "changed their mind", given that they understand that "real" is an essentially contested concept. Rather, they are distancing themselves from "their own" point of view in understanding this. Minds are broad enough to cope.

Let us examine the understandings of "real" that occur in this context. From the point of view of a contestant, the assertion, *A*, that he offers relates to the same thing as the assertion, *B*, offered by his opponent. The contestant holds that his assertion expresses reality, using whatever is his favoured concept to mark that claimed fact: for example, that the assertion is "true". His opponent, by contrast, makes a similar claim, but one that is false from the point of view of the first contestant. Reality, from the contestant's point of view, is expressed by his own assertion, but not by the assertion of his opponent. He accepts that the opponent's assertion conflicts with his own, and holds it false. This is not a dispassionate observation. The contestants each judge the other's assertion to be inconsistent with their own, and do so partly in virtue of a *commitment* to a *consistent* reality, which does not permit a pluralist approach. Given that each sees himself as contesting with the other, they *share* this commitment to a *shared* consistent reality.

There are other ways of putting the point: by analogy with Rawls's approach to the idea of "justice", the contestants share a "concept" of reality or truth but have conflicting "conceptions";[13] alternatively, they share a meta-criterion of reality but have conflicting criteria; alternatively, they may share a criterion for reality but differ in its application. Criteria for the application of the concepts of reality or truth are no more mechanical in their operation than is the application of any other rule.[14] The contestants cannot themselves be pluralists in this context and also committed to their own position as contestants. This is because to be a contestant is to try to *put down* the position of one's opponent, whereas to be a pluralist is to say that there is no need for this. The contestants' claims are inconsistent as judged by them both, and they share a requirement for consistency, wherever that may exactly be located in their shared understanding of reality.[15]

Certainly a contestant can use a *contingently* contested concept, for that merely involves recognition that the opponent contests his own use.[16] But one contestant cannot describe the situation as one in which his opponent counts reality differently from himself, without holding

---

13. Rawls, *A Theory of Justice*, 5.
14. See the material on the problem of "discretion" in H. Davies & D. Holdcroft, *Jurisprudence: Texts and Commentary* (London: Butterworth, 1991), 80ff.
15. It is possible that this is not so, and this possibility would arise in the different context where one person thought that their opponent's claim was inconsistent with their own and their opponent saw no inconsistency. However, that is not the situation dealt with here.
16. Note that the notion "contested concept" is itself ambiguous between something like "actually contested" (although with the implication that it should not be contested, because I believe myself to be right) and "acceptably contested", where in some sense I am prepared to live with that fact; this last is not formally identical with the notion of essential contestability but it may sometimes in practice amount to that.

also that the opponent does so falsely. He cannot *mean* that it is essential to understanding "real" that one recognizes valid alternatives. This means that only an observer can properly apply here the notion of an essentially contested concept. In not requiring a choice between the contested accounts, the observer is committed to a factual pluralism.

The meaning of "real" for each contestant is thus different from the meaning of "real" for the (philosophically observing) understander of the contest. Who "*really*" understands the meaning of "real"? It would be a philosophical prejudice – indeed, an *essentially* philosophical prejudice – to assume that it is the *observer*.[17] Moreover, it would be begging the question against pluralism to suppose that one point of view – even the observer's – involves a better understanding of "real" than another. There is no "best" understanding. The observer may seem to be better off philosophically, for he may be supposed "really" to understand the meaning of "real", in recognizing it as an essentially contested concept. However, he has no *commitment* to the application of the concept in the way the opponents do, and it is for this reason that he does not have the same *understanding* of the concept. Again, the contestants may seem to be better off philosophically, for they each grasp the connection between "reality" and "truth", and the opposition between "truth" and "falsehood", while the observer does not accept these in their situation. Yet their shared understanding yields inconsistency, disagreeing as they do. The upshot is that the concept of reality means to the observer something different from what it means to the contestants. No one here has a privileged grasp of the meaning. Even to describe a situation as involving an essentially contested concept is to adopt a partisan position.

The contestants, I have argued, are not factual pluralists, and only the observer can be. An exactly analogous argument has people contesting over their rights. Each contestant states a right claim as true, holding it to be inconsistent with the right claim of his opponent, and so sharing a commitment to the consistency of the reality that each is referring to. Yet in so far as "right" is an essentially contested concept, or, equivalently, in so far as the moral reality that makes right

---

17. On the other hand, it may be a *historical* prejudice. Historical understanding may be seen as essentially observer-centred, with historians understanding, better than those they are writing about, what is going on. That historical understanding is primary is a philosophical position shared by, for example, Vico, Hegel, Croce and Collingwood.

statements true is an inconsistent reality, then the observer who recognizes this is not committed to the consistency that the contestants believe in. Accepting this, and in order to clarify further this understanding of pluralism, the question now is what the concept of reality means for the philosophical observer, independent of the question of whether it is the same as or different from that used by the contestants. What is *his* use of the word "real", in particular for what rights there really are in this context? Is *that* use intelligible?

The observer will hold that the contestants offer two assertions about their rights that:

- are about the same thing;
- conflict with each other; and
- are both true.

We have noted that this set of descriptions can be interpreted as expressing at least two different points of view (that of a contestant plus that of an outsider to the contest), and it is possible to understand the observer merely as switching between these different viewpoints. However, this just repeats a conclusion already drawn, and does not take seriously the idea of the "observer". Assuming that we are trying to represent the observer as himself holding a single and internally consistent point of view then, when he says that the assertions "conflict", what does *he* mean? Given that he believes that both are true, he cannot consistently say that they conflict in the sense that one is true and the other false, and in any event to take this line would be to put himself in the position of one of the contestants. However, what *is* clearly assertible by him is that the *contestants* conflict. Since, on the observer's view, *both* assertions are true, despite any conflict, then he sees each contestant as claiming – in a totalitarian way – that theirs is the *sole truth* about the matter, or at least the sole truth expressed in that situation.

To put it another way, since the observer believes that both assertions are true, then he believes that each contestant is wrong, not in claiming truth, but in the totalitarian claim to uniqueness of truth that each makes. The observer believes that the two assertions are, by contrast with the beliefs of the contestants, *complementary* to each other: each is just part of the truth. In this way the assertions themselves do *not* conflict with each other; although the contestants – wrongly, from the observer's point of view – think that they do. So what actually conflict are not the two assertions but rather: claims *about* those two assertions; claims made at a meta-level; claims about what is or is not *the* truth, or otherwise, what is or is not the *whole* truth, or otherwise, what is or is not the *sole* truth about the rights or other matter being referred to. It is the claim to universality, of totality, of uniqueness, on the part of each of the contestants, that raises the problem.

So what makes the contestants conflict is their insistence on the privileged status of their own position and their refusal to accept the position of their opponent, and this contrasts with that *toleration* of alternative points of view that is embodied in the observer's understanding. Each contestant then has to *tolerate* the claim of the other in order to grasp what the observer understands, and indeed has to tolerate the observer's understanding also. Since it is the totalitarian drive to uniqueness on the part of any particular criterion for what is real in this context that yields inconsistency with alternatives, even the observer's tolerance is subject to this constraint: he will not fully understand the meaning of "real" unless he understands the commitment to conflict that, from a point of view different from his own, one may be committed to. Even the observer thinks the contestants wrong, but not because what is asserted as true is, according to the observer, false, but because what is asserted as true is asserted as the sole truth, so that an alternative is seen by the contestant as conflicting and therefore false. How the matter may be justly resolved will be discussed in Chapter 14.

The upshot is that a pluralist reality cannot be completely and consistently described within a single point of view, but it can be if a multiplicity of points of view is adopted. By this means we may achieve some intelligibility for the pluralism of reality, as an important way of structuring in particular our moral understanding. Yet while the idea of the inconsistency of moral reality and rights may be made intelligible by this means, none of this is an argument that rights actually are inconsistent; it is not an argument that beliefs need never be judged as conflicting, and, if they are judged to conflict, it is not an argument that no choices need be made. We have nevertheless reached the point of recognizing that human rights have no independent metaphysical existence, are not plausibly universal, may with reason change over time, and may be intelligibly inconsistent with each other. We nevertheless recognize the *value* that, like Hohfeld, we may give to the respect for consistency.

CHAPTER 11

Understanding rights

In Chapter 1 we observed that the concept of human rights in modern Western culture has a particular authority for us, as an ultimate standard of justification, which is an essential feature of both our moral and our legal standards. Much of Western moral and legal understanding has developed in terms of this concept, and we value the claims of human rights sufficiently strongly for the developing international world order to make explicit reference to them in declaration and in policy. We have here treated such rights in terms of their status as claimed by the 1948 Universal Declaration of Human Rights. We have presented human rights as if they set the overriding moral benchmark, and our major philosophical problem so far has been to examine the supposed independent and universal authority of these moral claims. We began with Plato, who presented us with an account of the independence and universality of a fundamental moral concept, such as "rights" purports to be, and through his arguments we isolated three features of such moral reality: that it is independent of us, that it is eternal or unchanging and that it is consistent. Each of these has been presented and assessed by reference to the major moral and political thinkers in the history of philosophy and by reference to Hohfeld's analysis of rights in the law. We have distinguished the human rights that raise our ultimate philosophical problems of justification from the moral or legal rights that may be contingently claimed within particular cultures and jurisdictions, and explained how the various kinds of rights relate to each other. We have concluded that human rights have no independent metaphysical existence, are not plausibly universal, may with reason be held to change over time, and may be intelligibly inconsistent with each other. We have noted that consistency is a value that is respected, and yet that we need to recognize different points of view if we are to encompass all our moral understanding.

We have, then, analysed the foundations of the justification of human rights and clarified their relationship with both other moral rights and legal rights. Yet despite the range of this material and the exactnesses of Hohfeld's analysis, philosophical problems of clarification remain. We still do not have an adequate understanding of rights, and in this chapter we will display the limitations of the present position and develop a way of improving it. We shall see that Hohfeld's position requires an understanding of the concepts of right and duty that is prior to his analysis. To display what is involved in a fuller understanding of rights I will present R. M. Hare's distinction between the meanings of moral terms and the criteria for their application. Hare's distinction risks unwanted metaphysical commitments, and we will show how these can be avoided by using Rawls's distinction between "concept" and "conception". I will conclude the chapter by showing that the further understanding of Hohfeld's right–duty links requires recognizing the different options as to which concept is actually prior: whether rights are prior to duties, duties prior to rights, or rights and duties are mutually supporting.

We have seen the various ways in which, accepting Hohfeld's general approach, we may understand "right", "duty" and their cognates as correlative terms: terms that are logically related to each other in specific ways. A particular example of Hohfeld's view of such logical relationships is this: "X has a claim-right against Y that p" implies that "Y has a duty towards X that p" and "Y has a duty towards X that p" implies that "X has a claim-right against Y that p". So understood, X's claim-right against Y can exist if and only if Y's correlated duty towards X exists, and a similar point can be made about the other correlated terms in Hohfeld's table (Table 7.1). Given the Hohfeldian position – that we have here a scheme of exact concepts that mutually support each other by logical implication – we may draw conclusions not only about the existence of rights and duties, but also about their place in our knowledge and indeed about their place in other issues. For example, given that one knows the logical implications involved, to *know* that X has a claim-right against Y is to *know* that Y has a duty towards X. Again, to *justify* the claim that X has a claim-right against Y is to *justify* the claim that Y has a duty towards X. Very generally, rights and duties stand or fall together throughout much of our best understanding, given Hohfeld's position.

Yet do these Hohfeldian analyses tell us enough about how rights are to be understood? The logical relationships that he describes can indeed make an important contribution to our reasoning about legal and moral issues but not only do they involve what we have seen may be a problematic evaluative commitment to consistency, but they presuppose a still prior understanding. This can be shown as follows. Suppose a word exists that you do not understand, a word that may be named with the letter R. A theorist tells you that you can understand R in the following way: R names a relationship between two different people, A and B. R relates the two people in such a way that, if A bears the relation R to B, then B bears the relation D to A, and if B bears the relation R to A, then A bears the relation D to B. Does this help? Plainly not. If you do not already know the meaning of D it is clear that nothing in the bare logical relationships specified between R and D will help you grasp the meaning of either R or D. Similarly, there has to be more to understanding the meaning of rights than is offered by Hohfeld's specification of logical equivalences.

What more is required? While you do not – before the theorist's explanation – understand the meaning of R, imagine that you do already know the meaning of D. To know D's meaning is at least in part to understand how D is used. If D is a word that you have no difficulty in understanding, then you will be able to reason with the word, recognize its usual synonyms or definitions, and be able to apply it to particular cases. Given that you know these things, then your imagined ignorance of the logical connection of D with the word R has to be of extremely limited importance. Precisely because of the logical connection between R and D, virtually everything that might be said by using R you can already say by using D.[1] This new knowledge of the meaning of R may nevertheless be extremely useful – at last you can understand those texts that use R – but what you are recognizing is little more than a new label that logically relates in a simple way to a conceptual core shared by R and D, a conceptual core that you already understand. The theorist's presentation of the logical connections between R and D is then helpful if you already understand D, but it is merely new labelling rather than new conceptual

---

1. Not quite everything. For example, the sentence "Sentences using D can be re-expressed using R" is not a sentence you are yet in a position to assert with justification.

content that is being provided. If you do not understand either *R* or *D*, it is a theorist's duty to explain at least one of these core terms in a way that goes beyond mere logical interrelationships with immediately associated terms and in a way that builds on other notions that we already understand.

This may seem a sufficiently general account of what more, beyond logical equivalences with *D*, is required for "understanding the meaning of *R*", but a further important point needs to be noted. If *R* is an *evaluative* word then its "meaning" may well involve the kind of complexity that was usefully spelled out by Hare. Distinguish, in accordance with Hare's examples, a "descriptive" remark, such as "this strawberry is large, red and juicy", from an "evaluative" remark, such as "this is a good strawberry".[2] We need to recognize, Hare points out, that an evaluative word like "good" – unlike a descriptive word like "red" – is used to *commend* things. There are perhaps serious philosophical difficulties in Hare's position: do "descriptive" and "evaluative" mark *categorical* distinctions between "fact" and "value", or do they overlap in some way? Can we derive an "ought" from an "is"?[3] While it may be true that "good" is used to "commend" things, is that always the case? Is it a defining characteristic of all "moral" terms? We need not investigate these difficulties here, but our recognition of these difficulties should not prevent our noting the important feature of moral language to which Hare has drawn our attention.

Usually we have criteria for distinguishing good from bad things, but not always. Imagine, with Hare, that two different people collect cacti and have the only cacti in the country. One may say to the other "I've got a better cactus than yours" but, Hare asks, "how does he know how to apply the word in this way? He has never learnt to apply 'good' to cacti; he does not even know any *criteria* for telling a good cactus from a bad one (for as yet there are none)."[4] Yet, Hare points out, both of these people know and share the meaning of the word "good" despite disagreeing about its application to particular cases. It is just because they share an understanding of the meaning of "good" that they are able to disagree in a meaningful way about which cases it should be applied to. We may therefore wish to follow Hare in distinguishing what may be called the "meaning" of an evaluative

---

2. R. M. Hare, *The Language of Morals* (Oxford: Oxford University Press, 1975), 111.

3. Hume, *A Treatise of Human Nature*, 469.

4. Hare, *The Language of Morals*, 97.

word from the "criteria for its application", and we may recognize, with Hare, that this distinction must be made just because – as his cacti example shows – we might know the meaning of "good" even when there are *no* criteria for its application. Even if there are criteria, the two people may disagree about these too, and each might attempt to *justify* to the other the criteria each uses. Your own criteria for the application of R may differ from everybody else's, so that you apply R to quite different things from other people and justify doing so in quite different ways. Yet, despite your difference in the application or use of R, you may still share with other people the same understanding of its meaning.

We have noted that if you fully understand a concept you will be able to reason with it, recognize its usual synonyms or definitions or logical equivalences, and be able to apply it to particular cases. "Application to particular cases" we can now see to be a complex notion. If you fully understand a concept you will also know, in so far as it is appropriate, how far there may be a "correct" use or uses: whether there is disagreement about its application to particular cases and how far different principles or rival criteria may be used for this purpose. A full understanding will include the complete range of such criteria. You should also recognize, if not in technical terms, whether the concept is "essentially contested": whether disagreement about its application is essential to its meaning. This may be evidenced in your practical expectation that disagreements will both occur and not be resolved. All this is needed for the full understanding of rights, but Hohfeld's analysis does not give it to us.

We have seen that Hohfeld's analysis logically relating types of right and types of duty is only helpful on the assumption that you already have some sufficient prior grasp of the "meaning" of one of the terms "right" or "duty", or one of the other related terms for which Hohfeld also provides logical connections. We can further conclude that Hohfeld's analysis is only helpful if you also have some sufficient prior grasp of the "range of criteria" for the application of "right" or "duty", for it is clear that "right", "duty" and their correlates have characteristics that make them fall in some way within the list of what Hare saw as "evaluative" terms, characteristics deriving from their central place in both moral and legal philosophy.

If Hare's approach is correct, then understanding rights requires grasping two different things: understanding the "meaning" of "rights" and understanding the "criteria for the application" of "rights". Understanding words, as we have said, requires in part that we understand how they are used. Language, Wittgenstein suggested, might be seen as a game with rules,[5] and, as he famously failed to say, "don't ask for the meaning, ask for the use".[6] Wittgenstein's position means that there is no immediately obvious difference between a set of rules for the use of a word and a set of criteria for the application of a word. How then can Hare distinguish "meaning" from "criteria for application"? It seems that Hare's distinction between "meaning" and "criteria for application" can only be won at the cost of making "meaning" utterly mysterious, something *different* from the way people use words, something that has no relation to the forms of life – which include their languages – that people actually have.

Does this matter? Since we seek "understanding" of rights we will seek to grasp both "meaning" and "criteria for application", and is it not merely an empty semantic issue – or at least an irrelevant issue – whether we choose to understand the word "meaning" as essentially specifying "criteria for application", or to understand "meaning" as distinct from "criteria for application"? Clarification of Hare's contrast here matters because we need to be careful not to prejudge metaphysical issues. We have already seen difficulties with the notion of the metaphysical independence of rights: difficulties with rights existing independently of us as rules in the natural order of things rather than as part of a rule-governed social practice. As we engage in further clarification of "rights" we must note the effect of our meta-physical argument on this clarification. The metaphysical argument will itself be clarified in this process.

The issue about the way concepts may be understood can be expressed in terms of the question of whether such understanding is "subjective" or "objective". Understanding may be held to be *subjective* in so far as its function is held to consist in the removal of ignorance, doubt or puzzlement on the part of those who have it.[7] Understanding may be held to be *objective* in so far as its function is held to be the achievement of a correct or truthful view of the way things really are or the way they actually work. It may be noted, assuming for the moment that these explanations of "subjective" and

---

5. See Wittgenstein, *Philosophical Investigations*, §§80ff. and *passim*, esp. §83.
6. The first score of sections of Wittgenstein's *Philosophical Investigations* are a good introduction to this view.
7. I have expressed this elsewhere, in particular in "Kellner on Language and Historical Representation", *History and Theory* 30 (1991), 356–68, and in "From History to Justice", in *Essays in Honor of Burleigh Wilkins: From History to Justice*, A. Jokic (ed.) (New York: Peter Lang, 2001), 19–69.

"objective" are correct, that the kind of understanding that successfully removes puzzlement may or may not give a true account of the
way things really are, while our best explanations of the way the
world works may be impossible for most people to understand –
indeed, we may imagine that the truth about things is such that no
human being can grasp it.

The contrast between "subjective" and "objective", as explained so
far, typically expresses a *realist* position: the view that there is a reality
or truth independent of what we believe it to be. On such an
approach, that we actually use the concept of "rights" in a certain way,
a way involving reference to "meanings" or to a particular range of
criteria for determining what rights we have, is no guarantee that we
are doing so correctly, that is, objectively rather than subjectively. On
such a realist approach, it is not our actual social practices that ground
the correctness of our understanding of rights but rather an external
and mysterious metaphysical something that has no necessary connection with those social practices. And yet if we too readily reject such
mystery and insist with Wittgenstein on limiting our understanding to
our actual use of words then we risk a relativism that may be quite
inappropriate to a proper understanding of rights and that would not
reflect the everyday sense that human rights, in particular, have some
kind of independence or objectivity that gives them the authority that
we commonly believe they have.

This realist approach has already been questioned. We note the
important issue of whether there are such things as human rights or
natural duties. Some theorists deny that there are, and believe that such
rights or duties are a subjective creation on the part of human beings.
But both the assertion and the denial of the existence of human rights
are ambiguous. To assert that human rights "exist" is an assertion that
can be interpreted both realistically and anti-realistically. To take an
example from contemporary physics, do extra dimensions exist?
Stephen Hawking expresses in a popular way an anti-realist approach
for physics, referring to what he calls a "positivist" approach: "Which
is reality, brane or bubble? They are both mathematical models that
describe the observations. One is free to use whichever model is most
convenient."[8] We may suppose such things to exist, but such a
supposition is no more than a claim that our best theory purports to
refer to them, and *we* choose which is "best". The philosophical
question is whether any sense is to be made of their "really" being there

8. S. Hawking, *The Universe in a Nutshell* (London: Bantam, 2001), 54, 198.

independently of what the theory says; summarily, the philosophical realist says yes, the anti-realist, no.

Our earlier argument against the metaphysical independence of human rights was an argument against their existence on a realist interpretation. But it may be that human rights exist in an anti-realist interpretation of existence. Similarly, if we deny that human rights exist, we may be denying a realistic interpretation of the existence of human rights and affirming an anti-realistic interpretation, or we may be denying their existence under any interpretation. In the light of this choice of denials, we may recall Hart's remark:

> Perhaps few would now deny, as some have, that there are moral rights; for the point of that denial was usually to object to some philosophical claim as to the "ontological status" of rights, and this objection is now expressed not as a denial that there are any moral rights but as a denial of some assumed logical similarity between sentences used to assert the existence of rights and other kinds of sentences.[9]

The "other kinds of sentences" here are those declarative sentences that, for Hart, might be more plausibly interpreted in a realistic way than are sentences referring to rights. Hart might be thinking of physics here, for example. Yet once we adopt an anti-realist interpretation of physics, we can no longer see a clear contrast between the ontological status of rights and that of the referents of physical theories: perhaps they all "exist" in *our* world. A Kantian approach permits this.

Rather than an external and mysterious metaphysical something, it may then be our actual social practices that ground the correctness of our understanding of rights. The contrast between "subjective" and "objective" therefore need not be taken to presuppose metaphysical realism in this context.[10] We have seen that whether there is such a thing as the way things actually are independently of human understanding is a central philosophical problem, and it is a familiar anti-realist response that the ultimate test of the merit of explanation or understanding may only be in terms of the removal of subjective doubt or puzzlement. The contrast between "subjective" and

---

9. H. L. A. Hart, "Are There Any Natural Rights?", reprinted in *Political Philosophy*, A. Quinton (ed.), 53–66 (Oxford: Oxford University Press, 1967), 54.

10. Some areas of discourse may be more appropriate to being interpreted realistically and others anti-realistically.

"objective" has to be explained differently if an anti-realist approach is adopted: typically, "subjectivity" may be taken to suggest that the relativistic and incommensurable positions of many different communities, or even the psychology of many particular individuals, can be the only standard for judging our rights or duties. By contrast, "objectivity" may be held to depend on some kind of worldwide inter-community commonality of standard or acceptance that is neutral with respect to different communities or individuals and that makes sense of the possibility of translation between different communities of belief and the possibility of external judgement of the approaches of particular communities or individuals.

An intermediate conclusion presupposing such contrasting communities was reached earlier, following which we may understand legal rights as belonging to particular jurisdictions and justified relative only to them, with moral rights understood as part of some comparatively localized system where the culture concerned need not be identical with a particular jurisdiction, and with human rights understood as part of a universal system, consistent or otherwise, and not identified with either a particular jurisdiction or a particular culture or practice. The present approach suggests that "human rights" in particular refers to some overriding conception that can be rationally justified as *universal* and that may be used to judge the merits of particular or jurisdiction-based or culture-based criteria, without adopting some approach where the meaning of "human rights" involves some metaphysical essence or natural reference that leaves behind the ways of human life. Hare's distinction between "meaning" and "criteria for application" must – if they are to be distinguished – both be made sense of without leaving behind our actual social practices. A full understanding of rights does not require reference to metaphysical essences, and we cannot permit Hare's distinction to have mysterious implications. We will see shortly how his distinction is best understood.

Hare's approach suggested a metaphysical difficulty, and Finnis raises a related one.[11] Both express themselves in such a way as to yield the same needless implication: that some mysterious entities exists when we talk about rights. In the explanation of Hohfeld's analysis of rights we noted Finnis's objection that Hohfeld's system permitted too complex an understanding of rights. According to

---

11. For the connection between natural rights and God see Finnis, *Natural Law and Natural Rights*, 48–9.

Finnis, lawyers may talk of rights simply in terms of two-place relationships between particular persons and the things they have a right to, rather than as three-place relationships between some particular persons, the things they have a right to, and some other particular persons against whom those rights are held. Recall Finnis's example of somebody, A, having, under some contract, a right to something against another person, B – a right that is then assigned so as to be held against a different person. In Hohfeld's system a right is essentially to be understood as a right–duty relationship, so that following assignment of the contract a different right–duty relationship comes into being. Such Hohfeldian understanding, observed Finnis, obscures the "intelligible unity" of the right throughout such changing assignments, a unity that reflects "one subsisting objective".[12] The idea of such a unity might be thought to be appropriate for our understanding of human rights. However, we argued earlier that a Hohfeldian approach gave detail that the legal reality required, and that talk of rights as two-place relationships was merely lawyers' superficial shorthand.

It should now be noted that Finnis wants to stress the "intelligible unity" of the *right*, and we may again recognize the mysterious metaphysical hint in this terminology, a hint that goes beyond everyday legal concerns. If there were such an intelligible unity, it is true, as Finnis claimed, that Hohfeld's system would obscure it. Yet not only is there no need to conclude that there are such curious entities as subsisting intelligible unities, but any attempt to specify these is completely arbitrary. After all, the Hohfeldian system would equally obscure the intelligible unity of the *duty*, if there were such a thing. Describing the assigned contract situation in Hohfeldian terms would at least have the advantage of being neutral between these unnecessary metaphysical suggestions.

The imagined contract between A and B gives A a right but also imposes on B a duty. In principle, contracts, understood as agreements imposing both rights and their correlated duties, may not permit assignment at all, or they may permit assignment of the right, or of the duty, or both. In a simple case I may rent a property. I have a right against the landlord to occupation and property maintenance, and I also owe a duty to pay rent to the landlord. The landlord has the correlated duties and rights. If we think particularly of the right to receive rent, then we may imagine an "intelligible unity" of this right

---

12. *Ibid.*, 201–202, 218ff.

persisting as one tenant replaces another. This, however, is a muddle. Apart from the contract itself, the one entity that has an "intelligible unity" here is the *landlord*, not the right; but this is a mere contingency.

It is also plain that the landlord may be able to sell the property and assign the right to receive my rent to a new landlord. If I remain as tenant throughout, then a series of such assignments between land-lords may equally lead us to think of the "intelligible unity of the duty" in this situation, but again we would do better to recognize that it is the *tenant*, not the duty, that has the continuity here. It is a contingent matter of the details of the contract that rights and duties can be assigned by whom and to whom. If a right or a duty has an "intelligible unity" – the kind of thing that gives it some kind of priority in our understanding here – then this cannot be argued for in terms of our everyday legal understanding with its concentration on the contingent details of particular contracts. The political merits, if such they are, of institutionalizing and understanding our relation-ships in terms of persisting rights with changing duties, rather than in terms of persisting duties with changing rights, needs a very different kind of argument, one that is not plausibly forthcoming. We need not dispute, however, that thinking in terms of "human rights" does – whether or not it is justified – imply some persistent unity to some rights; it also implies some persistent unity to some duties, given the Hohfeldian analysis.[13] Such unity would be due to a contingent universality, however, rather than to any mysterious way of existing.

Once we have explained away the metaphysical difficulties that Hare's and Finnis's presentations of their positions hint at,[14] we can move beyond them and interpret "meaning" and "criteria for applica-tion" more straightforwardly. As we noted in Chapter 10, Rawls made a useful distinction in his *A Theory of Justice* between a "concept" of justice and a "conception" of justice: people *share* the "concept" of

---

13. Whether the duties are, as the UN Declaration of Human Rights implies, duties on the part of states, or whether they would be better understood as the duties of individuals (as O'Neill suggests, in *A Question of Trust*), will not be dealt with here.

14. I am not claiming here that Hare and Finnis were committed to the mysteries I have referred to, only that their terminology – a common element in talk about rights – risks misunderstanding. "A belief in objective prescriptivity has flourished within the tradition of moral thinking, but in the end it cannot be defended", says J. L. Mackie, "Can There be a Right-based Moral Theory?", in *Theories of Rights*, Waldron (ed.), 168–71 (Oxford: Oxford University Press, 1984), esp. 171; also argued at length in his *Ethics, Inventing Right and Wrong* (Harmondsworth: Penguin, 1977).

justice when they agree (to use Rawls's example) that "institutions are just when no arbitrary distinctions are made between persons in the assigning of basic rights and duties and when the rules determine a proper balance between competing claims to the advantages of social life". Yet people may at the same time *differ* in their "conceptions" of justice in that, while they may agree that principles are required to determine exactly what counts as, for example, the "proper balance" between competing claims, they may disagree with each other over what those principles should be.[15]

We might then say of Rawls's position, if we follow Hare, that people know "the meaning of 'just'" but disagree over "the criteria for the application of 'just'". But this need not now leave us with any difficult metaphysical mysteries, for the matter can be described pragmatically, following Rawls, in terms of distinguishing things we may agree about from things we may disagree about.[16] This can be a matter of degree and need involve no categorical differences. "Rights", very obviously, is a word that we may know the "meaning" of – for example, in so far as we agree and share a Hohfeldian concept with its associated beliefs and are able to understand the word's range of normal functions – but it is also a word with respect to which we may have different "conceptions", in so far as we may disagree about what principles or criteria should be used to determine what rights we have, whether within a particular legal jurisdiction, a localized moral community or universally.

With these abstract but important considerations dealt with, we can return to what more is required, beyond Hohfeld's analysis, to understand rights and their associated duties in a full way. We noted earlier in this chapter that a full understanding involves a grasp of a concept's application to particular cases and of the range of rival or essentially contested criteria that may be used for this purpose. In the light of that earlier argument, one important way in which this issue can be approached is by asking which of the various terms is "prior". "Rights" will be "prior" to "duties" just when you need first to understand "rights" if you are to understand "duties", but not the other way around. "Duties" then get explained in terms of "rights", and "rights" – assuming you do not already understand them – have

---

15. Rawls, *A Theory of Justice*, 5.
16. Quine distinguishes in an analogous way, within what is pragmatically seen as the web of our beliefs, between those beliefs that form the "core" of the web and are in practice universally shared and unrevisable and those that form part of the periphery.

to get explained in terms of something else. Hobbes provided an example of this kind of explanation. We saw that, in his view, our natural situation was a state of war. "War" was explained by Hobbes as a period of time during which individual people were disposed to fight each other (although were not necessarily actually fighting against each other), and during which time there was nothing to block the operation of this disposition. "All other time is peace", he continued.[17] "Peace" was thus not "directly" explained, but rather explained in terms of its logical relationship to "war", while "war" was explained in terms of something else. Re-expressing this in the terms now introduced, the complexities of meaning and use and criteria for application are to be grasped and explained for "war" but need not be separately grasped and explained for "peace".

Hobbes also provides an example, together with Locke, of the importance of *alternative* directions of the "priority" of understanding. Consider the familiar question in philosophy of law, "Is there a necessary connection between law and morality?", a question that is sometimes used to distinguish legal positivism from natural law theory.[18] Briefly, one common view of the essence of legal positivism is that legal positivism essentially claims that there is *no* necessary connection between law and morality, while the essence of natural law theory is similarly perceived to be that there *is* such a necessary connection. Both Hobbes and Locke count as "natural law theorists" on this superficial approach, since each theorist holds that one cannot possibly have law without morality. This roughly outlined logical connection between law and morality that Hobbes and Locke broadly share nevertheless masks a critical difference between them about the relative priority of law and morality. Detail has been given above about Hobbes's and Locke's positions on this and, without being too misleading about their positions in making the present point, we can summarize Hobbes as regarding law as prior to morality in the following way: law, as the command of the sovereign, sets the standard of right and wrong and so of morality, which has no existence independently of the sovereign's command. By contrast, Locke's position, again in simple summary, is that an unjust law is not law; it is natural morality that is prior, and valid positive law exists and is understood as authoritative solely in virtue of and by reference to that natural morality.

---

17. Hobbes, *Leviathan*, Ch. 13.
18. See Hart, "Positivism and the Separation of Law and Morals", 17–37 and *The Concept of Law*, Ch. 5.

While it would not with full accuracy reflect the exact positions of Hobbes and Locke, we can imagine a theory that identified law with morality so as to yield the following analysis: the existence of positive law entails the existence of morality, and the existence of morality entails the existence of positive law. The symmetry of this imagined relationship between law and morality would nevertheless mask the asymmetry of the opposing positions that could be adopted with regard to the priority of each over the other, for identifying morality with law and vice versa still leaves open the question of whether our route into understanding the claimed morality–law pairing is by way of understanding morality or by way of understanding law. In an analogous way it is plain that a theory that accepts Hohfeld's analytical symmetries between rights and duties still leaves open the major issue of whether rights should be understood in terms of duties, or duties understood in terms of rights.

Which is prior? Should the complexities of meaning and use and criteria for application be grasped and explained for rights, with duties understood in terms of rights, or should the complexities of meaning and use and criteria for application be grasped and explained for duties, with rights understood in terms of duties? Or might there be no priority? Consider, with respect to this last suggestion, Rawls's understanding of "justice as fairness".[19] As it stands, this famous but ungrammatical expression is little better than a slogan. However, it marks Rawls's important idea of what he calls "reflective equilibrium".[20] As a first step to understanding this, we should follow Rawls and read "justice as fairness" as expressing the idea that the principles of justice are those principles that we would accept if we were fairly placed.[21] This hypothetical and counterfactual fair situation is called by Rawls the "original position". It is the *fairness* of such placing, the fairness of our decision situation, that for Rawls

---

19. Rawls, *A Theory of Justice*, esp. Ch. 1.
20. *Ibid.*, 20.
21. It is tempting to refer again to Hume: "philosophers may, if they please, extend their reasoning to the suppos'd *state of nature*; provided they allow it to be a mere philosophical fiction, which never had, and never cou'd have any reality" (*A Treatise of Human Nature*, 493). Rawls describes his theory as a "social contract" theory like Locke's (*A Theory of Justice*, 7), but I have argued elsewhere that this is misleading, since Locke's theory involved a social contract theory of political obligation and a natural rights theory of justice, whereas Rawls's theory involves a justice theory of political obligation and a social contract theory of justice; J. L. Gorman, "A Note on the Main Idea of Rawls's Theory of Justice", *Political Studies* **29** (1981), 282–3.

justifies the principles chosen in that situation as *just* principles; on the other hand, that the principles we choose are *just* principles would argue that the situation in which we produced them was indeed a *fair* situation. The explanation and justification is intended to work in both directions, and Rawls's theory is completed both by expressing the principles of justice and by characterizing what it is to be fairly placed. Both need to be understood in order fully to understand either.

Yet the conceptions of justice and fairness that mutually support each other in this way do not lack independent support, on Rawls's approach. The fairness of our decision situation is justified both on the basis of the just quality of the principles yielded and also on the basis of independent argument involving other intuitions and moral judgements, with the range of understanding, beliefs and criteria for application of concepts associated with those. Again, the justice of our chosen principles is similarly justified both on the basis of the fairness of the situation in which they were determined and also on the basis of independent argument involving other intuitions and moral judgements, again with the range of understanding, beliefs and criteria for application of concepts associated with those. An equilibrium of mutual support is thus imagined across a wide range of our concepts and beliefs, with neither justice nor fairness prior to the other. We might imagine, by analogy with this, that there be no priority of explanation, understanding or justification between rights and duties, but rather, first, that each not only analyses the other by way of Hohfeld's logical interconnections (if we stop just there we are in the empty situation of R and D) but in addition supports, justifies or explains the other and, secondly, that each is independently supported, justified or explained on other grounds. Only in this way would full understanding be achieved. In summary, there are three strands of approach, each of which in principle needs to be taken to frame the further understanding of Hohfeld's right–duty links on the basis of: rights being prior to duties; duties being prior to rights; or rights and duties being mutually supporting. A full understanding of rights requires mastery of all three strands of approach. The remaining chapters of this book will organize our understanding of rights in these terms.

CHAPTER 12

The rights-based approach

Our further understanding of rights depends on the further understanding of Hohfeld's right–duty links, and we have seen that in principle three approaches to this development are available: that rights may be understood as prior to duties; that duties may be understood as prior to rights; or that rights and duties may be mutually supporting.

The next step is to investigate and organize our understanding of rights and duties in these terms. In moving away from the question of what rights and duties metaphysically "really are" to the question of what our actual social practices disclose that they are, we are not escaping difficulties. After all, there is not a clear answer to the question of what "our social practices" say that rights and duties are. Is there a homogeneous "we" here? Are views held in the present more authoritative on this than views held in the past? Even if the "we" is interpreted as referring to some legally and morally educated or practising group within a particular jurisdiction or society during a particular period, a range of viewpoints will be disclosed. Or should we take a statistical survey of what people mean, and go with the majority? We do not seek such a survey, but rather seek what might be seen as "best practice", and we recognize this through the quality of its *justification*. It is for this reason that it is common in philosophy to select a particular *theorist* as authoritatively expressing "the view" from a particular time or place. This conceit is often used to drive the history of ideas, whether the history of philosophy or of political or legal theory, with its typical concentration on a series of great individuals each responding to his or her predecessors.

Moreover, referring to social or historical "facts" about our theories or practices can also be a philosophical step too far, raising as it does further metaphysical and epistemological issues about "facts" within social and historical understanding. Such issues will not be discussed here and we need no longer interpret these difficulties in a particularly abstract or metaphysical way, but it is important to recognize that the understanding of rights and duties has changed over time, however that "fact" might be dealt with philosophically. Etymological changes can be extreme: Quine, dealing with different concerns, says, a "startling example is black and the French blanc, 'white': it is conjectured that they are identical in prehistoric origin. The semantic link would have to do with fire – its soot on the one hand and its blaze on the other."[1] If "black" and "white" can have the same root, what difficulties might we face with the contingencies of our changing understanding of rights? We have seen that we cannot just take rights for granted as indubitable constants, as Robert Nozick does in *Anarchy, State and Utopia*: "Individuals have rights, and there are things no person or group may do to them (without violating their rights)".[2] Even Locke offered more than mere assertion.

We observe, then, that there has been historical change over long periods of time in "our" beliefs about what is morally correct and in particular about what our rights and duties are, including historical change in our beliefs about whether views about our rights and duties are to be interpreted realistically or anti-realistically. Law and public morality can change in the specification of their constraints and permissions in these matters, with sometimes duties and sometimes rights prior, and we saw such a change during the twentieth century. In one sense, therefore, it is a practical, contingent or historical matter which and when, if either, of "rights" or "duties" is understood to be prior to the other.

The three views about the direction of priority between rights and duties may be most usefully developed by a consideration of Finnis's presentation of the history of the word "right".[3] Here we will find exemplified a change of priority of understanding that will illuminate the notion of rights. Finnis proceeds by taking particular theorists as appropriately authoritative in expressing the meaning of "right",

---

1. W. V. O. Quine, *Quiddities: An Intermittently Philosophical Dictionary* (Harmondsworth: Penguin, 1990), 107, under "Kinship of Words".
2. Nozick, *Anarchy, State and Utopia*, ix.
3. Finnis, *Natural Law and Natural Rights*, 206ff.

illustrating this changing meaning of "right" in a move from the medieval philosopher St Thomas Aquinas (1224/5–74) to the sixteenth- and seventeenth-century legal thinker Francisco Suárez (1548–1617). Beginning with what he calls the "antecedent" of "right", the Latin "ius" (or "jus"), Finnis explains that Aquinas analysed "ius" as, primarily, covering acts, objects and states of affairs that are just or fair, situations in which those involved act "aright".[4] As Aquinas said, "the right in a work of justice, besides its relation to the agent, is set up by its relation to others".[5] For Aquinas, Finnis says, secondary or derivative meanings of "ius" include the art by which one knows and determines what is just (with the law consisting in the principles and rules of this art), they include the place in which justice is awarded, and they also include the award itself.[6]

> If we now jump about 340 years to the treatise on law by the Spanish Jesuit Francisco Suarez, written c.1610, we find another analysis of the meaning of "*jus*". Here the "true, strict and proper meaning" of *jus* is said to be: "a kind of moral power [*facultas*] which every man has, either over his own property or with respect to that which is due to him".[7]

There has been a shift in meaning here, described by Finnis as a "watershed", between understanding "ius" as a just state of affairs and understanding "ius" as "essentially something someone has, and above all (or at least paradigmatically) a *power* or *liberty*. If you like, it is Aquinas's primary meaning of '*jus*', but transformed by *relating it exclusively to the beneficiary* of the just relationship."[8] We see here a move from a justice-based to a rights-based approach: a change from the priority of justice to the priority of rights in our moral understanding.

---

4. "One could say that for Aquinas 'jus' primarily means 'the fair' or 'the what's fair'; indeed, if one could use the adverb 'aright' as a noun, one could say that his primary account is of 'arights' (rather than of rights)" Finnis, *Natural Law and Natural Rights*, 206.

5. T. Aquinas, *Summa Theologica*, 2nd rev. edn, Fathers of the English Dominican Province (trans.), online edn copyright © 2000 Kevin Knight, www.newadvent.org/summa (accessed May 2003), II-II, q. 57, "Whether right is the object of justice; I answer that . . .".

6. Finnis, *Natural Law and Natural Rights*, 206, referring to Aquinas, *Summa Theologiae* II-II, q. 57; see esp. "Reply to objection 1".

7. Finnis, *Natural Law and Natural Rights*, 206–207, referring to F. Suarez, *De Legibus* [1612] (Oxford: Clarendon Press, 1944), I, ii, 5.

8. *Ibid.*, 207 (original emphasis).

Finnis observes that in due course the law was no longer perceived to be an integral part of the determination of the benefit to be received by the beneficiary, for "within a few years Hobbes is writing: '*jus* and *lex*, *right* and *law* ... ought to be distinguished'".[9] As we have already seen, there is no law in Hobbes's state of nature, but there is a "right", understood to be a "liberty", with liberty understood "negatively" as the absence of external constraints. Finnis also translates from John Locke: "Right is predicated on this, that we have the free use of a thing",[10] and notes that Hobbes, Locke and Samuel von Pufendorf (1632–1694) agreed that a right is paradigmatically a liberty. Finnis continues, "their successors are those who defend the 'choice' theory of rights".[11]

Finnis's summary of "ius" in Suárez (and Hugo Grotius[12] (1583–1645)) as "essentially something someone has, and above all (or at least paradigmatically) a *power* or *liberty*" runs together in a single sentence two different points that require to be made and examined separately. Finnis's first point is to note the change from Aquinas's position of seeing "ius" as referring to a just state of affairs to Suárez's position of seeing "ius" exclusively from the point of view of the beneficiary. Finnis's second point is to interpret the move to the point of view of the beneficiary as being in some way a move towards the "choice" theory of rights. We will interpret next the suggestion that matters should be seen entirely from the point of view of the beneficiary. We will analyse this rights-based point of view, examining how far the beneficiary has to be an individual person and arguing that a group can be a beneficiary, and will also argue against the suggestion that rights are essentially connected to an individual independent self and against the consequential claim that they are therefore part of an essentially male-based morality. Finally in this chapter we will deal with Finnis's second point, distinguishing the "interest" from the "choice" theory of rights and showing that the point of view of the beneficiary does not imply the choice theory.

---

9. *Ibid.*, 208, referring to Hobbes, *Leviathan*, Ch. 14.

10. Finnis, *Natural Law and Natural Rights*, 208, n. 14, referring to Locke, *Essays on the Law of Nature*.

11. Finnis, *Natural Law and Natural Rights*, 208.

12. *Ibid.*, 207. "Suarez was the last great exponent of the Catholic theory of natural law. Grotius was the first Protestant to claim the same conceptual space", J. B. Schneewind, *The Invention of Autonomy* (Cambridge: Cambridge University Press, 1998), 59.

If we apply "right" and "duty" in terms of the understanding of Suárez, our understanding will be such that the just situation is to be understood entirely in terms of the right-holder. This is not a mere change of perspective, for as we have seen we are to understand the beneficiary as having "a kind of moral power" [*facultas*]. Apart from Suárez, Finnis rightly quotes in addition Grotius, for whom an important meaning of "ius" is "a moral quality of the person".[13] Rights are clearly to be understood as independently determined features of the just situation, and, given in addition Hohfeld's understanding, the duties that are logically related to those rights are derivative from our prior understanding of those rights.

On this approach, rights are prior to duties in our understanding, and prior also to our grasp of what justice consists in. We proceed on the temporary assumption that the just situation is to be understood *entirely* in terms of the right-holder. However, this priority need not be "absolute": while, necessarily on the present approach, the concept of rights is an independently determined element that takes priority in our moral understanding, it remains possible that, on what might be viewed by some as a morally worst-case scenario, rights and justice may be seen as *conflicting* ideals, so that, while the rights-based approach is offering a fundamental value, it is not the only value. This particular pluralist possibility does not affect the following argument and will be ignored throughout the rights-based, duty-based and justice-based presentations that follow.[14]

It may seem that the important term in the description "the point of view of the beneficiary" is "beneficiary", a word that may direct our philosophical attention to the nature of the benefit involved. The nature of the "benefit" will be discussed in Chapter 13. However, an important line of thought needs to be presented at this stage. Finnis summarized "ius" in Suárez as "essentially something someone has".[15] It is natural to understand Finnis here as suggesting that the beneficiary is some individual person, and he may well be right in so far as

13. Finnis, *Natural Law and Natural Rights*, 207, referring to H. Grotius, *De Jure Belli ac Pacis* [1625] (London: Sweet & Maxwell, 1922), I, I, iii.
14. Hohfeld's logical equivalencies block the possibility of rights and correlated duties themselves setting conflicting ideals. That does not mean that different rights may not involve conflicting ideals; we have already argued for the intelligibility of a pluralist view that rights may be in conflict with each other. In effect, the imaginary pluralist conflict is between right–duty pairs on the one hand and justice on the other, both conceived as expressing fundamental moral values.
15. Schneewind, *The Invention of Autonomy*, 207.

he intends to characterize the position of Suárez or Grotius. Yet must "the point of view of the beneficiary" be the point of view of an "individual person"? The notion of a "point of view" carries no such definite implication. This notion is complex and sometimes ambiguous: a "point of view" may indeed sometimes be taken as a metaphorical expression for an individual person, but it is often different from that.

We sometimes suggest "see things from his or her point of view" and we mean by it to characterize, not just an individual person's particular objective spatial position or, metaphorically, social situation within a wider world, but his or her *desires* with respect to some matter. Again, we may mean to characterize his or her *beliefs* with respect to some matter. Yet such specificity is not safely tied to an individual person. Desires and beliefs can be and commonly are *shared*, and the notion "point of view" is often used to refer to a particular *association* of people in terms of shared desires or beliefs, or even just for a set of desires or beliefs, for example, "from a Conservative point of view". The expression also has philosophical connotations that make Thomas Nagel's notion "the view from nowhere" both paradoxical and important.[16] In the present context, moving to "the point of view of the beneficiary" may inappropriately direct our attention to an analysis of rights that is centred on an independent individual self.

Instead, we should consider whether the beneficiary may be a group of people rather than an individual. The problem of group rights does not arise where groups are understood to be "nothing but" those individuals who compose them, for the rights of the group are then nothing but the rights of those individuals.[17] But can groups themselves have rights? Legally, of course they can. Thus I may rent property from a landlord, and the landlord may be, for example, a limited company. Such a company is typically recognized by the law as a single legal person, and has rights (and duties) just as any other landlord may have rights and duties deriving from the rental contract. Whether groups can have moral rights is a different question from whether they can have legal rights. In one sense, again, of course they can. Group personification may take place in our everyday moral

---

16. See J. L. Gorman, "Some Astonishing Things", *Metaphilosophy* 22 (1991), 28–40. See T. Nagel, *The View From Nowhere* (Oxford: Oxford University Press, 1986).

17. Note that a "right to associate" or a "right to self-determination" would not necessarily be group rights.

practices in addition to our legal practices and be based merely on our non-legal recognition of the social existence of some group.

However, as Roger Scruton points out, "Firms naturally lend themselves to the view that personification in law is a mere convenience, a device for protecting and limiting some 'common objective', and not the legal recognition of a new moral reality."[18] Finnis is committed to such a view.

> "Personality" is a distracting metaphor ... tugged between its two historic sources ... there is *persona* as mask; to this corresponds the law's carefree attribution of legal personality to *anything* that figures as the subject of legal relations ... On the other hand, there is *persona* as individual substance.[19]

Yet what counts as a "new moral reality" or a "substance" in this context? We have already moved away from the metaphysical suggestion that references to rights are references to independently existing things, and in a similar way we need not suppose that "groups", if they have rights, need to have some mysterious substantial existence over and above the existence of those individuals that compose them. We shall not repeat here arguments that parallel those given earlier about such matters. The fact remains that thinking in terms of groups is essential to our social understanding, and it is not easily or always reducible to thinking only in terms of the individuals that the group comprises.[20] Scruton agrees: "human individuals derive their personality in part from corporations".[21]

Groups, then, may have rights, legal or moral, even if that is no more than a metaphysically superficial claim; but can they have "human rights"? This question may seem more of a test for the idea of group rights. A typically supposed necessary condition for human rights is that they be held in virtue of being human. The question of whether there is a single or universal feature of being human is not of present relevance. Rather, can some *human* personality be ascribed to, or held by, a group? Some of the same theories of human nature that have been offered for the individual human being may also be offered

---

18. R. Scruton, "Corporate Persons", *Proceedings of the Aristotelian Society*, supp. vol. 63 (1989), 239–66, at 242.
19. J. Finnis, "Persons and Their Associations", *Proceedings of the Aristotelian Society*, supp. vol. 63 (1989), 267–74, at 274.
20. See J. O'Neill (ed.), *Modes of Individualism and Collectivism* (London: Heinemann, 1973).
21. Scruton, "Corporate Persons", 240–41.

for the group personification. As an example, just as we may suppose with Hobbes or Bentham that individual people are rational and desiring beings, so we may suppose that groups – in particular, firms – are rational and desiring beings. This view is supported by Milton Friedman's philosophy of economics.

Friedman asks us to think of a tree, with leaves, in the sunlight. Consider the density of the leaves around different parts of the tree. "I suggest", says Friedman:

> that the leaves are positioned as if each leaf deliberately sought to maximise the amount of sunlight it receives, given the position of its neighbours, as if it knew the physical laws determining the amount of sunlight that would be received in various positions and could move rapidly or instantaneously from any one position to any other desired and unoccupied position.[22]

This suggestion – Friedman stresses that it is no more than that, a mere hypothesis – does not state that leaves deliberately act in these ways, but rather, as he again stresses, act *as if* they did. The truth of this hypothesis enables us to predict how the leaves will move as the sunlight alters in intensity or direction.

The leaves do not "really" think like this, of course, but behave *as if* they did, and this gives us as much truth as we need. It is in just such a sense that we may understand groups: thus we have the "economic hypothesis that under a wide range of circumstances individual firms behave as if they were seeking rationally to maximise their expected returns ... and had full knowledge of the data needed to succeed in this attempt".[23] Crucially, it is in just such a sense that we may also understand individual people as so-called "rational economic men".[24] Thus firms act "as if" they were "rational economic men", it may be said; but then so do we act as individuals. Our understanding of others and of ourselves is in the light of such an approach, and this

22. M. Friedman, "The Methodology of Positive Economics", in *Philosophy and Economic Theory*, F. Hahn & M. Hollis (eds), 18–35 (Oxford: Oxford University Press, 1979), 30; originally published in *Essays in Positive Economics*, M. Friedman (Chicago, IL: University of Chicago Press, 1953).

23. Friedman, "The Methodology of Positive Economics", 32. For a detailed discussion of Friedman's views, and an excellent introduction to the philosophy of economic theory, see M. Blaug, *The Methodology of Economics* (Cambridge: Cambridge University Press, 1980).

24. See J. L. Gorman, *Understanding History: An Introduction to Analytical Philosophy of History* (Ottawa: University of Ottawa Press, 1992), Ch. 5.

understanding is no more and no less legitimate for groups than for some other entities. Individuals, firms, animals, the leaves on a tree – all may be "personified" in the same way, the only constraint being truth in predictable behaviour. What is "really" going on, if that is something different – assuming that any metaphysical sense can be made of that – is factually irrelevant. That, at least, is the way to understand the status of the theory of human nature exemplified here.

It should be noted that, while some of the theories of human nature that have been offered for the individual human being may be plausible for group personification in such a way, not all are clearly so. Thus a theory that sought to ground human rights in a universal capacity for physical suffering would not easily be applicable to personified groups, just because we think that firms cannot "really" suffer pain or even behave "as if" they did. (Animals, by contrast, can have human rights on this basis.) For a moment, the idea "pain" seems to reach beyond the mask or personification to the imagined hidden metaphysical reality beneath; and yet "pain" is an ordinary English word operating according to publicly available rules of language. Is it just a contingent feature of our language that we do not ascribe pain to corporations? Yet we can ascribe death to them. The nature of personhood remains an area fraught with philosophical difficulty.

It is plain that moving to "the point of view of the beneficiary" should not too quickly be taken to suggest that an analysis of rights should be centred on an independent individual self, and the assumption that moral understanding can or should be grounded in an independent individual self has been denied by many writers. Nevertheless some writers wishing to express a distinctively female moral experience have taken the view that, just because rights are grounded in an independent individual self, they are for that reason peripheral to a full moral understanding.

Consider Carol Gilligan's argument.[25] Beginning her book *In a Different Voice* with a summary of Nancy Chodorow's response to Sigmund Freud's understanding of female psychology, Gilligan observes that, given that children of both sexes are mainly brought up by women (at least in the very early years of life, which psychologically

---

25. C. Gilligan, *In a Different Voice: Psychological Theory and Women's Development* (Cambridge, MA: Harvard University Press, 1982). "It is my contention that Gilligan's work is both an indication of, and a major contributor to, a sea change that is under way in late twentieth-century intellectual thought", S. J. Hekman, *Moral Voices, Moral Selves* (Cambridge: Polity Press, 1995), 2.

matter most in this context), then, in order that a boy may develop his masculine gender identity, it is necessary that he sees himself as an individuated self separate from his mother. Such an individuated sense of self is a characteristic feature of the resulting male adult. For girls and women, by contrast, feminine gender identity does not require separation or personal individuation:

> girls, in identifying themselves as female, experience themselves as like their mothers, thus fusing the experience of attachment with the process of identity formation. ... Thus males tend to have difficulty with relationships, while females tend to have problems with individuation.[26]

Drawing on a number of other studies of the development of women, Gilligan suggests that women come to have a different moral understanding from men as a consequence of this contrast.

This particular theory of a cause of male–female differences need not be central to understanding Gilligan's position on morality. That children of both sexes are mainly brought up by women would appear to be a social (including economic) contingency, and there is no philosophical difficulty in imagining, with Plato, children being brought up in common rather than in narrowly nuclear circumstances, or in imagining their being brought up primarily by males. Indeed, however implausibly unstereotypical it may be, we may imagine a world in which it is females who tend to have difficulty with relationships and males who tend to have problems with self-individuation. However, we do not need either to form a view about the nature or causes of male–female social roles or attitudes or to speculate on alternatives to recognize Gilligan's hint here at a crucial distinction between a morality that is based on "relationships" and a morality that is based on "individuation". How far any such distinction may map on any male–female contrasts is not of direct relevance to a full understanding of rights.

Rights are understood by Gilligan as being on one side of the contrasting moral positions that she presents. For females, or at least for those on one side of her contrast, "the moral problem arises from conflicting responsibilities rather than from competing rights".[27] Male and female children both recognize the need to resolve conflict through agreement, "but see it as mediated in different ways – he

---

26. Gilligan, *In a Different Voice*, 7–8.
27. *Ibid.*, 19.

impersonally through systems of logic and law, she personally through communication in relationship",[28] yielding an "ethic of care" rather than a "logic of justice".

> Separation is justified by an ethics of rights while attachment is supported by an ethic of care. The morality of rights is predicated on equality and centered on the understanding of fairness, while the ethic of responsibility relies on the concept of equity, the recognition of differences in need. While the ethic of rights is a manifestation of equal respect, balancing the claims of other and self, the ethic of responsibility rests on an understanding that gives rise to compassion and care.[29]

Speaking of some of her research subjects:

> Thus in all of the women's descriptions, identity is defined in a context of relationship and judged by a standard of responsibility and care. ... {the subject Claire speaks:} "By yourself, there is little sense to things. It is like the sound of one hand clapping, the sound of one man or one woman, there is something lacking. It is the collective that is important to me."[30]

These two views of morality – rights versus care – may be complementary in outcome,[31] but at the level of practical reasoning they are very different: when asked how to choose between responsibility to oneself and responsibility to others in a case of conflict, a boy in Gilligan's study seeks rules to limit his own actions in the light of their effect upon others, whereas a girl seeks to extend her actions with positive acts of care. "She, assuming connection, begins to explore the parameters of separation, while he, assuming separation, begins to explore the parameters of connection."[32]

Claiming rights risks being *selfish*, which may lead to the abandonment of responsibility, of care.[33] Women may then support rights only at extremes, for example where they see their care roles as tantamount to slavery, as did early proponents of women's rights such

---

28. *Ibid.*, 29.
29. *Ibid.*, 164–5.
30. *Ibid.*, 160.
31. *Ibid.*, 30, 33.
32. *Ibid.*, 35–8.
33. *Ibid.*, 130.
34. *Ibid.*, 129.

as Mary Wollstonecraft.[34] Novels like George Eliot's *The Mill on the Floss* and Margaret Drabble's *The Waterfall*:

> demonstrate the continuing power for women of the judgment of selfishness and the morality of self-abnegation that it implies. ... the ethic of self-sacrifice is directly in conflict with the concept of rights that has, in this past century, supported women's claim to a fair share of social justice.[35]

The morality of responsibility, unlike the morality of rights, "blur[s] the distinction between self and other through the representation of their interdependence".[36] A different argument against rights as human rights is provided by Georgia Warnke: "efforts to secure substantive opportunities for women by emphasizing their innate or constructed needs [i.e. their biological or social difference] are undermined by demonstrations of their human sameness [i.e. with men]".[37]

Thus rights, so understood as contrasting with the morality of responsibility, are essentially connected to the individual independent self and therefore part of an essentially male-based morality. Rights are selfish: "the essential notion of rights, that the interests of the self can be considered legitimate";[38]

> the attempt to set up the [moral] dilemma as a conflict of rights turned it into a contest of selfishnesses, precluding the possibility of a moral decision, since either resolution could be construed as selfish from one or the other perspective. Consequently the concern with rights was overridden by a concern with responsibility ....[39]

Responsibilities set up a chain of expectations, so that "considerations of rights, based on an assumption of independence, threaten to interrupt the chain of relationships".[40] Thus there may be neither moral nor philosophical innocence in moving with Suárez and Grotius to understanding rights entirely from the point of view of the individual benefiting self. If rights are understood entirely in Gilligan's way then it is clear they are indeed morally secondary, if not peripheral.

---

35. *Ibid.*, 131–2.
36. *Ibid.*, 132.
37. G. Warnke, "Feminism and Democratic Deliberation", *Philosophy and Social Criticism* 26 (2000), 61–74, esp. 61–2.
38. Gilligan, *In a Different Voice*, 149.
39. *Ibid.*, 142.
40. *Ibid.*

Yet there are several different points to be distinguished in Gilligan's conception of rights. To begin with, she unnecessarily conceives rights as being based primarily on right-holders, and unnecessarily conceives right-holders as being individual people rather than groups. We have seen that three approaches may be taken to the "ius" of Aquinas: that rights may be understood as prior to duties; that duties may be understood as prior to rights; or that rights and duties may be mutually supporting. We shall shortly explain the alternatives at greater length, but it should be clear at this stage that the right–duty pairings that Hohfeld's analysis has disclosed need not force us to the view that our understanding must be primarily in terms of the individual beneficiary, since, for example, a justice-based view of rights like that of Aquinas may be held instead. Secondly, we have seen that, even if we do adopt a rights-based approach to understanding right–duty pairings, that does not of itself commit us to a narrow conception of the right-holder, since the right-holder need not be an individual at all. A right-holder or beneficiary can be a group, including perhaps women as a group. If women have a distinctive moral experience then they certainly have a right that this experience be accommodated in a theory of rights.

An important additional point is that Gilligan unnecessarily conceives "individuals" as beings defined by separation from others rather than by association with others, as if these two approaches conflicted.[41] We are to understand, with Gilligan, that in some way the self–other distinction does not need to be made as girls form their identity, but there is clearly confusion here about the meaning of "individual". There is no necessary theoretical conflict between individuality and association: on the contrary, it is clear that association with others, and the "ethics of care" that Gilligan relates to the female experience in this context, *presupposes* a sense of individual self, albeit a caring one. One cannot care *for others*, let alone contrast that with a selfish alternative, without presupposing a self–other distinction. It may well be that the individual duty-ower as understood within the theory of rights should be an individual with a sense of responsibility and care, just because the moral rights of others are best respected by individuals with such a sense.

Girls are imagined by Gilligan to fuse the experience of attachment to their mothers with the process of identity formation, but "attachment" here is unnecessarily ambiguous. The infant child, male or

---

41. What it is to be an "individual" is an important part of the theory of justice. See Kymlicka, *Contemporary Political Philosophy*, 199, 207–8.

female, is, in the ideal and hopefully widely typical case, both a receiver of love and a giver of it, and it is natural to read into this mutual love some unselfishness on both sides. Yet being selfish and being a self are not the same thing – in any event, girl-infants are not noticeably unselfish – and we have argued that a self–other distinction is required in this context. Gilligan unnecessarily conceives right-holders essentially to be individuals who have selfish desires, whereas it is plain that an individual may be altruistic and yet remain an individual: "it is the collective that is important to me".[42] Not all desires are selfish desires. Nevertheless, however mutual the *love* in parent–child attachment may be, the infant child – male or female – is a *receiver* of care and not a *giver* of it, and, as a *beneficiary* of the mother's care, the infant is analogous to a right-holder rather than a duty-ower. There is nothing intrinsically selfish about being a bene-ficiary. It is highly implausible to deny to the innocent infant beneficiary "the essential notion of rights, that the interests of the self can be considered legitimate".[43]

Yet there remains an important, although very partial, truth in what Gilligan is claiming. Just because the rights of one person are correlated with the duties of another, as Hohfeld shows, it may often seem appropriate to understand rights as held "against" others. To think of *oneself* as holding, and most certainly to think of oneself as choosing to exercise, a right may then be to think "against" those others, and this may conflict with an "ethic of care" for those others. It is always a moral question whether or not a right – either a legal or a moral right – *ought* to be exercised, and it is plain that rights can often be exercised, or for that matter waived, on selfish grounds. Equivalently, duties can be grudgingly undertaken. Just because it can be a moral question whether even a moral right ought to be exercised – there may be a conflict of moral rights, after all – the concept of rights cannot be solely fundamental in the moral domain. It is clear that the selfish exercise of a right may conflict with an ethic of care. But it is also clear that the selfish exercise of a right may conflict with a *duty* of care, and so with the right of another.

That to characterize rights as selfish is a very partial approach is shown in the following question: why think of *oneself* as holding or exercising a right? The very same conceptual apparatus can be properly used by a caring person in thinking instead of the *rights of*

---

42. Gilligan, *In a Different Voice*, 160.
43. *Ibid.*, 149.

others. We do a disservice to Suárez, Grotius and other contributors to our history of understanding rights if we interpret their positions in an unnecessarily selfish way. As Finnis noted, these thinkers transformed *"jus"* by "relating it exclusively to the beneficiary" of the just relationship,[44] but there is no reason here selfishly to imagine ourselves in that favoured position of beneficiary. By all means, let us imagine those for whom we care in that favoured position. As Aquinas said, "the right in a work of justice, besides its relation to the agent, is set up by its relation to others".[45] Seeing what is right entirely from the point of view of the beneficiaries of our actions in no way conflicts with an "ethic of care".

If the beneficiaries of our caring actions have rights to our care, then our caring will be a duty, given the correlation between them. It is said that many medical practitioners across the world dislike the move in recent years from the ethos of care that they once practised to the new climate of patients' rights. It is clear that caring may be a duty or it may not be, but it should not be assumed that caring *must* be a *supererogatory* moral quality that goes beyond a moral or legal duty. There is, in the typical parenting, medical or nursing contexts that are paradigmatic of caring relationships, a *duty* of care, both legal and moral. That is as it should be, and individual – although not necessarily selfish – rights exist in virtue of those duties. Gilligan seems incorrectly to be assuming that rights are essentially exercisable or waivable on selfish grounds; she is, in effect, presupposing the "will" theory of rights, and assuming that the choices in question must be exercised selfishly. We do not need to attribute such motives to those for whom we care.

Whether one sex is more or less likely than the other to adopt a selfish or caring attitude is not a matter that need be further addressed here. How far the theories of human nature that may be used in these contexts are currently too male-based remains an issue that is rightly a matter for further thought, but it is clear that understanding rights in terms of right-holders or beneficiaries does not in itself commit us to individualistic understanding, nor to some necessarily male-based individualistic understanding, nor to some conception of the individual as essentially selfish.

We saw earlier in this chapter that Finnis's summary of "ius" involved two different points: first, to note the change, from

---

44. Finnis, *Natural Law and Natural Rights*, 207.
45. Aquinas, *Summa Theologica* II-II, q. 57, "Whether right is the object of justice; I answer that . . ."

Aquinas's position of seeing "ius" as referring to a just state of affairs, to Suárez's position of seeing "ius" exclusively from the point of view of the beneficiary; secondly, to interpret the move to the point of view of the beneficiary as being in some way a move towards what Finnis called the "choice" theory of rights. We have noted the main difficulties associated with some individualist implications of the expression "the point of view of the beneficiary", and our next step is to see how this last may connect to the "choice", hereafter called in common with much current practice the "will", theory.

Our central concern at this stage of the rights-based approach is with what counts as a person – individual or group, male or female – being a "beneficiary", which means a person who is in receipt of something good for them. Recall Plato's position: that goodness is an abstract reality apprehended by the rational intellect. Only those who have self-mastery or rational self-control can know goodness. Reason expresses true worth, and we saw a variation on this position produced by Kant: a position in which the ultimate good is a "good will". Respect for this rational will in others – treating them as "ends in themselves" – is doing what is good for them. What is good for a person is then to be determined by objective reason, and the satisfaction of desire (let alone selfish desire) has no essential role in the assessment of what is good for a person. By contrast, recall the position in Plato's *Republic* expressed by Thrasymachus and Glaucon: that justice consists in the interests of the strong. It is their desires, not reason, that then determine what is good for people.

On a rights-based approach, with rights understood to express the benefit attaching to a particular person *vis-à-vis* the wider world – a situation that every individual person might be in, of course – the history of moral thought discloses two broad foundations for further understanding: rights as based on the *objective* good for a person, and rights as based on a person's *desires* or *choices*. It is these two broad approaches that, to an extent we will now examine, may be thought to lie behind the more specific and contrasting approaches of, respectively, the "interest" theory of rights and the "will" theory of rights.

Matthew H. Kramer presents these two specific approaches in a particularly clear way in the light of his own defence of a version of the interest theory.[46] The interest theory of rights holds that a right

---

46. Kramer, "Rights Without Trimmings".

essentially protects the right-holder's well-being or interests, and Kramer summarizes this theory in terms of two theses:

(1) Necessary but insufficient for the actual holding of a right by X is that the right, when actual, protects one or more of X's interests.

(2) The mere fact that X is competent and authorized to demand or waive the enforcement of a right will be neither sufficient nor necessary for X's holding of that right".[47]

Both of these theses, on Kramer's interpretation, are rejected by holders of the "will" theory, who mostly hold that a right's protecting an interest is neither necessary nor sufficient for its being a right, while:

X's competence and authorization to demand/waive the enforcement of a right are separately necessary and jointly sufficient for X's holding of that right. For the Will Theory, the essence of a right consists in opportunities for the right-holder to make normatively significant choices relating to the behaviour of someone else.[48]

Recognizing that there are these two approaches in this context, it is clear that Finnis is incorrect in thinking that there is an essential connection between understanding "right" purely from the point of view of the beneficiary and understanding "right" as a negative freedom or a choice.[49] By contrast with the latter, it is open to us to adopt a Platonic position and use an objective measure to determine what is good for a person. Such an approach would permit an "interest" theory of rights to be used. There is no commitment to the "will" theory of rights merely because a move is made to the point of view of the beneficiary. Nor is there any commitment here to the "interest" theory, of course. From Suárez we have the idea of "right" as an individual's "moral power"; from Grotius we have the idea of "right" as an individual's "moral quality". Finnis's own description, more neutrally, characterizes both as "from the point of view of the

---

47. M. H. Kramer, "Getting Rights Right", in *Rights, Wrongs and Responsibilities*, M. H. Kramer (ed.), 28–95 (Basingstoke: Palgrave, 2001), 28.

48. *Ibid.* As Hart puts it, "to have a right entails having a moral justification for limiting the freedom for another person" ("Are There Any Natural Rights?", 60).

49. See Scanlon, "Rights, Goals, and Fairness", 137: "Rights themselves need to be justified somehow, and how other than by appeal to the human interests their recognition promotes and protects?"

beneficiary". Taking rights as prior in any of these ways is not to be committed to the view that rights are to be understood as freedoms or choices nor to the view that the interest theory of rights is correct.

Choosing between the "interest" theory and the "will" theory of rights depends to a large extent on the theoretical views we adopt in the evaluation of rights–duties situations. An individual's interests may be objectively determined independently of the individual's perceptions of them, but may also be determined by individual choice: it is a typically utilitarian approach to hold that I am myself the best judge of my own interests. Rights that I may hold in virtue of these interests, whether the interests are objectively or subjectively determined, may in principle be waivable, but Kramer is right to hold that waivability is neither necessary nor sufficient for interest-based rights to exist. It is independent considerations – typically moral or political or legal – that justify the nature and content of the interests involved and that determine the merits of waivability.

Nevertheless, it seems clear that, in principle, background moral or political or legal considerations may stress the value of waivability more highly than the content of any other interest. Our value system may hold that a person's interest in being able to choose is the most important interest they have. It may then come to be true that the will theorist's view that a person's competence and entitlement to waive or insist upon a particular right's enforcement are in fact separately necessary and jointly sufficient for the holding of that right. This would be a contingent matter for a particular right, however, and not for rights in general, since it would be a contingency that varied with our changing views about the importance of autonomy or self-determination, notions that affect both individuals and groups.

It seems reasonable to conclude that the interest theory, given that it admits a subjective interpretation of "interest" that can permit a primary or overriding value to be given to "choice", may be *neutral* between these fundamentally different evaluative considerations, whereas the "will" theory, by contrast, is not plausible as a *general* theory of rights. For those, in particular, with an "ethic of care", moral relationships with others may well be more naturally understood in terms of those others' "rights" if rights are understood in terms of others' interests rather than their capacity for choice, with the opportunity the latter may give for selfishness. As Kramer rightly says of the interest theory, "its capaciousness enables its proponents to ascribe legal rights to sundry people and animals whose status as potential right-holders cannot be acknowledged by the Will

Theory".[50] The interest theory permits a wider range of criteria than does the will theory for determining what rights people may hold.

Neither will theory nor interest theory in itself tells us what rights we have, or ought to have; the answers to these questions depend on background considerations. These may be either legal or moral: the rules or principles of a particular jurisdiction may tell you what legal rights you have, if any, while more general moral theories – which may include political philosophies or theories of justice – may tell you what moral rights you have, if any. Such moral rights might be based on the promise of another person, correlated for example with what Rawls calls an "obligation";[51] or they might be – contingently – universally held, as natural or human rights are understood to be.

---

50. Kramer, "Getting Rights Right", 90.
51. See Ch. 13.

CHAPTER 13

Duty and justice

A full understanding of rights requires a grasp of the points of view of all involved in a right–duty situation, and so requires a grasp of rights-based, duty-based and justice-based approaches. Having outlined a rights-based approach to a situation in which those involved act "aright" (as Finnis puts it), let us next consider what a duty-based conception in this context can look like. Finnis described the move from Aquinas's conception of right as based on justice to Suárez's conception of right as related exclusively to the beneficiary, but he did not associate with this a parallel move that might be made in which Aquinas's position might be transformed by interpreting a just situation entirely from the point of view of the ower of the duty rather than from the point of view of the beneficiary.

As we saw in the earlier presentation of John Locke's position, Locke (unlike Hobbes) writes of "natural laws", which impose naturally enforceable duties in the required sense, and a duty-based approach is also central to Kant's moral philosophy. In the light of this, that which is "just" would appear to be a person-neutral term describing a good or fair situation, "right" would appear to be a term describing that situation entirely from the point of view of one of the protagonists in so far as that person is a beneficiary, with "duty" a term describing that situation entirely from the point of view of the other in so far as that person faces some demand or cost correlated with the right of the other. On the duty-based approach, as *mutatis mutandis* with the rights-based approach, adopting the point of view of the duty-holder is not merely a change of perspective but involves the claim that duties take priority in our moral understanding here.

169

Kant is the obvious main candidate for a position illustrating a duty-based approach. To begin with, duty is explained by Kant in clear assertions: "Nothing", he says:

> can possibly be conceived in the world, or even out of it, which can be called good without qualification, except a Good Will. ... A good will is good not because of what it performs or effects, not by its aptness for the attainment of some proposed end, but simply by virtue of the volition, that is, it is good in itself;[1]

> we will take the notion of duty, which includes that of a good will;[2]

> now an action done from duty must wholly exclude the influence of inclination;[3]

> duty is the necessity of acting from respect for the law.[4]

When we read Descartes's *Meditations*, with its approach typified by the suggestion "let us suppose, then, that we are dreaming",[5] we are invited to identify with the author in his examination of issues arising within what turns out to be the private space of the first-person singular point of view. The epistemological agenda for the next 300 years was set by this move, and even the empiricist Hume requires us to identify with him in his presentation of the first-person singular point of view of the nature of the mind; thus introspection of mental experience shows that simple ideas correspond to simple impressions, and "everyone may satisfy himself in this point by running over as many as he pleases".[6] Whether we are rationalist or empiricist in our philosophical approach, the Cartesian agenda requires us to begin with our individual mind and to construct the world, or construct an understanding of the world, on the basis of it.[7]

Kant's approach is, in such very general terms, in part very similar. He is concerned with the "universal laws of thought in general",[8] and

---

1. Kant, *Fundamental Principles*, 10–11.
2. *Ibid.*, 15.
3. *Ibid.*, 20.
4. *Ibid.*, 19.
5. R. Descartes, *Meditations on the First Philosophy* [1641] (London: Dent, 1965), 81.
6. Hume, *A Treatise of Human Nature*, 3–4.
7. "I have to think of myself as the world soul in humble disguise. In mitigation I can plead only that the same thought is available to any of you"; Nagel, *The View From Nowhere*, 61.
8. Kant, *Fundamental Principles*, 1.

these laws are not just illustrated by attending to the first-person singular point of view but are entirely constituted by the appropriate characteristics of that point of view. Thus Kant's "duty-based" approach to morality is "inward looking" in this way, and initially seeks an understanding entirely in terms of respect for the categorical imperative, that is, entirely in terms of the rational will of the agent. Following this, we might then imagine Aquinas's just situation, which is a public space in which things occur "aright", as characterizable in Kantian terms, not, as in Suárez, by moving to the point of view of the beneficiary, but rather by moving to the first-person singular point of view of the duty-ower.

However, in Chapter 6 we distinguished what it was to be a "moral agent" from what it was to be a "moral object". We noted, after our presentation of Plato, Hobbes, Locke and Hume, that a theory of human nature can tell us how we can know what is good and how we can be motivated to do what is good. In addition, we concluded, with our then presentation of Kant, a theory of human nature can tell us what it is that is valuable about other people, and on Kant's approach it is this that grounds the rights that we may think of as universal "human rights". It is thus an essential feature of Kant's moral philosophy that it offers a characterization of so-called "moral objects" and so requires you to address your attention to other entities and to what is valuable about them.

By presupposing, through the concept of universalizability, the contingent existence of other people (and so inconsistently offending against his own required purification from taint by experience), Kant's approach is "outward" looking as well as "inward" looking, and measures merit in terms of what is valuable about the moral object or beneficiary. We may recall the similar position of Grotius, mentioned above, for whom an important meaning of "right" was "a moral quality of the person".[9] Rights, so understood, may then be seen as expressing the moral quality of the moral object. We should also note that the moral quality of moral objects may – at least contingently, it has now been argued – lie in their capacity for choice, so that the will theory of rights may be justifiably held.

Duty, in Kant, cannot then be the whole story. It may be recalled that his position was expressed on the basis of two different foundations that did not fit completely consistently with each other.

---

9. Finnis, *Natural Law and Natural Rights*, 207, referring to Grotius, *De Jure Belli ac Pacis*, I, I, iii.

While one fundamental feature of Kant's moral philosophy is that nothing is perfectly good except a good will, a second fundamental feature of Kant's philosophy is that there is more than one good will, and respect for reason is not only respect for it in the nature of one's own principles of volition but respect for it in other people also, so that we must treat other people as ends in themselves. Yet Kant's position at this point is not – as perhaps, for consistency, it ought to be – that we should directly respect reason in others. To respect others is to respect them in particular as legislating members in the "Kingdom of Ends", and Kant thinks that it is the freedom and autonomy of the other person that we are to value here. Kant's move here is shared by some other writers on human rights: thus James Griffin, for example, wishes to ground human rights in a theory of the conditions for human agency.[10] Other people, we are to conclude, should be treated as ends in themselves even if they are not perfectly rational or perfectly good, for they may nevertheless have the freedom and autonomy and capacity for choice that Kant and others primarily wish us to value.[11] Whether this is consistent with Kant's other view that a rational "Good Will" is the only unconditional good is a question that can be put to one side. In any event, if we place this feature of Kant's position first, then we find that his moral philosophy places rights as prior to duties, rather than duties as prior to rights. Even Kant then has difficulty presenting a duty-based approach as prior in our moral understanding. Only, perhaps, if we understand morality and law entirely in terms of what can be *enforced* – which on one interpretation Locke does, as explained in Chapter 4: "the law of Nature would, as all other laws that concern men in this world, be in vain if there were nobody that in the state of Nature had a power to execute that law"[12] – are we able to make sense of our concerns in terms of duty as the prior concept in our understanding.

We turn next to the justice-based approach. Following Hohfeld, we understand "right" and "duty" as logically related to each other. Applying "right" and "duty" in terms of Finnis's presentation of Aquinas, our understanding is next such that neither "right" nor "duty" is prior to the other. Both terms are equally derivative from

10. Griffin, "Human Rights – The Very Idea".
11. It is a related difficulty that Rawls sees, following Sidgwick, in autonomy permitting the realization of the true self of the scoundrel; Rawls, *A Theory of Justice*, pp. 251, 254–5.
12. Locke, *Second Treatise*, §7. Should we understand law as having no existence or meaning if it cannot be enforced?

our prior understanding of what a just situation consists in. In other words, at this point we adopt not the point of view of the beneficiary or the point of view of the duty-ower, but a point of view that embraces the just situation involving both. Again, this is not merely an empty change of perspective, but a move that counts the justice of the situation as prior or foundational in our moral understanding. Given this, if we wish for a greater understanding of "rights", what we need is a greater understanding of what a just situation consists in: a greater understanding of what justice requires. On this Thomistic approach the theory of rights is then subordinate to the theory of justice.

The view that justice is prior to rights is an essential feature of Rawls's important position in *A Theory of Justice*. Rawls does, however, write in a way that suggests that it is duties rather than rights or justice that are prior, and as we move from a failed Kantian attempt to make duties fundamental towards understanding justice as fundamental we need to clarify this. Thus Rawls says, "there are many natural duties, positive and negative";[13] "a fundamental natural duty is the duty of justice";[14] and "if the basic structure of society is just ... everyone has a natural duty to do his part in the existing scheme. Each is bound to these institutions independent of his voluntary acts."[15] Rawls gives as examples of natural duties: the duty to help others when they are in need, provided excessive loss to oneself is not involved; the duty not to harm another; and the duty not to be cruel.[16] Natural duties hold between people "irrespective of their institutional relationships; they obtain between all as equal moral persons".[17] In similar vein, Locke says:

> The state of Nature has a law of Nature to govern it, which obliges every one, and reason, which is that law, teaches all mankind who will but consult it, that being all equal and independent, no one ought to harm another in his life, health, liberty or possessions.[18]

Locke here thus affirms that natural duties exist even when there is no society or organized state. The similarity of expression between Locke's and Rawls's positions here is striking, and indeed Rawls states

---

13. Rawls, *A Theory of Justice*, 114.
14. *Ibid.*, 115.
15. *Ibid.*
16. *Ibid.*, 114.
17. *Ibid.*, 115.
18. Locke, *Second Treatise*, §4.

that he "carries to a higher level of abstraction the familiar theory of the social contract ... in Locke, Rousseau and Kant".[19]

The similarity is nevertheless more apparent than real. For Locke, natural duties are expressed by natural laws that exist – they are binding on us and enforceable against us – independently of our voluntary acts, and so exist independently of the social contract into which we enter in order to escape the state of nature. For Rawls, by contrast, the expression "independent of his voluntary acts" has a seriously limited meaning, and this is apparent from the following heavily condensed claim that Rawls makes: "even though the principles of natural duty are derived from a contractarian point of view, they do not presuppose an act of consent ... in order to apply".[20]

Rawls makes an important distinction between natural duties and (non-natural) obligations.[21] Rawls's examples of "obligations" include those entered into by people accepting public office or getting married. "Obligations" are understood by him to arise as a result of voluntary acts such as promises. "The content of obligations is always defined by an institution or practice the rules of which specify what it is that one is required to do",[22] and the obligations or duties here may thus be thought of as attaching to an office or position that is voluntarily entered into. One of the things that a theory of justice has to do is specify the principles governing such institutions, offices or practices so that the relevant obligations can be binding when voluntarily assumed. Voluntary acts, for Rawls, do not give rise to obligations where unjust institutions are involved.[23] Prior to and necessary for the creation of obligations is the existence of just – or, at least, nearly just – institutions.[24] While necessary, such just institutions are not sufficient to create an obligation: the additional step required for sufficiency is the appropriate voluntary act.

Rawls's understanding of "natural duties", by contrast, is that these are not "obligations" as defined above. They are not, within society, voluntarily assumed when entering an institution, assuming an office

19. Rawls, *A Theory of Justice*, 11.
20. *Ibid.*, 115.
21. *Ibid.*, 111ff.
22. *Ibid.*, 113.
23. *Ibid.*, 112. See also Nozick, *Anarchy, State and Utopia*, 88ff and Ch. 6, n. 4.
24. One difficulty here is that issues of justice, rights and duties can also arise in unjust situations. Rawls makes clear that he is primarily arguing in terms of what he calls "strict compliance theory", a theory that examines "the principles of justice that would regulate a well-ordered society" (*A Theory of Justice*, 8). The principles of justice for an unjust society might then be different.

or engaging in a practice; "they do not presuppose an act of consent ... in order to apply".[25] Natural duties are prior to our voluntary acts in the same way as just institutions are prior to our voluntary acts. They apply to "persons generally", and it is this that "suggests the propriety of the adjective 'natural'".[26] Hart made a similar point for rights, in his claim that there is "at least one natural right, the equal right of all men to be free .... This right is not created or conferred by men's voluntary action; other moral rights are."[27] So far unqualified, Rawls's understanding of "natural duties" could still be consistent with Locke's position. However, Rawls's theory of justice is justly famous for the mode of reasoning that he offers in support of his characterization of just institutions.

In Chapter 11, I presented Rawls's notion of "justice as fairness"[28] and his general approach to moral justification expressed in the idea of "reflective equilibrium". We have seen that, for Rawls, the principles of justice are those principles that we would accept if we were fairly placed. What Rawls calls "the original position" is essentially characterized by agreement between those within it, and the agreement has the merit it does just in so far as those within it are fairly placed. It is, essentially, a voluntary agreement in just the same way as Locke's social contract is voluntary; Rawls stresses the merits of the "contract" terminology,[29] and its voluntary nature is also stressed.

> I have emphasized that this original position is purely hypothetical. It is natural to ask why, if this agreement is never actually entered into, we should take any interest ... The answer is that the conditions embodied in the description of the original position are ones that we do in fact accept. Or if we do not, then perhaps we can be persuaded to do so by philosophical reflection.[30]

It should be observed that the "voluntary" acceptance here characterized as occurring in the hypothetical original position has to have a quite different status from the voluntary act of consent that, if actually undertaken within a (nearly) just society, yields an obligation.

---

25. Rawls, *A Theory of Justice*, 115.
26. *Ibid.*
27. Hart, "Are There Any Natural Rights?", 53–4.
28. Rawls, *A Theory of Justice*, esp. Ch. 1.
29. *Ibid.*, 16.
30. *Ibid.*, 21.

Importantly, the former acceptance is claimed as universal, which is what in Rawls's view warrants the description of the duties resulting from it as "natural" duties. Parallel reasoning for universality by Hart involves the claim that a natural right requires, among other things, that it be held by "all men ... if they are capable of choice: they have it qua men".[31]

It is clear that Rawls's position differs from Locke's position in the crucial respect that, for Rawls, "natural duties" are part of the *outcome* of the agreement in the original position, whereas for Locke they are *presupposed* in the social contract situation. As Rawls says, "the principles of natural duty ... are those that would be acknowledged in the original position. These principles are understood as the outcome of a hypothetical agreement."[32] "It suffices to show that the parties in the original position would agree to principles defining the natural duties which as formulated hold unconditionally",[33] that is, independently of "voluntary acts". The parties in the original position are, of course, "fairly placed". The conditions of fairness include various assumptions, such as a view about what information it would be fair for people to have (the so-called "veil of ignorance"[34]), "a principle of equal liberty"[35] and other formal weaker constraints.[36] There are no presupposed duties, however, not even a natural duty to support just institutions.[37]

The principles of justice are essentially a way of stating or defining what our basic rights and duties are, and "the principles of right, and so of justice" frame and restrict what can be a reasonable conception of an individual person's good, that is, they define which desires are proper.[38] "It is assumed that the members of society are rational persons able to adjust their conceptions of good to their situation."[39]

---

31. Hart, "Are There Any Natural Rights?", 53.
32. Rawls, *A Theory of Justice*, 28, 115.
33. *Ibid.*, 116.
34. *Ibid.*, 136–42.
35. *Ibid.*, 31.
36. *Ibid.*, 130–36.
37. *Ibid.*, 334. We may note a contrast between Kant and Rawls: "the principles of justice are not derived from the notion of respect for persons, from a recognition of their inherent worth or dignity" (*ibid.*, 585). Such notions are "not suitable" (*ibid.*, 586).
38. *Ibid.*, 31; 4, 10. The close link here is evident also in the expression: "an inviolability founded on justice or, as some say, on natural right" (*ibid.*, 28).
39. *Ibid.*, 94. The assumed separation here between an "individual" and his or her situation is problematic. See Kymlicka, *Contemporary Political Philosophy*, 199, 202, 207–8.

One of Nozick's very influential arguments in his *Anarchy, State and Utopia* was as follows: "If D_1 was a just distribution, and people voluntarily moved from it to D_2 ..., isn't D_2 also just?"[40] Nozick means that D_2 is thereby just *no matter what it is*, so long as it is justly derived from a just distribution, and so a "patterned" theory of social justice like Rawls's, which specifies principles saying what a just distribution has to look like, cannot be right. Nozick's position presupposes that the voluntary transfers involved in moving from D_1 to D_2 are exercises of a fundamental right to liberty, which, to use Dworkin's word, "trumps" justice. Using Rawls's point against this, some voluntary choices cannot be just if a distributively unjust pattern results; which rights are held in the process and how far they may constrain voluntary transfers are determined by the principles of justice. If all concerned understand that, rational persons may adjust their choices accordingly. "Everyone is assured an equal liberty to pursue whatever plan of life he pleases as long as it does not violate what justice demands."[41] For Rawls, justice is prior to rights; not so for Nozick.

We therefore see in Rawls's approach a view similar to that of Aquinas, that rights and duties are founded in justice. Arguments about what rights and duties we have, or alternatively ought to have, are then grounded in arguments about what justice requires. The nature and demands of justice have been much discussed in recent decades, and, having presented the foundation of that discussion in Rawls's position, I leave further explanation of theories of justice to other writings on that subject.[42]

---

40. Nozick, *Anarchy, State and Utopia*, 161.
41. Rawls, *A Theory of Justice*, 94.
42. An excellent introduction is T. Campbell, *Justice*, 2nd edn (Basingstoke: Macmillan, 2001).

Conclusion

In Chapter 1 I outlined a wide range of uses of the concept of rights in modern Western culture. We noted the concept's growing importance as a way of organizing our moral and legal understanding, and noted that the concept of human rights in particular is authoritative for us, providing an ultimate standard of justification in both morality and law. Noting too the 1948 Universal Declaration of Human Rights, I presented human rights as if they set the overriding moral benchmark. We saw that a range of questions might be asked: how can human rights be justified as authoritative? How can our individual and social choices be "constrained" by rights, as if they were independent of us? How can we be motivated by such moral considerations? How are rights located in the rest of our morality and law? What rights do we have?

Contrasting philosophical concerns with the concerns that other disciplines might have about rights, we isolated two interrelated major issues: justification and understanding. We have taken as central to the above range of problems the problem of how to justify and understand the supposed independent and universal authority of human rights. We have characterized the foundations of the apparent authority that human rights have for us, and have shown the ways in which different philosophers use such foundations to answer the range of questions posed above.

We began with Plato's theory, which presented us with an account of the independence and universality of a fundamental moral concept such as "rights" purports to be. Perhaps the most important feature of Plato's philosophy in this context was the method of *development* of his answer to the question "What is justice?" Socrates sought an answer through dialogue with opponents whose own philosophical presuppositions were presented and criticized, and his conclusion was that the ethical forms a single internally consistent idea, an idea that could be separately accessed by members of a particular class of people. Particularly distinctive of Plato's characterization of Socratic dialogue was the view that there are *mutually shared standards of reasoning* involved. In addition to involving shared standards of consistency, reason provided knowledge of the ethical, which was conceived as an *independent* and *unchanging* reality. We thus isolated through Plato's arguments three features of such moral reality: that it is *independent* of us, that it is *eternal* or unchanging, and that it is *consistent*. Plato also helped us to locate the ways in which the fundamental disciplines of philosophy – ethics, logic, metaphysics and epistemology – relate to each other in understanding our moral concerns about rights.

We saw next that Hobbes expressed views about human nature, society and the state that were radically different from and opposed to those of Socrates. An explicit reference to rights contrasted with Plato's amorphous reference to justice. Hobbes affirmed just one theory of human nature rather than Plato's three, and for him we are all equal in our fundamental characteristics. Hobbes's epistemology and metaphysics stressed in a way quite opposed to Plato the view that reality is something material and experienceable rather than abstract and intellectually apprehended. Even reason seemed comparatively weak and indeterminate, since it was merely instrumental in achieving our desires. Moreover, Hobbes stressed that different people had different views about what did or did not conform to the requirements of reason. Yet while this was so, we also saw that essential to Hobbes's theory was his presentation of reason as setting all of humanity a *common standard*. At the foundation of Hobbes's philosophical approach, just as in Plato's, we found the idea of reason as setting a mutually shared standard, an external and unchanging standard expressing demands for consistency independent of us many error-prone individuals. The details of Hobbes's own understanding of rights were explained in terms of his assumption of the independent eternal authority of reason, sharing with Plato a perception of geometry as the paradigm case of this, as "the only science that it hath pleased God hitherto to bestow on mankind".[1]

---

1. Hobbes, *Leviathan*, Ch. 4.

We saw Locke using this same understanding of reason to express with particular explicitness his different idea of natural rights. Natural rights were grounded in God-given, and so authoritative, reason as setting a mutually shared, external and unchanging moral standard for us all. Locke took such reason for granted, and gave in his *Essay* only the most cursory justification for his very exact claims about natural rights. Plato, Hobbes and Locke thus shared the view that reason provided an external authority for us, and all shared the view that the ethical and the legal had their foundation in this. Human rights, in so far as they might have any real authority for us, had to be understood on the same presuppositions concerning their independent, unchanging and consistent character.

Having presented the main philosophical features of rights theories in terms of their background in Plato, Hobbes and Locke, we examined one by one the elements of the assumptions made about the nature of reason. The first assumption to be attacked was that of the *independence* or *externality* of reason. It was Hume who cast doubt on this. How can we be motivated by external standards of reason? We cannot. Even if not motivating, how can reason give us the content of any standards independent of personal desires or experience? It cannot. If reason cannot express an externally authoritative eternal standard, then how can natural rights – or indeed any ethical standard supposedly derived from reason – exist in such a way? As Hume's follower Bentham expressed it, they cannot – the idea must be "nonsense on stilts".

But Hume's approach on this issue had in due course to face a much more sophisticated philosophical opponent than Plato, Hobbes or Locke. Kant responded to Hume in a way that made a crucial contribution to our current understanding. For Kant, Hume was partly right: reason is indeed not an external abstraction existing in some fairylike metaphysical way outside our experienced world, let alone an abstraction that has some direct external motivating force on us. Rather, reason is an essential feature of our construction as human beings, and it is also an essential feature of our construction of the experienced world. That we find reason in the "external" world is because of our own rational input into the formation of that world as we understand and know it to be. Reason is not something external to and independent of us, but intrinsic to us.

Far from it being difficult to understand how we might be motivated by reason, reason characterizes the essence of human will and so of morality. Moreover, reason not only grounds moral knowledge and moral motivation, it also expresses what is valuable about us as human beings. If we accept this rationalist approach rather than Hume's empiricism, then we can keep a notion of human rights as expressing eternal rational standards, just because of the unchanging rationality of human nature. Such rights are a way of expressing and protecting our dignity and autonomy as rational human beings. Of the three elements of Plato's moral reality – independence, eternity and consistency – we lose *independence* by following Hume, but regain a version of it in terms of *universality* by following Kant. So it is the universal and unchanging and essentially rational structures of our own understanding that are then seen as foundational to human rights.

Kant's detailed understanding of the rational structures of the human mind was importantly based on his analysis of the structures of human language, because the way we use language expresses the structures of our minds. Given this, further philosophical understanding required more extensive analysis of our concepts, for concepts are common to both language and mind. We explained the "scientific" presuppositions of twentieth-century advances in conceptual analysis and presented Hohfeld's analysis of the language of rights as an instance of this. Hohfeld's exercise in analytical jurisprudence was offered as a solution to legal problems and was seen by approving contemporaries as a branch of pure science. Hohfeld began by claiming that the notions of "right" and "duty" are ambiguous, and he analysed and clarified these terms. Hohfeld aimed to specify and if necessary to stipulate a scheme of precise concepts, all mutually supporting each other by logical implication, and in a form intended to make sense of the entire category of our practical legal concerns.

Hohfeld's approach was intended to answer legal problems, but it was difficult to see in what sense his answers could be *true*. It had earlier been argued that there was no metaphysically independent reality for them to be true of, and it seemed appropriate to see his answers as true of a particular rule-governed social practice. Using this idea we were able to distinguish the human rights that raise our ultimate philosophical problems of justification from the moral or legal rights that may be contingently claimed within particular cultures and jurisdictions, and we explained how the various kinds of rights relate to each other. However, as Hohfeld's kind of philosophical analysis developed in the twentieth century, it became apparent that a choice had to be made between two different interpretations of the status of analysis. The suggestion that Hohfeld's answers were true of a particular rule governed social practice did not work. Hohfeld's approach partly sought to *describe* an existing linguistic practice but partly sought to *prescribe* corrected use of the language of rights according to *standards of consistency*. We showed his conceptual analysis to be a confused mixture of deference to legal practice and judicial authority and to universal demands of reason. Ultimately, the stipulative recommendations of his refined distinctions of legal terminology were justified by him by an appeal to consistency, thus carrying through the Kantian commitment to rationality in the analysis of language, yet also expressing values associated with predictability, which he thought the courts and the legal profession should foster.

That reason is a *value* permits doubt; perhaps there are opposing values. Earlier we had noted with Plato's help three features of moral "reality" that might express the nature of the authority of human rights: that it is independent of us, that it is eternal or unchanging, and that it is consistent. First we objected to independence. Our next stage of argument, in Chapter 9, was to object to the eternal or unchanging nature of reason. Chapter 10 showed that the recommendation of consistency that Hohfeld's approach presupposed is problematic, not merely because it gives reason an overriding value but because reason, quite apart from Hume's response to it, involves weaknesses that Kant himself argued for. These objections with regard to *eternity* and to *consistency* had a common source in Kant.

We often disobey what is morally required of us, but how can essentially rational beings act wrongly? There was, in unacknowledged fact, a serious dislocation in Kant's philosophy between "human beings" and "rational beings". Kant was optimistic about the human condition, and argued in his "Idea of a Universal History" that we may expect our proto-rational nature to develop both in our moral understanding and in our moral behaviour. But we saw that this is not an adequate answer. It implies that people now are not worthy of respect, and that the end justifies the means. This is inconsistent with Kant's main moral philosophy and also with our common-sense moral judgements. Moreover, the view implies that morality changes over time and that reason changes over time. Thus the attempts to ground human rights in unchanging human nature must fail just because, and in so far as, there is no such thing as unchanging human nature. We thus lose the second Platonic requirement, that of the *eternal* nature of ultimate moral values like human rights.

Having lost independence and eternity, we lose the third value too. If reason changes over time then reality must be *inconsistent*. While a sense of unchanging rationality has been seen as essential to the ethical since before Socrates, we noted Berlin's pluralistic view that moral reality is inherently and essentially inconsistent and also Dworkin's view that inconsistent legal and moral principles, while having to be weighed in particular cases so that one might be overridden, did not lose their ultimate validity thereby. Characterizing the expression of these positions as largely metaphorical, we developed an intelligible expression of this pluralistic approach by analysing the idea that reality might be an essentially contested concept. We argued that a pluralist reality cannot be completely and consistently described within a single point of view, but that it can be if a multiplicity of points of view are adopted and tolerated. We concluded that human rights have no independent metaphysical existence, are not plausibly universal, may with reason change over time, and may be intelligibly inconsistent with each other. We need to recognize different points of view if we are to encompass all our moral understanding. We nevertheless recognized the value that, like Hohfeld, we may give to the respect for consistency, and indeed this book has attempted to respect that value in full.

At the beginning we presented the interrelated issues of justification and of understanding as central to our philosophical concerns. Having reached the conclusions specified in the last paragraph, we recognized that philosophical problems of the clarification of rights still remained. We saw that, with or without the assumption of consistency, Hohfeld's position required an understanding of the concepts of right and duty that was *prior* to his analysis. We distinguished with Hare the meanings of moral terms from the criteria for their application, and showed how unwanted metaphysical commitments suggested by his and others' terminology could be avoided by using Rawls's distinction between "concept" and "conception". Three strands for presenting a prior grasp of rights and duties were introduced: that understanding rights is prior to understanding duties; that understanding duties is prior to understanding rights; and that understanding rights and understanding duties might be mutually supporting. We argued that a full understanding of rights would require an understanding of the central theories that may respectively support each of these three approaches.

There has been historical change over long periods of time in our beliefs about what our rights and duties are. Finnis's presentation of the history of the word "right" exemplified, in the change from Aquinas to Suárez, a change of priority of understanding from a justice-based to a rights-based approach. We used this to analyse the rights-based approach in which the point of view of the beneficiary of a just situation is primary. We looked at the nature of the "individuals" who might be bearers of such rights, examining first how far the beneficiary has to be an individual person. We concluded that both groups and, more generally, non-humans might have human rights in so far as they might be treated "as if" they were human. We argued, secondly, against the suggestion that rights are essentially held by individual independent selves who are selfish and incapable of full association with others, and against the consequential claim that rights are therefore part of an essentially male-based morality. We distinguished the "interest" from the "will" theory of rights and showed that the point of view of the beneficiary does not imply the will theory. We observed that the interest theory of rights permits a wider range of criteria than does the will theory for determining what rights people may hold.

We next tried to make sense of a duty-based conception of rights. Kant's position is often seen as grounding morality in duty, but we showed that only part of his philosophy permitted this. The duty-based approach in Kant involves adopting the first-person singular point of view, but Kant also told us what it is to be a "moral object". It is the freedom and autonomy of the other person that we are to value. We showed that measuring merit in terms of what is valuable about the moral object or beneficiary contrasted with measuring merit in terms of the inherent rationality of the duty-ower's will. If we placed this former feature of Kant's position first, then we found that his moral philosophy placed rights as prior to duties, rather than duties as prior to rights. Even Kant then had difficulty presenting a duty-based approach as prior in our moral understanding. We suggested that only if we understand morality and law entirely in terms of what can be *enforced* might we be able to make sense of duty as the prior concept in our understanding.

Finally, we examined the view that rights and duties are in some way mutually supporting features of a just situation. The view that justice is prior to rights is an essential feature of Rawls's *A Theory of Justice*, and we presented and analysed this, showing that Rawls's references to "natural duties" indeed depended on an understanding of justice as prior. With the understanding of the place of theories of justice we concluded our presentation of the rights-based, duty-based and justice-based points of view in understanding rights, and thereby located the central philosophical issues and theories involved in a full understanding of rights.

It is apparent that the argument neither begins nor ends with the concerns of justice. Just as there are arguments about the content of human rights, and just as there are myriad claims to various rights across the world, whether by individuals or by other entities, so there are pluralities of theories that offer some understanding of the moral and legal realm and of the places that rights may hold in it. We earlier made intelligible the suggestion that moral reality may be inherently inconsistent, and, whatever the truth of this view may be, it is apparent that moral argument, if not moral "reality", does display an essential contestability.

We have to choose between arguments for rights because different arguments justify different rights. Philosophical argument in this context would be dead, in practical terms, if we all agreed on what all our rights were in all actual situations. That different explanations or justifications might be available would then be merely of theoretical interest. Even if we had a complete agreement specifying our rights in general, however, there would always be particular situations in which discretion would be called for; there would be some point at which our explicit principles ran out. At such a point we would need philosophical theory, if only to guide the conclusion by placing the burden of proof one way rather than another in the uncertain context. In fact there is no such agreement, and we have conflicting claims about rights with conflicting supporting arguments. In the actual situation, it is a mere matter of degree how far we may have to decide between different conflicting rights and how far we may have to decide between different conflicting theories of rights. Deciding between different theories of rights involves the same issues as deciding between different rights.

We cannot, then, ignore moral views that are opposed to our own, and all views contribute to moral understanding, even if only so that we can define our own against them. Must we just tolerate alternative moral philosophies? We are now in the familiar position that the concept of toleration involves: surely not any alternative should be tolerated. Yet where should any line be drawn, and on what ground? "Toleration" is a notoriously elusive concept, and at this point we have a situation where what is tolerated and what is not may at best be arbitrary, and at worst may involve a situation where, as we have seen, reason cannot constrain our choices at all. In other words, the plurality of philosophies seems to allow us to believe what we like about good and bad, and we may never need to choose between inconsistent beliefs, or even to judge them inconsistent.

It is not only the proliferation of opposing rights and their theories that raises the philosophical difficulty: it is also the widely held view that rights, particularly human rights, are themselves the ultimate ground for determining the ordering of conflicting moral demands. As we noted in Chapter 1, human rights have a pre-eminent place in current political, social, legal and moral thinking, to such an extent that one might even think them totalitarian in their force; the Chinese, for example, with whatever moral sincerity I will not enquire, have sometimes claimed the international human rights agenda to be yet another example of Western imperialism. Again, it is a familiar conservative complaint in Britain that new systems of institutionalizing human rights in British law are part of the route towards a European super-state. The totalitarian implications of that last expression are knowingly part of the rhetoric that is used.

One way of avoiding the proliferation of rights is, as we have seen, to follow Kant. In jurisprudence, says Kant, we want "to know exactly (with mathematical precision) what the property of everyone is".[2] Property rights are, as we have seen with Hohfeld's analysis, very complex but, very simply understood, are typically not in conflict. I can *claim* a right to ownership of a house owned by you, but we cannot both get the money if you sell it, and, since the money follows the right in the simple case, we cannot both have the right to ownership of it. Actual property rights, again understood very simply, do form a consistent set. We may imagine a map with different areas spatially distinguished by boundary lines, with the owner's name inscribed in each space. It would make little sense for both your name and mine to appear in the same space, except as representing some partnership. There can indeed be something mathematically – or at least geometrically – exact about this. We know that Kant's view of rights in general is like this. To establish what rights there are is to establish a consistent set. Rights, thus understood, cannot be in conflict. If such a philosophical understanding is correct then the proliferation of opposing moral demands that "come wrapped in the garb of rights", as Steiner put it, may be removed, because "real" rights do not conflict.

Followers of Kant believed:

> that reason could determine a set of principles which represents the mutual compatibility of individual wills: in this way, each

---

2. Quoted by Steiner, "Working Rights", 270 n. 60, from Kant, *Metaphysical Elements of Justice*, J. Ladd (trans.) (Indianapolis: Bobbs-Merrill, 1965), 38–9.

person's freedom might be reconciled with the freedom of everyone else, and the content of the necessary system of rules could be determined without privileging the will and preferences of any individual.[3]

The individual autonomous and rational will is thus seen, in the Kantian tradition, as grounding the nature of rights. That rights are in some way grounded in the will is reflected, as we have seen, in the familiar everyday intuition that rights are in some sense freedoms. Freedoms do not have to be exercised, and a related intuition is that rights can be waived. To repeat an earlier point, "right", Kant said, "is ... the sum of the conditions under which the choice of one can be united with the choice of another in accordance with a universal law of freedom".[4]

Yet we have seen difficulties with the Kantian view. Various thinkers have thought that rights should be seen not as domains of protected freedom of will but as protected interests.[5] Moreover, not only people have interests, but animals too, and it is typically interest theories of rights, rather than will theories of rights, that permit us to ascribe rights to animals (and children and foetuses and corporations) in an understandable way. Again, as we know, people's and animals' interests can conflict, and it is the huge range of interests that different beings have that can be taken to warrant the generation of rights, so understood, in such an incontinent way. Rights are not then the kind of thing that can act as ultimate arbiters of moral conflict, but rather are themselves the kind of thing that typically gives rise to such conflict, and are thus subordinate to whatever overarching principle it may be that properly ranks and orders them,[6] a principle that might be broadly economic, expressing the purposes of the state, or whatever, and that risks understanding judicial decisions on such matters as being the exercise of unlimited discretion. Yet the overarching principles available also form an inconsistent plurality.

Can we in practice, and recognizing cultural, legal and geographical limitations, rely on our ordinary common-sense intuitions

---

3. As N. E. Simmonds usefully summarized it in his "Rights at the Cutting Edge", in *A Debate Over Rights: Philosophical Enquiries*, M. H. Kramer, N. E. Simmonds & H. Steiner (eds), 113–232 (Oxford: Clarendon Press, 1998), 123.
4. Quoted by Steiner, "Working Rights", 276 n. 71, from Kant *The Metaphysics of Morals*, 56.
5. Simmonds, "Rights at the Cutting Edge", 129.
6. See Steiner, "Working Rights", 290–92.

in the face of these difficulties? Not even this. Our ordinary intuitions about rights typically include the idea that rights are often waivable by the right-holder. Yet if, by contrast, rights are seen as based upon our objective interests then the possibility of their waivability seems less acceptable, and the interest theory risks paternalism. Again, our ordinary intuitions about rights include the idea that, for example, infants have rights, but the will theory typically rejects as right-holders those who are not capable of exercising will at the appropriate level of rational choice. Can rights be both authoritative moral truths and also waivable at the will of the individual? There are many other conflicting intuitions in our ordinary moral and legal understanding of rights, and it is widely agreed that, whichever theory of rights we opt for, we have to reject certain ordinary intuitions about rights if we seek consistency. James Griffin has held that, in the face of conflicting intuitions, we can only stipulate.[7] We have already seen, in Hohfeld's work, how different values can be imported by this move, and if different intuitions have, as it were, a right to be heard, we can see how question-begging such a move is.

Steiner can be helpful here, although first we need to clarify a difficulty in his position. One of the most familiar roles for rights, Steiner notes, is that they figure in circumstances where there is disagreement between people.[8] If everyone always agreed with each other, he continues, the need for rights would disappear. This assertion, however, is implausible and needs clarification. Given that rights correlate with duties, it amounts to saying that, where there is no disagreement there is no need for duties either, and this is even more obviously implausible. In the ideal case, just because we all agree with each other, we will all agree with each other about what ought to be done, and rights and duties may certainly exist and may well be needed in virtue of that.[9] Yet just because we all agree with each other about what our rights and duties are does not mean that we will carry

---

7. At a conference held in his honour on the occasion of his retirement from the chair of moral philosophy: "Human Rights – The Very Idea", Human Rights Colloquium, Corpus Christi College, Oxford, 6 July 2000.
8. Steiner, "Working Rights", 236. Compare, and perhaps contrast, this with a position expressed by Dworkin: "We need rights, as a distinct element in political theory, only when some decision that injures people nevertheless finds prima-facie support in the claim that it will make the community as a whole better off on some plausible account of where the community's general welfare lies", "Rights as Trumps", 166.
9. The "will" theory and the "interest" theory of rights will generate these in different ways.

out our duties willingly, and a right-holder may need to *enforce* a right held. Is this "disagreement"? We need not accept Steiner's further point that disagreement at some level is necessary or sufficient for characterizing a situation where reference to rights is required. Rather, what Steiner wishes to do is draw our attention to a situation that he calls "deadlock": one that is *adversarial*. Such a circumstance is one in which "two disagreeing persons' chosen courses of action *intersect*: . . . their two courses of action are jointly unperformable".[10]

Discussion or other means of eliminating the disagreement can resolve a deadlock, Steiner continues, but he asserts:

> the distinctive function of [rights] thinking is to secure the elimination of deadlocks *without* eliminating the disagreements that generate them. Rights supply adversaries with reasons to back off from interference when they have no other reason to allow the performance of the actions they're interfering with.[11]

He describes the attitude required as one of "toleration", adding that whoever backs down "gets a round of applause for being tolerant".[12] That is not much of a reason. On the other hand, it is *justice* that grounds the ascription of rights, Steiner continues,[13] but he eventually admits, "I've offered no reasons as to why we should *be* just. Nor do I think that any can be found".[14] It is not, however, quite as bad as that, for "offering a reason to be just" is ambiguous between offering a reason to a contestant to tolerate his opponent's position, and offering a reason to the observer to decide justly between the two opponents. This last is more easily achievable.

"The rights rule", says Steiner, "has to be such that, in any conceivable deadlock, only one of the parties is within his/her rights. And the way in which this is guaranteed is by having a rights rule that generates only rights which are *compossible*".[15] This claim is a version of Kant's requirement of consistency, and it is clearly too strong, in that it begs the question in favour of a Kantian approach. Clearly a situation in which two courses of action are jointly unperformable may need to be resolved, and while not all truths have a direct link to

---

10. Steiner, "Working Rights", 237.
11. *Ibid.*, pp. 237–8. Note that the "choice" of action which an adversary may have does not imply a "will" theory of the rights involved.
12. *Ibid.*, 195.
13. Steiner, *An Essay on Rights*, 193.
14. Steiner, "Working Rights", 282.
15. *Ibid.*, 200–201.

action, there is no doubt that some do. Peter Lipton put the pragmatic point as follows: "beliefs are guides to action that help us to get what we want and avoid trouble".[16] Yet just because some disagreements must be resolved rather than, pragmatically, "shelved", it does not follow that all rights must be compossible, as we saw in Chapter 10.

Interpreting Steiner further and arguing somewhat by analogy with his own argument, we find him characterizing an adversarial situation in terms of three moral points of view that map onto the points of view we have already pointed out in our discussion of the consistency and inconsistency of moral reality: the moral code of one contestant, the moral code of the other contestant, and a code of justice that is externally applied. "All I'm doing", says Steiner, "is describing what's involved *if* you [act justly ...]".[17] On his view, where there is deadlock and a right exists then an external adjudicator with the capacity for enforcement exists. We expressed a position like this in Chapter 10 in recognizing the need to make intelligible a pluralist view of reality by referring to an observer who was external to the contestants.

The "reality" version of the argument is as follows. We are not to ask which of the opposing beliefs of the contestants is true, for that involves appealing to contestant-centred criteria for truth. We may even imagine that one of our contestants is an empiricist and the other a rationalist. We can not, without bias, rely on such criteria. Rather, we need an external observer-centred criterion for truth. However, this criterion cannot have the content of contestant-centred criteria. Indeed, *no* ranking order for contestant-centred criteria exists, for any such order could form part of the contestant-centred criteria and would then beg the question. Grotius saw the point clearly: in international law, and as summarized by J. B. Schneewind:

> if the nations in a dispute are as widely divided on the particulars of religion as the Protestant Dutch and the Catholic Portuguese and the Catholic Portuguese and the Catholic Portuguese and the Catholic Portuguese and Spanish, then no appeal to the Bible or to specific Christian doctrines will help. Each side interprets the Bible in its own way ....[18]

Again by analogy with Steiner's argument, since no criterion for relevantly differentiating contestant-centred criteria can be eligible to serve as a standard of choice, it follows that no contestant-centred

---

16. P. Lipton, *Inference to the Best Explanation* (London: Routledge, 1991), 23.
17. Steiner, "Working Rights", 203.
18. Schneewind, *The Invention of Autonomy*, 71.

criteria can be regarded by the observer as relevantly different; that is, all contestant-centred criteria are relevantly alike. We cannot refer to rights as a way of choosing between contestants claiming different and conflicting rights, and we have to regard claims to rights, and also their justifying theories, as equivalent. No criterion for determining truth in a sense appropriate for an individual contestant – reason or experience, for example – can serve as a standard for that reality shared between the contestants, and the same point goes for the determination of rights. The upshot is that everyone is entitled to equal freedom of belief, just because and in so far as there is no shared criterion for distinguishing between them.[19] The observer has to ask, just as Steiner asks in a different context, who should have the freedom here? It is no surprise that truth, realistically understood, would constrain such freedom, for that was where the relevant point in Chapter 10 began, with Foucault's view that truth is a censor. By contrast, equal freedom to believe is the foundation of moral truth and so of inconsistent rights, if we recognize the pluralist assumptions involved here. Again – although not a pluralist – Grotius saw the conclusion to be drawn, following on from the point that it is question-begging to rely on contestant-centred criteria:

> Just as, in fact, there are many ways of living, one being better than another, and out of so many ways of living each is free to select that which he prefers, so also a people can select the form of government it wishes; and the extent of its legal right in the matter is not to be measured by the superior excellence of this or that form of government, in regard to which different men hold different views, but by its free choice.[20]

The concluding point is this: that the content of a right and its justifying rights theory cannot be provided by the content of what the contestants disagree about, since the disagreement remains to be decided even when one contestant admits that the rights of his opponent provide him with a reason to tolerate the position of that opponent. Where it is rights or their theories that are disagreed about, then the very fact of conflict means that neither contestant's moral

---

19. Contrast with Dworkin's contrast: "my hypothesis, that the rights which have traditionally been described as consequences of a general right to liberty are in fact the consequences of equality instead, may in the end prove to be wrong", "Rights as Trumps", 167.
20. Quoted from Grotius, *De Jure Belli ac Pacis*, by Schneewind, *The Invention of Autonomy*, 73.

code contains a reason to accept, as opposed to tolerate, the relevant part of the moral code of the other. Where a right occurs which requires toleration, then it is – just as Kant said – a *formal* demand for freedom without moral content that justifies the right.

In the end, we find that a pluralist account of inconsistent rights and rights theories is possible, relative to which a narrowly understood "theory of justice" is required to determine which rights take priority in specific conflict situations. Such determinations are not general ranking orders for rights such as Rawls might offer, but – in a pluralist context – localized procedures for resolving jointly unperformable conflicting actions.[21] Beyond freedom without moral content, there is no general philosophical answer available here for prioritizing rights just because there is no philosophy for prioritizing philosophies, not even reason itself, for that begs the question in favour of reason. Since philosophy rightly ends in uncertainty between different philosophies here, so will this book.

---

21. That such procedures – and particularly legal procedures – should be localized in this way justifies the view that judges should, as they traditionally do, speak to the particular case rather than to the universal principle. We may then agree with the relevant part of the judgement of Lord Hutton, in *R. v Attorney-General, Ex parte Rusbridger and another*, House of Lords, 26 June 2003, referring to Lord Justice-Clerk Thomson in *Macnaughton v Macnaughton's Trustees* [1953] SC 387, 392, that "it is not the function of the courts to decide hypothetical questions which do not impact on the parties before them".

United Nations
Universal Declaration of Human Rights

Adopted and proclaimed by General Assembly resolution 217 A (III) of 10 December 1948.

On December 10, 1948 the General Assembly of the United Nations adopted and proclaimed the Universal Declaration of Human Rights the full text of which appears in the following pages. Following this historic act the Assembly called upon all Member countries to publicize the text of the Declaration and "to cause it to be disseminated, displayed, read and expounded principally in schools and other educational institutions, without distinction based on the political status of countries or territories."

Preamble

Whereas recognition of the inherent dignity and of the equal and inalienable rights of all members of the human family is the foundation of freedom, justice and peace in the world,

Whereas disregard and contempt for human rights have resulted in barbarous acts which have outraged the conscience of mankind, and the advent of a world in which human beings shall enjoy freedom of speech and belief and freedom from fear and want has been proclaimed as the highest aspiration of the common people,

Whereas it is essential, if man is not to be compelled to have recourse, as a last resort, to rebellion against tyranny and oppression, that human rights should be protected by the rule of law,

Whereas it is essential to promote the development of friendly relations between nations,

Whereas the peoples of the United Nations have in the Charter reaffirmed their faith in fundamental human rights, in the dignity and worth of the human person and in the equal rights of men and women and have determined to promote social progress and better standards of life in larger freedom,

Whereas Member States have pledged themselves to achieve, in co-operation with the United Nations, the promotion of universal respect for and observance of human rights and fundamental freedoms,

Whereas a common understanding of these rights and freedoms is of the greatest importance for the full realization of this pledge,

Now, Therefore THE GENERAL ASSEMBLY proclaims THIS UNIVERSAL DECLARATION OF HUMAN RIGHTS as a common standard of achievement for all peoples and all nations, to the end that every individual and every organ of society, keeping this Declaration constantly in mind, shall strive by teaching and education to promote respect for these rights and freedoms and by progressive measures, national and international, to secure their universal and effective recognition and observance, both among the peoples of Member States themselves and among the peoples of territories under their jurisdiction.

Article 1.
All human beings are born free and equal in dignity and rights. They are endowed with reason and conscience and should act towards one another in a spirit of brotherhood.

Article 2.
Everyone is entitled to all the rights and freedoms set forth in this Declaration, without distinction of any kind, such as race, colour, sex, language, religion, political or other opinion, national or social origin, property, birth or other status. Furthermore, no distinction shall be made on the basis of the political, jurisdictional or international status of the country or territory to which a person belongs, whether it be independent, trust, non-self-governing or under any other limitation of sovereignty.

Article 3.
Everyone has the right to life, liberty and security of person.

Article 4.
No one shall be held in slavery or servitude; slavery and the slave trade shall be prohibited in all their forms.

Article 5.
No one shall be subjected to torture or to cruel, inhuman or degrading treatment or punishment.

Article 6.
Everyone has the right to recognition everywhere as a person before the law.

Article 7.
All are equal before the law and are entitled without any discrimination to equal protection of the law. All are entitled to equal protection against any discrimination in violation of this Declaration and against any incitement to such discrimination.

Article 8.
Everyone has the right to an effective remedy by the competent national tribunals for acts violating the fundamental rights granted him by the constitution or by law.

Article 9.
No one shall be subjected to arbitrary arrest, detention or exile.

Article 10.
Everyone is entitled in full equality to a fair and public hearing by an independent and impartial tribunal, in the determination of his rights and obligations and of any criminal charge against him.

Article 11.
(1) Everyone charged with a penal offence has the right to be presumed innocent until proved guilty according to law in a public trial at which he has had all the guarantees necessary for his defence.
(2) No one shall be held guilty of any penal offence on account of any act or omission which did not constitute a penal offence, under national or international law, at the time when it was committed. Nor shall a heavier penalty be imposed than the one that was applicable at the time the penal offence was committed.

Article 12.

No one shall be subjected to arbitrary interference with his privacy, family, home or correspondence, nor to attacks upon his honour and reputation. Everyone has the right to the protection of the law against such interference or attacks.

Article 13.

(1) Everyone has the right to freedom of movement and residence within the borders of each state.

(2) Everyone has the right to leave any country, including his own, and to return to his country.

Article 14.

(1) Everyone has the right to seek and to enjoy in other countries asylum from persecution.

(2) This right may not be invoked in the case of prosecutions genuinely arising from non-political crimes or from acts contrary to the purposes and principles of the United Nations.

Article 15.

(1) Everyone has the right to a nationality.

(2) No one shall be arbitrarily deprived of his nationality nor denied the right to change his nationality.

Article 16.

(1) Men and women of full age, without any limitation due to race, nationality or religion, have the right to marry and to found a family. They are entitled to equal rights as to marriage, during marriage and at its dissolution.

(2) Marriage shall be entered into only with the free and full consent of the intending spouses.

(3) The family is the natural and fundamental group unit of society and is entitled to protection by society and the State.

Article 17.

(1) Everyone has the right to own property alone as well as in association with others.

(2) No one shall be arbitrarily deprived of his property.

Article 18.

Everyone has the right to freedom of thought, conscience and religion; this right includes freedom to change his religion or belief, and freedom, either alone or in community with others and in public or private, to manifest his religion or belief in teaching, practice, worship and observance.

Article 19.

Everyone has the right to freedom of opinion and expression; this right includes freedom to hold opinions without interference and to seek, receive and impart information and ideas through any media and regardless of frontiers.

Article 20.

(1) Everyone has the right to freedom of peaceful assembly and association.

(2) No one may be compelled to belong to an association.

Article 21.

(1) Everyone has the right to take part in the government of his country, directly or through freely chosen representatives.

(2) Everyone has the right of equal access to public service in his country.

(3) The will of the people shall be the basis of the authority of government; this will shall be expressed in periodic and genuine elections which shall be by universal and equal suffrage and shall be held by secret vote or by equivalent free voting procedures.

Article 22.

Everyone, as a member of society, has the right to social security and is entitled to realization, through national effort and international co-operation and in accordance with the organization and resources of each State, of the economic, social and cultural rights indispensable for his dignity and the free development of his personality.

Article 23.

(1) Everyone has the right to work, to free choice of employment, to just and favourable conditions of work and to protection against unemployment.

(2) Everyone, without any discrimination, has the right to equal pay for equal work.

(3) Everyone who works has the right to just and favourable remuneration ensuring for himself and his family an existence worthy of human dignity, and supplemented, if necessary, by other means of social protection.

(4) Everyone has the right to form and to join trade unions for the protection of his interests.

Article 24.

Everyone has the right to rest and leisure, including reasonable limitation of working hours and periodic holidays with pay.

Article 25.

(1) Everyone has the right to a standard of living adequate for the health and well-being of himself and of his family, including food, clothing, housing and medical care and necessary social services, and the right to security in the event of unemployment, sickness, disability, widowhood, old age or other lack of livelihood in circumstances beyond his control.

(2) Motherhood and childhood are entitled to special care and assistance. All children, whether born in or out of wedlock, shall enjoy the same social protection.

Article 26.

(1) Everyone has the right to education. Education shall be free, at least in the elementary and fundamental stages. Elementary education shall be compulsory. Technical and professional education shall be made generally available and higher education shall be equally accessible to all on the basis of merit.

(2) Education shall be directed to the full development of the human personality and to the strengthening of respect for human rights and fundamental freedoms. It shall promote understanding, tolerance and friendship among all nations, racial or religious groups, and shall further the activities of the United Nations for the maintenance of peace.

(3) Parents have a prior right to choose the kind of education that shall be given to their children.

Article 27.

(1) Everyone has the right freely to participate in the cultural life of the community, to enjoy the arts and to share in scientific advancement and its benefits.

(2) Everyone has the right to the protection of the moral and material interests resulting from any scientific, literary or artistic production of which he is the author.

Article 28.
Everyone is entitled to a social and international order in which the rights and freedoms set forth in this Declaration can be fully realized.

Article 29.
(1) Everyone has duties to the community in which alone the free and full development of his personality is possible.
(2) In the exercise of his rights and freedoms, everyone shall be subject only to such limitations as are determined by law solely for the purpose of securing due recognition and respect for the rights and freedoms of others and of meeting the just requirements of morality, public order and the general welfare in a democratic society.
(3) These rights and freedoms may in no case be exercised contrary to the purposes and principles of the United Nations.

Article 30.
Nothing in this Declaration may be interpreted as implying for any State, group or person any right to engage in any activity or to perform any act aimed at the destruction of any of the rights and freedoms set forth herein.

Council of Europe Convention for the Protection of Human Rights and Fundamental Freedoms, as amended by Protocol No. 11 Rome, 4.XI.1950

The governments signatory hereto, being members of the Council of Europe,

Considering the Universal Declaration of Human Rights proclaimed by the General Assembly of the United Nations on 10th December 1948;

Considering that this Declaration aims at securing the universal and effective recognition and observance of the Rights therein declared;

Considering that the aim of the Council of Europe is the achievement of greater unity between its members and that one of the methods by which that aim is to be pursued is the maintenance and further realisation of human rights and fundamental freedoms;

Reaffirming their profound belief in those fundamental freedoms which are the foundation of justice and peace in the world and are best maintained on the one hand by an effective political democracy and on the other by a common understanding and observance of the human rights upon which they depend;

Being resolved, as the governments of European countries which are like-minded and have a common heritage of political traditions, ideals, freedom and the rule of law, to take the first steps for the collective enforcement of certain of the rights stated in the Universal Declaration,

Have agreed as follows:

Article 1 – Obligation to respect human rights

The High Contracting Parties shall secure to everyone within their jurisdiction the rights and freedoms defined in Section I of this Convention.

Section I – Rights and freedoms

Article 2 – Right to life

1 Everyone's right to life shall be protected by law. No one shall be deprived of his life intentionally save in the execution of a sentence of a court following his conviction of a crime for which this penalty is provided by law.
2 Deprivation of life shall not be regarded as inflicted in contravention of this article when it results from the use of force which is no more than absolutely necessary:
a in defence of any person from unlawful violence;
b in order to effect a lawful arrest or to prevent the escape of a person lawfully detained;
c in action lawfully taken for the purpose of quelling a riot or insurrection.

Article 3 – Prohibition of torture

No one shall be subjected to torture or to inhuman or degrading treatment or punishment.

Article 4 – Prohibition of slavery and forced labour

1 No one shall be held in slavery or servitude.
2 No one shall be required to perform forced or compulsory labour.
3 For the purpose of this article the term "forced or compulsory labour" shall not include:
a any work required to be done in the ordinary course of detention imposed according to the provisions of Article 5 of this Convention or during conditional release from such detention;
b any service of a military character or, in case of conscientious objectors in countries where they are recognised, service exacted instead of compulsory military service;
c any service exacted in case of an emergency or calamity threatening the life or well-being of the community;
d any work or service which forms part of normal civic obligations.

Article 5 – Right to liberty and security

1 Everyone has the right to liberty and security of person. No one shall be deprived of his liberty save in the following cases and in accordance with a procedure prescribed by law:

a the lawful detention of a person after conviction by a competent court;

b the lawful arrest or detention of a person for non-compliance with the lawful order of a court or in order to secure the fulfilment of any obligation prescribed by law;

c the lawful arrest or detention of a person effected for the purpose of bringing him before the competent legal authority on reasonable suspicion of having committed an offence or when it is reasonably considered necessary to prevent his committing an offence or fleeing after having done so;

d the detention of a minor by lawful order for the purpose of educational supervision or his lawful detention for the purpose of bringing him before the competent legal authority;

e the lawful detention of persons for the prevention of the spreading of infectious diseases, of persons of unsound mind, alcoholics or drug addicts or vagrants;

f the lawful arrest or detention of a person to prevent his effecting an unauthorised entry into the country or of a person against whom action is being taken with a view to deportation or extradition.

2 Everyone who is arrested shall be informed promptly, in a language which he understands, of the reasons for his arrest and of any charge against him.

3 Everyone arrested or detained in accordance with the provisions of paragraph 1.c of this article shall be brought promptly before a judge or other officer authorised by law to exercise judicial power and shall be entitled to trial within a reasonable time or to release pending trial. Release may be conditioned by guarantees to appear for trial.

4 Everyone who is deprived of his liberty by arrest or detention shall be entitled to take proceedings by which the lawfulness of his detention shall be decided speedily by a court and his release ordered if the detention is not lawful.

5 Everyone who has been the victim of arrest or detention in contravention of the provisions of this article shall have an enforceable right to compensation.

Article 6 – Right to a fair trial

1 In the determination of his civil rights and obligations or of any criminal charge against him, everyone is entitled to a fair and public hearing within a reasonable time by an independent and impartial tribunal established by law. Judgment shall be pronounced publicly but the press and public may be excluded from all or part of the trial in the interests of morals, public order or national security in a democratic society, where the interests of juveniles or the protection of the private life of the parties so require, or to the extent strictly necessary in the opinion of the court in special circumstances where publicity would prejudice the interests of justice.

2 Everyone charged with a criminal offence shall be presumed innocent until proved guilty according to law.

3 Everyone charged with a criminal offence has the following minimum rights:

a to be informed promptly, in a language which he understands and in detail, of the nature and cause of the accusation against him;

b to have adequate time and facilities for the preparation of his defence;

c to defend himself in person or through legal assistance of his own choosing or, if he has not sufficient means to pay for legal assistance, to be given it free when the interests of justice so require;

d to examine or have examined witnesses against him and to obtain the attendance and examination of witnesses on his behalf under the same conditions as witnesses against him;

e to have the free assistance of an interpreter if he cannot understand or speak the language used in court.

Article 7 – No punishment without law

1 No one shall be held guilty of any criminal offence on account of any act or omission which did not constitute a criminal offence under national or international law at the time when it was committed. Nor shall a heavier penalty be imposed than the one that was applicable at the time the criminal offence was committed.

2 This article shall not prejudice the trial and punishment of any person for any act or omission which, at the time when it was committed, was criminal according to the general principles of law recognised by civilised nations.

Article 8 – Right to respect for private and family life

1 Everyone has the right to respect for his private and family life, his home and his correspondence.

2 There shall be no interference by a public authority with the exercise of this right except such as is in accordance with the law and is necessary in a democratic society in the interests of national security, public safety or the economic well-being of the country, for the prevention of disorder or crime, for the protection of health or morals, or for the protection of the rights and freedoms of others.

Article 9 – Freedom of thought, conscience and religion

1 Everyone has the right to freedom of thought, conscience and religion; this right includes freedom to change his religion or belief and freedom, either alone or in community with others and in public or private, to manifest his religion or belief, in worship, teaching, practice and observance.

2 Freedom to manifest one's religion or beliefs shall be subject only to such limitations as are prescribed by law and are necessary in a democratic society in the interests of public safety, for the protection of public order, health or morals, or for the protection of the rights and freedoms of others.

Article 10 – Freedom of expression

1 Everyone has the right to freedom of expression. This right shall include freedom to hold opinions and to receive and impart information and ideas without interference by public authority and regardless of frontiers. This article shall not prevent States from requiring the licensing of broadcasting, television or cinema enterprises.

2 The exercise of these freedoms, since it carries with it duties and responsibilities, may be subject to such formalities, conditions, restrictions or penalties as are prescribed by law and are necessary in a democratic society, in the interests of national security, territorial integrity or public safety, for the prevention of disorder or crime, for the protection of health or morals, for the protection of the reputation or rights of others, for preventing the disclosure of information received in confidence, or for maintaining the authority and impartiality of the judiciary.

Article 11 – Freedom of assembly and association

1 Everyone has the right to freedom of peaceful assembly and to freedom of association with others, including the right to form and to join trade unions for the protection of his interests.

2 No restrictions shall be placed on the exercise of these rights other than such as are prescribed by law and are necessary in a democratic society in the interests of national security or public safety, for the prevention of disorder or crime, for the protection of health or morals or for the protection of the rights and freedoms of others. This article shall not prevent the imposition of lawful restrictions on the exercise of these rights by members of the armed forces, of the police or of the administration of the State.

Article 12 – Right to marry

Men and women of marriageable age have the right to marry and to found a family, according to the national laws governing the exercise of this right.

Article 13 – Right to an effective remedy

Everyone whose rights and freedoms as set forth in this Convention are violated shall have an effective remedy before a national authority notwithstanding that the violation has been committed by persons acting in an official capacity.

Article 14 – Prohibition of discrimination

The enjoyment of the rights and freedoms set forth in this Convention shall be secured without discrimination on any ground such as sex, race, colour, language, religion, political or other opinion, national or social origin, association with a national minority, property, birth or other status.

Article 15 – Derogation in time of emergency

1 In time of war or other public emergency threatening the life of the nation any High Contracting Party may take measures derogating from its obligations under this Convention to the extent strictly required by the exigencies of the situation, provided that such measures are not inconsistent with its other obligations under international law.

2 No derogation from Article 2, except in respect of deaths resulting from lawful acts of war, or from Articles 3, 4 (paragraph 1) and 7 shall be made under this provision.

3 Any High Contracting Party availing itself of this right of derogation shall keep the Secretary General of the Council of Europe fully informed of the measures which it has taken and the reasons therefor. It shall also inform the Secretary General of the Council of Europe when such measures have ceased to operate and the provisions of the Convention are again being fully executed.

Article 16 – Restrictions on political activity of aliens
Nothing in Articles 10, 11 and 14 shall be regarded as preventing the High Contracting Parties from imposing restrictions on the political activity of aliens.

Article 17 – Prohibition of abuse of rights
Nothing in this Convention may be interpreted as implying for any State, group or person any right to engage in any activity or perform any act aimed at the destruction of any of the rights and freedoms set forth herein or at their limitation to a greater extent than is provided for in the Convention.

Article 18 – Limitation on use of restrictions on rights
The restrictions permitted under this Convention to the said rights and freedoms shall not be applied for any purpose other than those for which they have been prescribed.

Section II – European Court of Human Rights

Article 19 – Establishment of the Court
To ensure the observance of the engagements undertaken by the High Contracting Parties in the Convention and the Protocols thereto, there shall be set up a European Court of Human Rights, hereinafter referred to as "the Court". It shall function on a permanent basis.

Article 20 – Number of judges
The Court shall consist of a number of judges equal to that of the High Contracting Parties.

Article 21 – Criteria for office
1 The judges shall be of high moral character and must either possess the qualifications required for appointment to high judicial office or be jurisconsults of recognised competence.

2　The judges shall sit on the Court in their individual capacity.

3　During their term of office the judges shall not engage in any activity which is incompatible with their independence, impartiality or with the demands of a full-time office; all questions arising from the application of this paragraph shall be decided by the Court.

Article 22 – Election of judges

1　The judges shall be elected by the Parliamentary Assembly with respect to each High Contracting Party by a majority of votes cast from a list of three candidates nominated by the High Contracting Party.

2　The same procedure shall be followed to complete the Court in the event of the accession of new High Contracting Parties and in filling casual vacancies.

Article 23 – Terms of office

1　The judges shall be elected for a period of six years. They may be re-elected. However, the terms of office of one-half of the judges elected at the first election shall expire at the end of three years.

2　The judges whose terms of office are to expire at the end of the initial period of three years shall be chosen by lot by the Secretary General of the Council of Europe immediately after their election.

3　In order to ensure that, as far as possible, the terms of office of one-half of the judges are renewed every three years, the Parliamentary Assembly may decide, before proceeding to any subsequent election, that the term or terms of office of one or more judges to be elected shall be for a period other than six years but not more than nine and not less than three years.

4　In cases where more than one term of office is involved and where the Parliamentary Assembly applies the preceding paragraph, the allocation of the terms of office shall be effected by a drawing of lots by the Secretary General of the Council of Europe immediately after the election.

5　A judge elected to replace a judge whose term of office has not expired shall hold office for the remainder of his predecessor's term.

6　The terms of office of judges shall expire when they reach the age of 70.

7   The judges shall hold office until replaced. They shall, however, continue to deal with such cases as they already have under consideration.

Article 24 – Dismissal

No judge may be dismissed from his office unless the other judges decide by a majority of two-thirds that he has ceased to fulfil the required conditions.

Article 25 – Registry and legal secretaries

The Court shall have a registry, the functions and organisation of which shall be laid down in the rules of the Court. The Court shall be assisted by legal secretaries.

Article 26 – Plenary Court

The plenary Court shall
   a   elect its President and one or two Vice-Presidents for a period of three years; they may be re-elected;
   b   set up Chambers, constituted for a fixed period of time;
   c   elect the Presidents of the Chambers of the Court; they may be re-elected;
   d   adopt the rules of the Court, and
   e   elect the Registrar and one or more Deputy Registrars.

Article 27 – Committees, Chambers and Grand Chamber

1   To consider cases brought before it, the Court shall sit in committees of three judges, in Chambers of seven judges and in a Grand Chamber of seventeen judges. The Court's Chambers shall set up committees for a fixed period of time.
2   There shall sit as an ex officio member of the Chamber and the Grand Chamber the judge elected in respect of the State Party concerned or, if there is none or if he is unable to sit, a person of its choice who shall sit in the capacity of judge.
3   The Grand Chamber shall also include the President of the Court, the Vice-Presidents, the Presidents of the Chambers and other judges chosen in accordance with the rules of the Court. When a case is referred to the Grand Chamber under Article 43, no judge from the Chamber which rendered the judgment shall sit in the Grand Chamber, with the exception of the President of the Chamber and the judge who sat in respect of the State Party concerned.

Article 28 – Declarations of inadmissibility by committees

A committee may, by a unanimous vote, declare inadmissible or strike out of its list of cases an application submitted under Article 34 where such a decision can be taken without further examination. The decision shall be final.

Article 29 – Decisions by Chambers on admissibility and merits

1 If no decision is taken under Article 28, a Chamber shall decide on the admissibility and merits of individual applications submitted under Article 34.

2 A Chamber shall decide on the admissibility and merits of inter-State applications submitted under Article 33.

3 The decision on admissibility shall be taken separately unless the Court, in exceptional cases, decides otherwise.

Article 30 – Relinquishment of jurisdiction to the Grand Chamber

Where a case pending before a Chamber raises a serious question affecting the interpretation of the Convention or the protocols thereto, or where the resolution of a question before the Chamber might have a result inconsistent with a judgment previously delivered by the Court, the Chamber may, at any time before it has rendered its judgment, relinquish jurisdiction in favour of the Grand Chamber, unless one of the parties to the case objects.

Article 31 – Powers of the Grand Chamber

The Grand Chamber shall

1a determine applications submitted either under Article 33 or Article 34 when a Chamber has relinquished jurisdiction under Article 30 or when the case has been referred to it under Article 43; and

b consider requests for advisory opinions submitted under Article 47.

Article 32 – Jurisdiction of the Court

1 The jurisdiction of the Court shall extend to all matters concerning the interpretation and application of the Convention and the protocols thereto which are referred to it as provided in Articles 33, 34 and 47.

2 In the event of dispute as to whether the Court has jurisdiction, the Court shall decide.

Article 33 – Inter-State cases

Any High Contracting Party may refer to the Court any alleged breach of the provisions of the Convention and the protocols thereto by another High Contracting Party.

Article 34 – Individual applications

The Court may receive applications from any person, non-governmental organisation or group of individuals claiming to be the victim of a violation by one of the High Contracting Parties of the rights set forth in the Convention or the protocols thereto. The High Contracting Parties undertake not to hinder in any way the effective exercise of this right.

Article 35 – Admissibility criteria

1 The Court may only deal with the matter after all domestic remedies have been exhausted, according to the generally recognised rules of international law, and within a period of six months from the date on which the final decision was taken.
2 The Court shall not deal with any application submitted under Article 34 that
a is anonymous; or
b is substantially the same as a matter that has already been examined by the Court or has already been submitted to another procedure of international investigation or settlement and contains no relevant new information.
3 The Court shall declare inadmissible any individual application submitted under Article 34 which it considers incompatible with the provisions of the Convention or the protocols thereto, manifestly ill-founded, or an abuse of the right of application.
4 The Court shall reject any application which it considers inadmissible under this Article. It may do so at any stage of the proceedings.

Article 36 – Third party intervention

1 In all cases before a Chamber or the Grand Chamber, a High Contracting Party one of whose nationals is an applicant shall have the right to submit written comments and to take part in hearings.
2 The President of the Court may, in the interest of the proper administration of justice, invite any High Contracting Party which is not a party to the proceedings or any person concerned

who is not the applicant to submit written comments or take part in hearings.

Article 37 – Striking out applications

1 The Court may at any stage of the proceedings decide to strike an application out of its list of cases where the circumstances lead to the conclusion that

a the applicant does not intend to pursue his application; or

b the matter has been resolved; or

c for any other reason established by the Court, it is no longer justified to continue the examination of the application.

However, the Court shall continue the examination of the application if respect for human rights as defined in the Convention and the protocols thereto so requires.

2 The Court may decide to restore an application to its list of cases if it considers that the circumstances justify such a course.

Article 38 – Examination of the case and friendly settlement proceedings

1 If the Court declares the application admissible, it shall

a pursue the examination of the case, together with the representatives of the parties, and if need be, undertake an investigation, for the effective conduct of which the States concerned shall furnish all necessary facilities;

b place itself at the disposal of the parties concerned with a view to securing a friendly settlement of the matter on the basis of respect for human rights as defined in the Convention and the protocols thereto.

2 Proceedings conducted under paragraph 1.b shall be confidential.

Article 39 – Finding of a friendly settlement

If a friendly settlement is effected, the Court shall strike the case out of its list by means of a decision which shall be confined to a brief statement of the facts and of the solution reached.

Article 40 – Public hearings and access to documents

1 Hearings shall be in public unless the Court in exceptional circumstances decides otherwise.

2 Documents deposited with the Registrar shall be accessible to the public unless the President of the Court decides otherwise.

Article 41 – Just satisfaction

If the Court finds that there has been a violation of the Convention or the protocols thereto, and if the internal law of the High Contracting Party concerned allows only partial reparation to be made, the Court shall, if necessary, afford just satisfaction to the injured party.

Article 42 – Judgments of Chambers

Judgments of Chambers shall become final in accordance with the provisions of Article 44, paragraph 2.

Article 43 – Referral to the Grand Chamber

1   Within a period of three months from the date of the judgment of the Chamber, any party to the case may, in exceptional cases, request that the case be referred to the Grand Chamber.

2   A panel of five judges of the Grand Chamber shall accept the request if the case raises a serious question affecting the interpretation or application of the Convention or the protocols thereto, or a serious issue of general importance.

3   If the panel accepts the request, the Grand Chamber shall decide the case by means of a judgment.

Article 44 – Final judgments

1   The judgment of the Grand Chamber shall be final.

2   The judgment of a Chamber shall become final

a   when the parties declare that they will not request that the case be referred to the Grand Chamber; or

b   three months after the date of the judgment, if reference of the case to the Grand Chamber has not been requested; or

c   when the panel of the Grand Chamber rejects the request to refer under Article 43.

3   The final judgment shall be published.

Article 45 – Reasons for judgments and decisions

1   Reasons shall be given for judgments as well as for decisions declaring applications admissible or inadmissible.

2   If a judgment does not represent, in whole or in part, the unanimous opinion of the judges, any judge shall be entitled to deliver a separate opinion.

Article 46 – Binding force and execution of judgments

1   The High Contracting Parties undertake to abide by the final

judgment of the Court in any case to which they are parties.

2   The final judgment of the Court shall be transmitted to the Committee of Ministers, which shall supervise its execution.

Article 47 – Advisory opinions

1   The Court may, at the request of the Committee of Ministers, give advisory opinions on legal questions concerning the interpretation of the Convention and the protocols thereto.

2   Such opinions shall not deal with any question relating to the content or scope of the rights or freedoms defined in Section I of the Convention and the protocols thereto, or with any other question which the Court or the Committee of Ministers might have to consider in consequence of any such proceedings as could be instituted in accordance with the Convention.

3   Decisions of the Committee of Ministers to request an advisory opinion of the Court shall require a majority vote of the representatives entitled to sit on the Committee.

Article 48 – Advisory jurisdiction of the Court

The Court shall decide whether a request for an advisory opinion submitted by the Committee of Ministers is within its competence as defined in Article 47.

Article 49 – Reasons for advisory opinions

1   Reasons shall be given for advisory opinions of the Court.

2   If the advisory opinion does not represent, in whole or in part, the unanimous opinion of the judges, any judge shall be entitled to deliver a separate opinion.

3   Advisory opinions of the Court shall be communicated to the Committee of Ministers.

Article 50 – Expenditure on the Court

The expenditure on the Court shall be borne by the Council of Europe.

Article 51 – Privileges and immunities of judges

The judges shall be entitled, during the exercise of their functions, to the privileges and immunities provided for in Article 40 of the Statute of the Council of Europe and in the agreements made thereunder.

Section III – Miscellaneous provisions

Article 52 – Inquiries by the Secretary General
On receipt of a request from the Secretary General of the Council of Europe any High Contracting Party shall furnish an explanation of the manner in which its internal law ensures the effective implementation of any of the provisions of the Convention.

Article 53 – Safeguard for existing human rights
Nothing in this Convention shall be construed as limiting or derogating from any of the human rights and fundamental freedoms which may be ensured under the laws of any High Contracting Party or under any other agreement to which it is a Party.

Article 54 – Powers of the Committee of Ministers
Nothing in this Convention shall prejudice the powers conferred on the Committee of Ministers by the Statute of the Council of Europe.

Article 55 – Exclusion of other means of dispute settlement
The High Contracting Parties agree that, except by special agreement, they will not avail themselves of treaties, conventions or declarations in force between them for the purpose of submitting, by way of petition, a dispute arising out of the interpretation or application of this Convention to a means of settlement other than those provided for in this Convention.

Article 56 – Territorial application
1   Any State may at the time of its ratification or at any time thereafter declare by notification addressed to the Secretary General of the Council of Europe that the present Convention shall, subject to paragraph 4 of this Article, extend to all or any of the territories for whose international relations it is responsible.
2   The Convention shall extend to the territory or territories named in the notification as from the thirtieth day after the receipt of this notification by the Secretary General of the Council of Europe.
3   The provisions of this Convention shall be applied in such territories with due regard, however, to local requirements.
4   Any State which has made a declaration in accordance with paragraph 1 of this article may at any time thereafter declare on

behalf of one or more of the territories to which the declaration relates that it accepts the competence of the Court to receive applications from individuals, non-governmental organisations or groups of individuals as provided by Article 34 of the Convention.

Article 57 – Reservations

1 Any State may, when signing this Convention or when depositing its instrument of ratification, make a reservation in respect of any particular provision of the Convention to the extent that any law then in force in its territory is not in conformity with the provision. Reservations of a general character shall not be permitted under this article.

2 Any reservation made under this article shall contain a brief statement of the law concerned.

Article 58 – Denunciation

1 A High Contracting Party may denounce the present Convention only after the expiry of five years from the date on which it became a party to it and after six months' notice contained in a notification addressed to the Secretary General of the Council of Europe, who shall inform the other High Contracting Parties.

2 Such a denunciation shall not have the effect of releasing the High Contracting Party concerned from its obligations under this Convention in respect of any act which, being capable of constituting a violation of such obligations, may have been performed by it before the date at which the denunciation became effective.

3 Any High Contracting Party which shall cease to be a member of the Council of Europe shall cease to be a Party to this Convention under the same conditions.

4 The Convention may be denounced in accordance with the provisions of the preceding paragraphs in respect of any territory to which it has been declared to extend under the terms of Article 56.

Article 59 – Signature and ratification

1 This Convention shall be open to the signature of the members of the Council of Europe. It shall be ratified. Ratifications shall be deposited with the Secretary General of the Council of Europe.

2 The present Convention shall come into force after the deposit of ten instruments of ratification.

3 As regards any signatory ratifying subsequently, the Convention shall come into force at the date of the deposit of its instrument of ratification.

4 The Secretary General of the Council of Europe shall notify all the members of the Council of Europe of the entry into force of the Convention, the names of the High Contracting Parties who have ratified it, and the deposit of all instruments of ratification which may be effected subsequently.

Done at Rome this 4th day of November 1950, in English and French, both texts being equally authentic, in a single copy which shall remain deposited in the archives of the Council of Europe. The Secretary General shall transmit certified copies to each of the signatories.

Bibliography

Ankersmit, F. R. 1994. *History and Tropology: The Rise and Fall of Metaphor*. Los Angeles, CA: University of California Press.

Aquinas, T. 1920. *Summa Theologica*, 2nd rev. edn, Fathers of the English Dominican Province (trans.). Online edn copyright © 2000 Kevin Knight, www.newadvent.org/summa (accessed May 2003).

Aristotle, 1976. *The Nicomachean Ethics*, J. A. K. Thompson (trans.), H. Tredennick (rev.). Harmondsworth: Penguin.

Austin, J. 1832. *The Province of Jurisprudence Determined*. London: John Murray.

Austin, J. L. 1970. *Philosophical Papers*, 2nd edn, J. O. Urmson & G. J. Warnock (eds). Oxford: Oxford University Press.

Ayer, A. J. 1971. *Language, Truth and Logic*. Harmondsworth: Penguin.

Bamforth, N. 2001. "Hohfeldian Rights and Public Law". In *Rights, Wrongs and Responsibilities*, M. H. Kramer (ed.), 1–27. Basingstoke: Palgrave.

Benn, S. I. & R. S. Peters 1959. *Social Principles and the Democratic State*. London: Allen & Unwin.

Bentham, J. 1968. *The Collected Works of Jeremy Bentham*, J. H. Burns (ed.). London: Athlone Press.

Berlin, I. 1953. *The Hedgehog and the Fox*. London: Weidenfeld & Nicolson.

Berlin, I. 1980. "The Purpose of Philosophy". In *Concepts and Categories: Philosophical Essays* [1960], I. Berlin, 1–11. Oxford: Oxford University Press.

Berlin, I. 1980. "Logical Translation". In *Concepts and Categories: Philosophical Essays* [1960], I. Berlin, 56–80. Oxford: Oxford University Press.

Berlin, I. 1996. *The Proper Study of Mankind: An Anthology of Essays*, H. Hardy & R. Hausheer (eds). London: Chatto & Windus.

Blaug, M. 1980. *The Methodology of Economics*. Cambridge: Cambridge University Press.

Burke, P. 1985. *Vico*. Oxford: Oxford University Press.

Campbell, T. 2001. *Justice*, 2nd edn. Basingstoke: Macmillan.

Coady, C. A. J. 1992. *Testimony*. Oxford: Clarendon Press.

Collingwood, R. G. 1933. *An Essay on Philosophical Method*. Oxford: Clarendon Press.

Collingwood, R. G. 1946. *The Idea of History*. Oxford: Oxford University Press.

217

Cook, W. W. 1919. "Introduction". In *Fundamental Legal Conceptions as Applied in Judicial Reasoning*, W. N. Hohfeld, W. W. Cook (ed.). New Haven, CT: Yale University Press.

Corbin, A. L. 1919. "Foreword". In *Fundamental Legal Conceptions as Applied in Judicial Reasoning*, W. N. Hohfeld, W. W. Cook (ed.). New Haven, CT: Yale University Press.

Cotterrell, R. 1989. *The Politics of Jurisprudence*. London: Butterworth.

Crossman, R. H. S. 1937. *Plato Today*. London: Allen & Unwin.

Davidson, D. 1968. "Actions, Reasons and Causes". Reprinted in *The Philosophy of Action*, A. R. White (ed.), 79–94. Oxford: Oxford University Press.

Davidson, D. 1984. "What Metaphors Mean" [1978]. In *Inquiries into Truth and Interpretation*, D, Davidson, 245–64. Oxford: Clarendon Press.

Davies, H. & D. Holdcroft 1991. *Jurisprudence: Texts and Commentary*. London: Butterworth.

Descartes, R. 1965. *Meditations on the First Philosophy* [1641], J. Veitch (trans.). London: Dent.

Dworkin, R. M. 1977. "Is Law a System of Rules?". In *The Philosophy of Law*, R. M. Dworkin (ed.), 38–65. Oxford: Oxford University Press.

Dworkin, R. M. 1977. *Taking Rights Seriously*. London: Duckworth.

Dworkin, R. M. (ed.) 1977. *The Philosophy of Law*. Oxford: Oxford University Press.

Dworkin, R. M. 1981. "Is There a Right to Pornography?", *Oxford Journal of Legal Studies* 1: 177–212.

Dworkin, R. M. 1984. "Rights as Trumps". See Waldron (ed.) (1984), 153–67.

Dyke, C. 1981. *Philosophy of Economics*. Englewood Cliffs, NJ: Prentice-Hall.

Finnis, J. 1980. *Natural Law and Natural Rights*. Oxford: Clarendon Press.

Finnis, J. 1989. "Persons and Their Associations", *Proceedings of the Aristotelian Society* supp. vol. 63: 267–74.

Foucault, M. 1981. *Power/Knowledge*. New York: Pantheon.

Friedman, M. 1979. "The Methodology of Positive Economics", in *Philosophy and Economic Theory*, F. Hahn & M. Hollis (eds), 18–35. Oxford: Oxford University Press. Originally published in M. Friedman, *Essays in Positive Economics* (Chicago, IL: University of Chicago Press, 1953).

Gallie, W. B. 1955–56. "Essentially Contested Concepts", *Proceedings of the Aristotelian Society* 56: 167.

Gewirth, A. 1978. *Reason and Morality*. Chicago, IL: University of Chicago Press.

Gilligan, C. 1982. *In a Different Voice: Psychological Theory and Women's Development*. Cambridge, MA: Harvard University Press.

Goodin, R. E. & P. Pettit (eds) 1997. *Contemporary Political Philosophy: An Anthology*. Oxford: Blackwell.

Gorman, J. L. 1981. "A Note on the Main Idea of Rawls's Theory of Justice", *Political Studies* 29: 282–3.

Gorman, J. L. 1991. "Kellner on Language and Historical Representation", *History and Theory* 30: 356–68.

Gorman, J. L. 1991. "Some Astonishing Things", *Metaphilosophy* 22, 28–40.

Gorman, J. L. 1992. *Understanding History: An Introduction to Analytical Philosophy of History*. Ottawa: University of Ottawa Press.

Gorman, J. L. 1999. "On Hedgehogs and Foxes", *Philosophical Inquiry* 21: 61–86.

Gorman, J. L. 2001. "From History to Justice". In *Essays in Honor of Burleigh Wilkins: From History to Justice*, A. Jokic (ed.), 19–69. New York: Peter Lang.

Griffin, J. P. 2000. "Human Rights – The Very Idea". Paper delivered at Human Rights Colloquium held in his honour, Corpus Christi College, Oxford, 6 July.

Grotius, H. 1922. *De Jure Belli ac Pacis* [1625]. London: Sweet & Maxwell.

Hahn, F. & M. Hollis (eds) 1979. *Philosophy and Economic Theory*. Oxford: Oxford University Press.

Hare, R. M. 1975. *The Language of Morals*. Oxford: Oxford University Press.

Hart, H. L. A. 1967. "Are There Any Natural Rights?". Reprinted in *Political Philosophy*, A. Quinton (ed.), 53–66. Oxford: Oxford University Press.

Hart, H. L. A. 1977. "Positivism and the Separation of Law and Morals". In *The Philosophy of Law*, R. M. Dworkin (ed.), 17–37. Oxford: Oxford University Press. Also in F. A. Olafson (ed.), *Society, Law and Morality* (Englewood Cliffs, NJ: Prentice-Hall, 1961).

Hart, H. L. A. 1994. *The Concept of Law* [1961], 2nd edn. Oxford: Clarendon Press.

Hawking, S. 2001. *The Universe in a Nutshell*. London: Bantam.

Hekman, S. J. 1995. *Moral Voices, Moral Selves*. Cambridge: Polity Press.

Hempel, C. G. 1966. *Philosophy of Natural Science*. Englewood Cliffs, NJ: Prentice-Hall.

Hobbes, T. 1962. *Leviathan* [1651], J. Plamenatz (ed.). London: Collins. Also published as *Leviathan*, R. Tuck (ed.) (Cambridge: Cambridge University Press, 1991).

Hohfeld, W. N. 1919. *Fundamental Legal Conceptions as Applied in Judicial Reasoning*, W. W. Cook (ed.). New Haven, CT: Yale University Press.

Holmes, O. Wendell, Jr 1920. *Collected Legal Papers*. New York: Harcourt, Brace and Co.

Hume, D. 1888. *A Treatise of Human Nature* [1739], L. A. Selby-Bigge (ed.). Oxford: Clarendon Press.

Hume, D. 1965. *An Enquiry Concerning the Principles of Morals*, sect. V (1752). In *Hume's Ethical Writings*, A. MacIntyre (ed.). London: Collier-Macmillan.

Jenkins, K. 1991. *Re-thinking History*. London: Routledge.

Kant, I. 1929. *A Critique of Pure Reason* [1787], 2nd edn, N. Kemp Smith (trans.). London: Macmillan.

Kant, I. 1953. *Prolegomena to Any Future Metaphysics* [1783], P. G. Lucas (trans.). Manchester: Manchester University Press.

Kant, I. 1959. "Idea of a Universal History from a Cosmopolitan Point of View", W. Hastie (trans.). In *Theories of History*, P. Gardiner (ed.), 22–34. New York: The Free Press. Also published as "Idea for a Universal History with a Cosmopolitan Purpose", H. B. Nisbet (trans.), in, *Kant: Political Writings*, 2nd edn, H. Reiss (ed.), 41–53, (Cambridge: Cambridge University Press, 1991).

Kant, I. 1962. *Fundamental Principles of the Metaphysic of Ethics* [1785], 10th edn, T. Kingsmill Abbott (trans.). London: Longman.

Kant, I. 1965. *Metaphysical Elements of Justice*, J. Ladd (trans.). Indianapolis: Bobbs-Merrill.

Kant, I. 1991. *The Metaphysics of Morals*, M. Gregor (trans.). Cambridge: Cambridge University Press.

Kellner, H. 1989. *Language and Historical Representation*. Madison, WI: University of Wisconsin Press.

Kelly, J. M. 1992. *A Short History of Western Legal Theory*. Oxford: Clarendon Press.

Kramer, M. H. 1998. "Rights Without Trimmings". See N. E. Kramer *et al.* (eds) 1998, 7–111.

Kramer, M. H. 1999. *In the Realm of Legal and Moral Philosophy: Critical Encounters*. London: Macmillan.

Kramer, M. H. 2001. "Getting Rights Right". In *Rights, Wrongs and Responsibilities*, M. H. Kramer (ed.), 28–95. Basingstoke: Palgrave.

Kramer, M. H. (ed.) 2001. *Rights, Wrongs and Responsibilities*. Basingstoke: Palgrave.

Kramer, M. H., N. E. Simmonds, H. Steiner (eds) 1998. *A Debate Over Rights: Philosophical Enquiries*. Oxford: Clarendon Press.

Kuhn, T. S. 1962. *The Structure of Scientific Revolutions*. Chicago, IL: The University of Chicago Press.

Kymlicka, W. 1990. *Contemporary Political Philosophy: An Introduction*. Oxford: Clarendon Press.

Lee, S. 1988. *Judging Judges*. London: Faber & Faber.

Lipton, P. 1991. *Inference to the Best Explanation*. London: Routledge.

Locke, J. 1924. "An Essay Concerning the True Original, Extent and End of Civil Government". *On Civil Government: Two Treatises*, vol. 2 [1690]. London: Dent. Also called the *Second Treatise*.

Locke, J. 2002. *Essays on the Law of Nature*, W. von Leyden (ed.). Oxford: Oxford University Press.

Mackie, J. L. 1977. *Ethics: Inventing Right and Wrong*. Harmondsworth: Penguin.

Mackie, J. L. 1984. "Can There be a Right-based Moral Theory?" See Waldron (ed.) (1984), 168–71.

Marshall, T. H. 1997. "Citizenship and Social Class". In *Contemporary Political Philosophy: An Anthology*, R. E. Goodin & P. Pettit (eds), 291–319. Oxford: Blackwell.

Masterman, M. 1970. "The Nature of a Paradigm". In *Criticism and the Growth of Knowledge*, I. Lakatos & A. Musgrave (eds), 59–89. Cambridge: Cambridge University Press.

Mill, J. S. 1987. *Utilitarianism* [1863]. Reprinted in *John Stuart Mill and Jeremy Bentham: Utilitarianism and Other Essays*, A. Ryan (ed.). Harmondsworth: Penguin.

Milne, A. J. M. 1968. *Freedom and Rights*. London: Allen and Unwin.

Milne, A. J. M. 1986. *Human Rights and Human Diversity*. London: Macmillan.

Nagel, T. 1986. *The View From Nowhere*. Oxford: Oxford University Press.

Nozick, R. 1974. *Anarchy, State and Utopia*. Oxford: Basil Blackwell.

Olafson, F. A. (ed.) 1961. *Society, Law and Morality*. Englewood Cliffs, NJ: Prentice-Hall.

O'Neill, J. (ed.) 1973. *Modes of Individualism and Collectivism*. London: Heinemann.

O'Neill, O. 2002. *A Question of Trust*, BBC Reith Lectures 2002. Cambridge: Cambridge University Press.

Passmore, J. 1972. *The Perfectibility of Man*. London: Duckworth.

Plato 1975. *Phaedo*, D. Gallop (ed. and trans.). Oxford: Oxford University Press.

Plato 1987. *Republic*, H. D. P. Lee (trans.). London: Penguin. Also *The Republic of Plato*, 2nd edn, with notes and an interpretive essay by A. Bloom (trans.) (New York: Basic Books, 1991).

Plato 1991. *Meno*, R. W. Sharples (ed. and trans.). Warminster: Aris & Phillips.

Pompa, L. 1975. *Vico: A Study of the "New Science"*. Cambridge: Cambridge University Press.

Popper, K. R. 1966. *The Open Society and Its Enemies* [1945]. London: Routledge & Kegan Paul.

Pörn, I. 1970. *The Logic of Power*. Oxford: Basil Blackwell.

Quine, W. V. O. 1960. *Word and Object*. Cambridge, MA: MIT Press.

Quine, W. V. O. 1961. "On What There Is". In *From a Logical Point of View*, 2nd edn.

W. V. O. Quine, 1–19. New York: Harper & Row.

Quine, W. V. O. 1969. "Ontological Relativity". In *Ontological Relativity and Other Essays*, W. V. O. Quine, 26–68. New York: Columbia University Press.

Quine, W. V. O. 1990. *Quiddities: An Intermittently Philosophical Dictionary*. Harmondsworth: Penguin.

Rawls, J. 1972. *A Theory of Justice*. Oxford: Oxford University Press.

Rorty, R. 2001. "The Continuity Between the Enlightenment and 'Postmodernism'". In *What's Left of Enlightenment? A Postmodern Question*, K. M. Baker & P. H. Reill (eds), 19–36. Stanford, CA: Stanford University Press.

Scanlon, T. M. 1984. "Rights, Goals, and Fairness". See Waldron (ed.) (1984), 137–52.

Schneewind, J. B. 1998. *The Invention of Autonomy*. Cambridge: Cambridge University Press.

Scruton, R. 1983. *A Dictionary of Political Thought*. London: Macmillan.

Scruton, R. 1989. "Corporate Persons", *Proceedings of the Aristotelian Society* supp. vol. **63**: 239–66.

Sen, A. 1987. *On Ethics and Economics*. Oxford: Basil Blackwell.

Simmonds, N. E. 1998. "Rights at the Cutting Edge". See N. E. Kramer *et al.* (eds) (1998), 113–232.

Smith, A. 1997. "Thoughts for the Day". Review of I. Berlin, *The Proper Study of Mankind: An Anthology of Essays*, H. Hardy & R. Hausheer (eds) (London: Chatto & Windus, 1996), *The Observer*, 23 February.

Smith, M. 1987. "The Humean Theory of Motivation", *Mind* **96**: 36–61.

Steiner, H. 1994. *An Essay on Rights*. Oxford: Blackwell.

Steiner, H. 1998. "Working Rights". See N. E. Kramer *et al.* (eds) (1998), 233–301.

Suárez, F. 1944. *De Legibus* [1612]. Oxford: Clarendon Press.

Sumner, L. W. 1987. *The Moral Foundation of Rights*. Oxford: Clarendon Press.

Thomson, J. J. 1990. *The Realm of Rights*. Cambridge, MA: Harvard University Press.

Tuck, R. 1991. "Introduction" to Thomas Hobbes, *Leviathan*. Cambridge: Cambridge University Press.

Vico, G. 2002. *The First New Science* [1725–1744], L. Pompa (ed.). Cambridge: Cambridge University Press.

Vlastos, G. 1973. "The Unity of the Virtues in the *Protagoras*". In *Platonic Studies*, G. Vlastos, 221–69. Princeton, NJ: Princeton University Press.

Vlastos, G. 1984. "Justice and Equality". See Waldron (ed.) (1984), 41–76.

Waldron, J. (ed.) 1984. *Theories of Rights*. Oxford: Oxford University Press.

Warnke, G. 2000. "Feminism and Democratic Deliberation". *Philosophy and Social Criticism* **26**: 61–74.

Wilkins, B. T. 1974. *Hegel's Philosophy of History*. Ithaca, NY: Cornell University Press.

Wittgenstein, L. 1968. *Philosophical Investigations*, 3rd edn, G. E. M. Anscombe (trans.). Oxford: Basil Blackwell.

Wittgenstein, L. 2001. *Tractatus Logico-Philosophicus* [1922]. London: Routledge.

Wolff, J. 1991. *Robert Nozick: Property, Justice and the Minimal State*. Cambridge: Polity Press.

Wyman, B. 1909. *Cases on Public Service Companies, Public Carriers, Public Works, and Other Public Utilities*, 2nd edn (Cambridge, MA: The Harvard Law Review Association).

Index